The Treaty of Paris in a Changing States System

D0887178

PAPERS FROM A CONFERENCE
January 26-27, 1984

DATE DUE

10-31-05	

Prosser Gifford
Editor

GAYLORD · PRINTED IN U.S.A.

WOODROW WILSON INTERNATIONAL CENTER FOR SCHOLARS

UNIVERSITY PRESS OF AMERICA

Barry University Library
Miami, Fla. 33161

Copyright © 1985 by

The Woodrow Wilson International
Center for Scholars

University Press of America,® Inc.

4720 Boston Way
Lanham, MD 20706

3 Henrietta Street
London WC2E 8LU England

All rights reserved

Printed in the United States of America

Library of Congress Cataloging in Publication Data
Main entry under title:

The Treaty of Paris (1783) in a changing states
  system.

  Conference organized by the Wilson Center and the
Folger Library's Center for the History of British
Political Thought.
  Bibliography: p.
  1. United States—History—Revolution, 1775-1783—
Peace—Conference. 2. Treaty of Paris (1783)—
Congresses. I. Gifford, Prosser. II. Woodrow,
Wilson International Center for Scholars. III. Center
for the History of British Political Thought (Folger
Shakespeare Library)
E249.T74 1985   973.3'17   85-9139
ISBN 0-8191-4752-4 (alk. paper)
ISBN 0-8191-4753-2 (pbk. : alk. paper)

The Woodrow Wilson International Center for Scholars subscribes to a
policy of equal educational and employment opportunities.

The Wilson Center is a nonpartisan institution committed to the
exploration of a broad range of scholarship and ideas. It does not
necessarily endorse these or any other statements presented at its
conferences and meetings.

Co-published by arrangement with
The Woodrow Wilson International Center for Scholars,
Smithsonian Institution Building, Washington, D.C. 20560

E
349
.T74
1985

Contents

SECTION III

REVERBERATIONS IN THE AMERICAS: DOES THE REVOLUTION CONTINUE?

This volume is a collection of the papers presented at a bicentennial symposium commemorating American ratification in January 1784 of the Treaty of Paris. Organized by The Wilson Center and the Folger Institute's Center for the History of British Political Thought, both of which are located in Washington, D.C., the symposium was devoted to a central question: Did the successful revolt of the American colonies change relations among the then-existing nations of Europe between the early 1780s and the outbreak of the Napoleonic Wars?

Little changed, James Hutson observes in his opening overview of period diplomacy. American politicians of the new nation, ever cognizant of both the vulnerability of the United States and its potential commercial power, perpetuated balance-of-power politics in an attempt to stop the British from expanding still further their mercantile strength and military power. Whether or not American negotiators in Paris in 1783 at first tried to overturn the diplomatic status quo, as Jack Greene notes in response to Hutson, relations among nations altered little following ratification of the Treaty of Paris.

Adam Smith, interestingly enough, put his finger on why this was so. Smith had found, writes A.S. Skinner, that the colonies were unnecessarily fettered by British regulation, and that the growth rate of the mother country was held down by the colonial relationship. Moreover, Britain's sluggish growth was the result of "self-imposed costs and restrictions," the very factors that helped the colonies attain a relatively high growth rate. These economic realities made war inevitable only insofar as Britain dealt with the situation by needing to save face at home and abroad. A more rational response would have been either union or simple recognition of America as a separate state, Smith noted. Either course would have again put relations with America on a more profitable footing. Thus, the Treaty of Paris represented a correction in the old ways of doing things, not a transformation to a new set of rules by which international trade and diplomacy would be conducted.

Nowhere was this more evident than in Europe. In England, while the Revolution contributed to an increase in parliamentary power, to the rise of provincial consciousness, and to a decline in patronage, it had little bearing on the rise of interest groups, and on how both ministerial and opposition parties came to rely on them for support as there were fewer favors to dispense. This new pattern, Alison Olson writes, "probably would have happened without the American Revolution," though she acknowledges that independence for the colonies "certainly speeded the changes along."

In Ireland, too, the Revolution proved to be little more than a catalyst. Able to anticipate change faster than the Irish demanded it, the British recognized Irish rights in mid-April 1783 under the Constitution of 1782; British timing, according to A.P.W. Malcomson, whose essay contrasts the British treatment of the American and Irish cases, was such that "Ireland experienced no political reaction to the Treaty of Paris." But the Irish experiment in political autonomy was short-lived, because by 1795 the British had reversed direction. The French also, according to Claude Fohlen, had expectations that went unfulfilled. They fought against the British in the Revolution primarily to avenge their humiliating defeat at British hands in 1763. They had high hopes of dislodging the new United States from the commercial linkages of the "first British empire." But for a variety of reasons the French could not capitalize on their opportunity before internal political troubles preoccupied them. No significant political or commercial realignment resulted.

The third section of this volume deals with the effects of the American Revolution in the Western Hemisphere. Perhaps it is not surprising, in retrospect, that the greater impact of the Treaty of Paris occurred in the colonial possessions north and south of the former British colonies. More surprising is the direction of change: the Spanish Empire moving to modernize and liberalize its governance; the Canadians, augmented by a number of Loyalists fleeing from the United States, turning more conservative by choice.

But what of the American, the so-called new man? How did he conceive of the cultural legacy and identity of the United States? Marcus Cunliffe addresses this question by examining the degree of cultural continuity and free speech of Americans.

The volume returns finally to the effect of the American Revolution upon British political perceptions, assumptions, and arrangements for empire. J.G.A. Pocock, the principal organizer of the Folger Institute Center for British Political Thought at the Folger Shakespeare Library, closes the volume with his comments on the changes in British political culture. The experiments in imperial relationships represented by the American colonies, the Caribbean islands, Ireland, and Canada later continued with Asian and African territories. It is in these relationships that the changes signaled by the treaty in 1783 and ratified at Annapolis in 1784 reverberated longer.

Constraints on space make it impossible to include the remarks of commentators for all of the conference papers, and I wish to convey my appreciation to Gordon J. Schochet, Rutgers University; Peter P. Hill, George Washington University; Thomas Garvin, University College of Dublin; and Robert Webb, University of Maryland Baltimore County, for their contributions to the symposium. Those who chaired panels helped to give the symposium point and structure. We are grateful to Joan Challinor, National Committee for the Bicentennial of the Treaty of Paris; Elizabeth Eisenstein, University of Michigan; Philip Knachel, Folger Shakespeare Library; and Peter Klaren, George Washington University.

The conference would not have been possible without the assistance of the steering committee of the Folger Institute Center for the History of British Political Thought. In addition to J.G.A. Pocock, Gordon J. Schochet of Rutgers University and Louis G. Schwoerer of George Washington University participated in planning and shaping the intellectual agenda from the outset. John F. Andrews and Lena C. Orlin of the Folger Institute contributed both intellectually and materially to the conference, the first day of which took place in the Folger Shakespeare Library's theater. Finally, we are all indebted to the ambassador, Sir Oliver Wright, and Hugh Crooke of the British Embassy for their involvement in the conference and for the ambassador's reception following Marcus Cunliffe's presentation. Sir Oliver's gracious remarks suggest that the Treaty of Paris still provides an occasion for cordial continuity in British-American relations.

My special thanks go to David Kolkebeck, who undertook the detailed burdens of polishing the manuscript; Patricia Sheridan, who typed it; and Margaret Ferguson, who played an important part in its production and design.

Prosser Gifford

Contributors

ANN GORMAN CONDON has taught history at the University of New Brunswick, Saint John, since 1977. She is the author of The Envy of the American States: The Loyalist Dream for New Brunswick and a piece in Esmond Wright's Red, White, and True Blue, "Marching to a Different Drummer—The Ideology of the American Loyalists."

MARCUS CUNLIFFE, University Professor at George Washington University, has taught at Manchester University, the University of Sussex, and at Harvard. He is the author of George Washington: Man and Monument and The Nation Takes Shape, 1789-1837.

CLAUDE FOHLEN started the American history program at the Sorbonne in 1967. A former Wilson Center fellow and instructor in French history at Yale, he is author of L'industrie en France sous le Second Empire, Histoire de Besançon, and, most recently, l'Amérique de Franklin Roosevelt.

JACK GREENE, a former Wilson Center fellow, is professor in the humanities at Johns Hopkins University. He is author of The Ambiguity of the American Revolution and Colonies to Nation, 1763-1789 and editor of All Men are Created Equal.

JAMES H. HUTSON is chief of the Manuscripts Division at the Library of Congress. A former history instructor at Yale, he was assistant editor of the Papers of Benjamin Franklin there. He has written Pennsylvania Politics, 1746-1770 and edited John Adams and the Diplomacy of the American Revolution.

FRANKLIN KNIGHT, professor of history at Johns Hopkins University, is a native of Jamaica. A former associate professor of history at the State University of New York at Stony Brook, he is author of Slave Society in Cuba during the Nineteenth Century and The African Dimension in Latin American Societies.

PEGGY K. LISS is an independent scholar based in Washington, D.C. She has been a lecturer at Swarthmore and at Hiram College, and is a member of the Conference of Latin American History. Her books include Mexico under Spain, 1521-1556: Society and the Origins of Nationality and Atlantic Empires.

A.P.W. MALCOMSON serves as keeper of the Public Records Office of Northern Ireland, in Belfast. Among his books are John Foster: The Politics of the Anglo-Irish Ascendancy and The Extraordinary Career of the Second Earl of Massereene, 1743-1805.

ALISON G. OLSON, professor of history at the University of Maryland, has taught history at American University and Rutgers. Her books include The Radical Duke: Career and Correspondence of Charles Lennox, Third Duke of Richmond and Anglo-American Politics.

J.G.A. POCOCK is professor of history at Johns Hopkins University. He has been a resident fellow of St. John's College at Cambridge University, a senior lecturer in political science at the University of Canterbury, and a Wilson Center fellow. He has written The Machiavellian Moment: Florentine Political Thought and the Atlantic Republican Tradition and edited Three British Revolutions: 1641, 1688, 1776.

A.S. SKINNER, professor of political economy at the University of Glasgow, is a specialist on Adam Smith. Coeditor of Essays on Adam Smith and the Glasgow edition of Wealth of Nations, he is the author of Adam Smith and the Role of the State.

I

Contemporary Politics and Trade: Did the Treaty Have Any Impact?

THE TREATY OF PARIS AND THE
INTERNATIONAL STATE SYSTEM

James H. Hutson

On the morning of September 3, 1783, at the Hotel d'York in Paris, John Adams, Benjamin Franklin, and John Jay signed a treaty of peace with representatives of George III, thereby recognizing the independence of the United States. Since independence was the goal for which the American Revolution had been conducted, the Treaty of Paris affirmed the success of the Revolution before the powers and principalities of the earth. What was the impact of the American Revolution—after having been given the international seal of legitimacy by the Treaty of Paris—on contemporary politics among nations?

This question must be handled with care, for it has acted as an intoxicant on otherwise sober American historians, expanding their minds to vast and dramatic dimensions. Ask an American historian about the effect of the Revolution on the world and he might answer, as Forrest McDonald did in 1965, that it was "only a beginning in teaching men the process [of revolution], but once it was done—once the vulgar overstepped the bonds of propriety and got away with it—there was no logical stopping place. Common Sense led unerringly to Valmy, and Valmy to Napoleon, and Napoleon to the Revolution of 1830, and that to the Revolutions of 1848, and those to the Paris Commune of 1871, and that to the Bolshevik Revolution, and that to the African and Asian Revolutions in Expectations, and those to eternity."[1] Richard B. Morris yields little to Professor McDonald in estimating the reach of the Revolution, seeing in it the yeast of worldwide political fermentation throughout the 19th and 20th centuries and detecting its influence on such figures as Ho Chi Minh, Mao Tse Tung, Kwame Nkrumah, and the leaders of Burma.[2] That the advent of a revolutionary American state had a long-range impact on the international political system is a proposition that will be examined later in this paper. First, however, its immediate influence on the state system will be considered.

Here, too, scholars have made large claims for the Revolution. One influential thesis, proposed by Felix Gilbert, holds that American officials in Europe were "representatives of a new diplomacy," favoring "proposals which were entirely alien to the spirit and practice of the time." They are pictured as believing that "traditional diplomacy and power politics [were] elements of a past epoch." Their objective, according to Gilbert, was nothing less than the destruction of the European balance-of-power system.[3] Richard

4

Morris, among others, adopted the Gilbert thesis. Morris wrote that
in the negotiations at Paris in 1782 and 1783, Franklin, Jay, and
company were "instruments of a new revolutionary society which confronted the Old Order...governed by its balance of power politics,
its pseudo-Machiavellian ethics, and its objectives of limited
gains." The Americans, he claimed, represented a break with "the
traditional politics of the balance of power." "Under the 'new
diplomacy'" they espoused, "obstacles to free commercial intercourse
among nations would be removed, expansion would be replaced by
friendship and cooperation, double-dealing by candor."[4] European
statecraft would be turned upside down by the Treaty of Paris as
decisively as European arms had been on the field of Yorktown.

Nothing of the sort happened. The Treaty of Paris did not produce the millenium in international relations. It did not usher in
a new era of diplomacy. Nor did it reform power politics. Business
was conducted as usual in Europe before, during, and after the negotiation of the treaty. In 1778-79, for example, Austria, using a
flimsy claim, invaded Bavaria. Prussia retaliated by invading Bohe-
mia. Peace was then arranged, with France and Russia mediating, at
the expense of the small states that had been the victims of aggres-
sion. In 1782, insurgents, having seized control in Geneva in the
name of popular sovereignty, were crushed by a Franco-Sardinian
expedition acting at the request of a handful of dispossessed pa-
tricians. In 1783, Russia, using pretexts no better or worse than
her neighbors', invaded the Crimea and detached it from the Ottoman
Empire; Austria's response was to propose to help itself to other
Turkish properties in the area so that the balance of power in
Eastern Europe would be preserved. In 1787, the Dutch Patriot
movement was liquidated by Prussian armies invading the Netherlands
under the pretext of avenging an insult to a Prussian princess.
Although this foray did not prompt the Spanish minister Alberini's
remark that in the 18th century the powers of Europe "cut and pared
states like Dutch cheeses,"[5] it was characteristic of the "cynical
and brutal" political environment in which the Treaty of Paris was
signed. Why did the "new diplomacy" of the American Revolution
fail to change this system? The answer is that there was no "new
diplomacy." Professor Gilbert's thesis is unsupportable. To come
to grips with our topic, it is necessary to explain why.

According to Gilbert, Americans intended to use free trade to
banish balance-of-power politics. He alleges that the Americans
were converted to the gospel of free trade by the philosophes and
adopted it as their guideline in foreign relations by writing it
into their Model Treaty of 1776, which would govern their negotiators in the future. The philosophes, Gilbert argued, taught the
Americans that free trade would produce a "new age of peace" in
which "relations between nations would become purely commercial contacts, and the need for a political diplomacy with alliances and
balance of power would disappear from the international scale."[6]
The influence of the philosophes on late 18th-century statecraft is

a perennial topic of debate. European leaders flattered them and pretended to be instructed by them. The philosophes persuaded themselves that they were influencing their princes. In diplomacy, however, there is little evidence that Europe followed their precepts. What was the situation in America?

Since historians of the American Revolution have never ascribed much influence to the philosophes, Gilbert's thesis, unsupported as it is by any evidence from the 1770s, would seem to be suspect on its face. In the past decade we have had, moreover, an authoritative investigation of the ideas behind the American Revolution by Bernard Bailyn, who has concluded that the mentality of the American Revolutionary leaders was formed principally by English Opposition writers.[7] Nowhere in his delineation of the intellectual sources of the Revolution does Bailyn so much as mention the French philosophes.[8] There is also contemporary testimony about the absence of the philosophes' influence in Revolutionary America. In his Notes on Virginia, written in 1781-82, Thomas Jefferson conceded that French thinkers were virtually unknown in America; "we are but just becoming acquainted with her [France]," Jefferson wrote.[9] More important for our purposes is John Adams, the draftsman of the Model Treaty of 1776. Gilbert called Adams "the chief architect of the Model Treaty";[10] Adams regarded himself as the architect of the whole of early American foreign policy, the man "who refin'd it first and show'd its use, as really as Dean Swift did irony."[11] Therefore, his scorn for the French philosophers is especially significant. Their system, he wrote Benjamin Rush on December 22, 1806, "I took some pains, more than five and twenty years ago, to understand; but could not find one Gentleman among the Statesmen, Philosophers, and Men of Letters, who pretended to understand it. I procured the Books of Quanay [Quesnay] and I could not understand much of them, and much of what I understood I did not believe...."[12] The utter lack of influence of the philosophes on Adams is demonstrated by his 1777 reply to a friend who was seeking to inform himself about political economy, about commerce and money in particular. Read Locke, Postlethwait, and Newton, Adams advised him.[13]

It seems possible that Gilbert assumed that the American Revolutionary leaders were under the influence of the philosophes because he mistook what the Americans meant by "free trade"—the panacea of the philosophes. The Model Treaty of 1776, which established the guidelines of American foreign policy, proposed commercial equality, not commercial freedom. Americans wanted nothing more than to compete with other nations in world trade on equal terms, no matter how onerous. So far were they from being doctrinaire free traders that in 1783 they contemplated subjecting themselves once more to the rigors of the British Navigation Acts in the interest of reviving their commercial prosperity, pending the negotiation of a new commercial treaty with the British.

But Great Britain refused to grant a commercial treaty to the United States. American statesmen responded, not by turning the other cheek and attempting to disarm British hostility with free trade, but with projects of countervailing navigation acts, excluding British shipping from American ports.[14] Thomas Jefferson himself, who under the spell of the French intellectual world as minister to Versailles made a handful of statements in the late 1780s that seemed to support free trade, "helped to draft the congressional address of April 30, 1784, recommending that the states 'vest Congress with so much power over their commerce...to enable them...to pass something like the British navigation act.'"[15] And it was Jefferson's partisans, led by Madison, who fought in Congress throughout the 1790s for a system of discriminatory commercial duties.[16] The notion that American leaders were committed to free trade, as the philosophes understood it, is--it should be clear by now--a mirage.

Americans viewed trade from the perspective of mercantilism, which undergirded the British Empire in which they had matured. They subscribed to the mercantilist dogma that monetary wealth was power and that commerce was the parent of wealth and hence of power. With their burgeoning population--Americans accepted Franklin's estimate that it was doubling every 20 years--they regarded themselves as an insatiable market for European commercial goods and an engine of power in international politics. In 1760 Franklin declared that the "foundations of the future grandeur and stability of the British empire lie in America,"[17] a refrain that other American writers immediately picked up. "The Foundations of the Power and Glory of Great Britain are Based in America," claimed John Dickinson in 1765.[18] America, declared George Wythe in 1774, "is one of the Wings upon which the British Eagle has soared to the Skies."[19] The union of Britain with the American colonies has raised her, the Second Continental Congress affirmed, "to a power the most extraordinary the world had ever known."[20] "The English," wrote John Adams on August 4, 1779, "by means of their commerce and extensive settlements abroad, arose to a degree of opulence and naval power" that had allowed them to tyrannize the world.[21]

These statements--and they could be pyramided endlessly--demonstrate more than the mercantilistic slant of American thinking; they also show that in the years before independence Americans believed that, by raising Britain to the pinnacle of power she enjoyed as a result of the Seven Years' War, they were the key component in the European balance of power. As Robert Morris wrote: "[F]rom my knowledge of the Commerce of this Country with Europe I dare assert that whatever European Power possesses the presumption of it, must of consequence become the richest and most potent in Europe."[22] American leaders believed, in fact, that if the connection between the colonies and Britain continued, the European balance of power would be annihilated in favor of total British hegemony. For the power of the British Empire would not, in the

American view, be static. As America's population relentlessly increased, so would the power of the empire. "Our trade was rapidly increasing with our increase of people, and in greater proportion," a committee of Congress declared in March 1776.[23] With these facts in mind, John Adams concluded that in another war the power of the united British Empire would have destroyed France's "existence as a maritime and commercial power," would have been "fatal" to her.[24] Nor, in Adams's opinion, would the commerce and even the independence of the Netherlands have survived against an indivisible British Empire.[25] And the freedom of the seas, any place in the world, would have been an impossibility in the face of such a coalition.[26] On the other hand, Adams believed that for America, upon becoming independent, to deny her commerce to Britain would be "fatal" to the mother country, would "ruin" her, and these were sentiments in which all of his colleagues agreed.[27] The kingdom, declared Richard Henry Lee at the First Continental Congress, "could not exist" without the commercial connection with America;[28] the dissolution of this connection, the Second Continental Congress informed the inhabitants of Great Britain, would "deliver you, weak and defenceless, to your natural enemies,"[29] would reduce you, a correspondent of Franklin's predicted, "to a State of being a Province of France."[30] It was indisputable, then, to Adams and the other American leaders, that the power the united colonies possessed made them the arbiter of the European balance of power. A "Connection with America," Adams wrote Patrick Henry on July 9, 1778, "must in the future decide the Ballance of Maritime Power in Europe."[31]

The following statement by John Adams on May 20, 1783, illustrates the American attitude toward the existing state system:

> Gentlemen can never too often [be] requested to recollect the Debates in Congress in the Years 1775 and 1776, when the Treaty with France was first in Contemplation. The Nature of those Connections, which ought to be formed between America and Europe, will never be better understood than they were at that time. It was then said, there is a Ballance of Power in Europe. Nature has formed it. Practice and Habit have confirmed it, and it must exist forever. It may be disturbed for a time, by the accidental Removal of a Weight from one Scale to the other; but there will be a continual Effort to restore the Equilibrium....if We give exclusive priviledges in Trade, or form perpetual Alliances offensive and defensive with the Powers in one Scale, we infallibly make enemies of those in the other....Congress adopted these Principles and this System in its purity....[32]

Despite the alliance concluded with France in 1778, Americans, having fought, hated, and derided the French for as long as any of them could remember, could not refrain from regarding the subjects of the Most Christian King with fear and suspicion. As Carter Braxton put it, France was a nation "famous for Intrigue and Deception," sentiments that the successful wartime collaboration with Louis XVI failed to stanch.[33] "Neither England nor America," wrote John Adams on May 20, 1783, "could depend upon the Moderation of such absolute Monarchies and such ambitious Nations" as France and Spain.[34] Perhaps John Dickinson best expressed the American attitude toward France, in his July 1, 1776 speech opposing the Declaration of Independence: "Suppose we shall ruin her [Great Britain]. France must rise on her Ruins. Her Ambition. Her Religion. Our Dangers from thence. We shall weep at our Victory."[35]

If American leaders were apprehensive about the future behavior of France, they were certain that Britain would be inimical toward them. "They hate us, universally, from the throne to the footstool and would annihilate us, if in their power," John Adams wrote John Jay on August 13, 1782.[36] That the definitive treaty of 1783 left Canada in Britain's hands was regarded as particularly ominous by American leaders, for, as Hamilton declared in Federalist No. 6, "it has...become a sort of axiom in politics, that vicinity, or nearness of situation, constitutes nations natural enemies."[37] Neighboring nations, asserted Edmund Randolph, "were bound to clash in 'bloodshed and slaughter.'"[38] Richard Henry Lee predicted that "British possession of Canada, N. Sco. and the Floridas will inevitably produce" a "War in 7 years."[39] The sea, where Britain reigned as the imperious master, was also considered a point of certain friction. Since Americans would be engaging in sea-borne commerce, "wars then must sometimes be our lot," Jefferson prophesied.[40] Expecting trouble from Britain, Americans heeded Adams when, as minister to London from 1785 to 1788, he warned them that they should "keep up a constant Expectation of War," that Britain would "make war immediately against us" whenever an opportunity arose.[41]

The world, as Americans in the Revolutionary era saw it, presented a somber spectacle: The United States was confronted at the same time with the enmity of two of the most powerful nations in the world, who were themselves implacable foes. The Revolutionary leaders responded to this situation by trying to use their principal resource—commerce—to create a balance of power between the two antagonists, so that each would be able to restrain the aggressions of the other against the United States. This does not mean that in formulating the liberal trade provisions of the Model Treaty Adams and his colleagues expected to create an exact parity of power between Britain and France. If Britain availed herself of the terms offered by the Model Treaty, she would, Adams believed, obtain "more of American Trade...than France" and would derive from it "more support" for her Navy than the French would. She would, he believed, "recover...much of her Commerce, and perhaps equal Consideration and Profit and Power from [America] as ever."[42] This was a remarkable policy since Britain was regarded as America's "natural Enemy for the future," one that "would clean the wooden shoes of the

French upon Condition that they would permit them to wreck their Vengeance on us."[43] Yet, conceding British enmity in its fullest measure, Adams considered it folly to enfeeble Britain vis-à-vis France. The United States, he contended, "ought with the utmost Firmness to Resist every thought of giving to France any unequal advantage in our Trade even over England, for it never could be our Interest to ruin England, or annihilate their maritime Power, if we could possibly save our Liberty and independence without it."[44] And in 1783 Adams asserted that he had "laid it down as a first principle that...above all...it could never be our interest to ruin Great Britain, or injure or weaken her any further than should be necessary to our independence and our alliance."[45] Why should Britain not be injured excessively? Because "the time might come," Benjamin Rush recalled Adams saying in 1776, "when we should be obliged to call upon Britain to defend us against France."[46] The draftsman of the Model Treaty did not see all of its benefits going to Britain, however. Giving France freedom to trade with the United States would extend her "navigation and Trade, augment her resources of naval Power...and place her on a more equal footing with England."[47] Thus strengthened, France would be better able to discourage British designs on America.

This examination of the principles of Revolutionary foreign policy is designed to refute Professor Gilbert's thesis and to demonstrate that the recognition of the independence of the United States at the Treaty of Paris did not convulse or even challenge the conduct of international relations. The Americans were conformists and conservatives. They accepted the international state system based on the balance of power and tried to manipulate it for their own benefit.

We should not be deceived in this regard by the orders that Jefferson and Adams received in 1784 to negotiate commercial treaties, grounded in reciprocity of privileges, with the several powers of Europe. This was not a singular commission. Commercial treaties were a kind of fad in late 18th-century Europe. As conservative a statesman as the Count de Vergennes negotiated 17 of them during his tenure (1774-87) as French foreign minister,[48] including one in 1786 with his arch rival, Great Britain. But the count's motives were not humanitarian or altruistic. He and his negotiating partners wanted to use commerce to increase national power. Even as Vergennes bargained over commerce with the British, he was expecting the imminent outbreak of hostilities with them.[49]

Vergennes had more success in negotiating treaties than did Adams and Jefferson. Their failure during the 1780s to conclude a commercial treaty with Britain was particularly disappointing and galling. Hopes were high when Lord Shelburne was directing the peace negotiations. In 1782 he prepared an American Intercourse Bill that would have permitted citizens of the independent United States to participate in British trade on essentially the same terms

as they had enjoyed as British subjects. The Shelburne ministry
fell during the winter of 1783, however, and politicians believing
in the sanctity of the British Navigation Acts came to power. On
July 2, 1783, an order-in-council was issued that confined trade
with the British colonies to British subjects. Other orders followed throughout the decade, unilaterally regulating trade with the
United States. Having shown no inclination to conclude a commercial
treaty with the Americans, some Britishers feared retaliation, but
the government of the Confederation had no power to regulate commerce and did nothing. Lord Sheffield and other British pundits
had predicted as much. These men had, in fact, argued that American
self-interest would be so well served by trading with Great Britain
that, treaty or no, Britain would monopolize the commerce of the
new nation and would retain its power and military prowess--a view
shared by Adams and other architects of American foreign policy,
although they assumed that Britain would secure her position through
the medium of a treaty. Figures proved the Sheffields and the
Adamses correct: In 1787, Britain held 80 percent of the foreign
tonnage entering Philadelphia; two years later it held 98 percent
of that entering New York.[50] Despite the efforts of France throughout the 1780s to increase her participation in American trade by
offering attractive commercial opportunities in the West Indies,
her position vis-à-vis Britain in 1787 was little better than it
had been before the American Revolution began. The advent of an
independent United States did not, then, appreciably alter Britain's
position in the maritime balance of power, as Britons feared and
Frenchmen hoped.

Nor did American independence weaken Britain by wounding her
in Ireland. American Revolutionary leaders tried to create a second
front in Ireland by inflaming the natives' resentment of their British overlords. The Continental Congress sent a spirited Address to
the People of Ireland in July 1775 and never relinquished the hope
that trouble could be brewed up there. The American Revolution did,
in fact, lead to a relaxation of controls imposed on the most op-
pressed segment of the Irish population, the Catholics, but the
benefits obtained by the Catholics were not conferred by American
intervention but rather by the British as a reward for their loyalty
in opposing the rebellion. Overwhelmingly--almost monolithically--
supporting the Crown, Catholics enlisted in British expeditionary
forces with "large Expectations by the forfeited estates and culti-
vated lands which may fall to them when the Troubles subside."
Britain granted other political reforms to the Irish during the war
--most conspicuously autonomy to the Irish Parliament in 1782--and
thereby succeeded in keeping problems under control and preserving
her power from the erosion it must have offered from a revolt or
upheaval in Ireland.[51]

Closer to the United States, the Revolutionary War populated
the Canadian Maritime provinces with Loyalists for whom unsatisfactory arrangements (from their point of view) were made in the Treaty

of Paris. Britain tried to incorporate Canada into a reconstructed navigation system in the New World, in which the Maritime provinces would perform the role of suppliers of provisions, lumber, and other raw materials to the West Indies, as the revolted colonies to the south had formerly done. Although the new system did not immediately answer the expectations of its most optimistic proponents, it contributed some support to the British marine and appeased the true believers in the Navigation Act.

In Ireland and Canada British power suffered as little from American independence as it did in its access to the commerce of the new nation. Dean Tucker and other critics predicted before the outbreak of hostilities with the Americans that colonial independence would not be detrimental to Britain's position in international politics. The results of the Treaty of Paris proved the dean and his associates correct.

Some Americans in the 1780s were ambivalent, and many more were uncomfortable, about boasting of the potential of their commerce and calculating its effect on the balance of power. Many Revolutionary statesmen, in fact, delivered passionate denunciations of commerce. Pennsylvania Congressman James Searle asserted, for example, "that commerce had injured us, that the merchants of America were without example such vile rogues and speculators that it would be happy for America if they were instantly extirpated...."[52] Americans, however, preferred to extirpate foreign trade rather than those who participated in it. Jefferson's assertion that "it might be better for us to abandon the ocean altogether" and his wish that "there were an ocean of fire between us and the old world" were characteristic of a broad band of American opinion. As David Rittenhouse put it: Let nature "raise her everlasting bars between the new and old world...and make a voyage to Europe as impracticable as one to the moon."[53]

The problem with commerce was that it threatened to subvert republicanism, next to independence the primary goal of the Revolution. "Commerce produces money, money luxury and all three are incompatible with Republicanism," wrote John Adams. Or, as Silas Deane explained, "only by banishing wealth and luxury, and holding commerce the parent of both in abhorrence" would it be possible to preserve republican government.[54] Eighteenth-century political science was clear about the incompatibility of republicanism with commerce, luxury, and wealth. For a republican government to succeed, it required an unusual population, one dedicated to virtue—understood in the civic sense as a commitment to the public welfare—to equality, simplicity, and frugality. Such a population existed in America, her leaders believed (by 1787 they were less confident), but it existed nowhere else in the world.

Africa and Asia were so benighted, it was thought, that they were not worth mentioning; Europe had descended into "cancerous corruption."[55] Thomas Paine articulated these attitudes in Common Sense: "Freedom hath been hunted round the globe, Asia and Africa have expelled her. Europe regards her like a stranger, and England hath given her warning to depart."[56] Before the Revolution began, America gave up on England, too, accepting the indictments of various British Jeremiahs who lamented a nation "rolling to the brink of a precipice that must destroy us" and denounced the "vain, luxurious, and selfish effeminacy" of the British people.[57] America was not immune from European corruption, for it could spread, through commerce, like a contagion, infect the people, sap their virtue, and destroy the experiment in republicanism. Hence the diatribes against commerce with Europe and even the suggestion made by Elbridge Gerry in November 1783 that the United States refuse diplomatic relations with Europe, lest Americans be "gradually divested of our virtuous republican principles," a suggestion endorsed by a congressional committee a month later.[58]

Europe, then, and the world at large were so corrupt that they could not sustain a republican revolution; therefore, the virtuous American Revolution had to remain at home, for it could not flourish in regions of vice. There was, accordingly, no missionary impulse in American leaders, sharing, as they did, the attitude reflected both in John Adams's famous statement that one might as well try to establish a republic over the animals in the royal menagerie at Versailles as over the people of France and in John Randolph's remark that "you cannot make liberty out of Spanish matter—you might as well try to build a seventy four out of saplings."[59] Revolutionaries found little encouragement in the United States, as many Latin Americans could attest. It was perhaps too much to expect a slaveholding nation to warm to the rebellion in Santo Domingo in the 1790s, but Americans were scarcely more hospitable to the Venezuelan patriot Miranda, whose followers were prosecuted by Jefferson's administration in 1806, or to later Latin revolutionaries seeking aid and recognition.

Convictions about the uniqueness of the American Revolution and its unsuitability for transmission elsewhere, passed along by Revolutionary leaders to generations of their posterity, have been criticized recently by Richard B. Morris, who contends that for "too long" such views have allowed Americans "to ignore the libertarian currents that the event set off through the world." For Morris the American Revolution was one of the transforming episodes in history; in his view, it "provoked" the French Revolution and influenced the subsequent revolutions that worked their way through the 19th century and agitate the world today.[60] If this is so, the long-range impact of the American Revolution—and of the Treaty of Paris—was profound, even cataclysmic, although its immediate impact was imperceptible.

Professor Morris does not produce any new evidence to illustrate the relationship of the American to the French Revolution.

The case for the impact of the one upon the other rests now, as it has for at least a half-century, upon three propositions: One, France's participation in the American Revolution brought it to the brink of bankruptcy, which compelled political decisions that led inexorably to conflagration; two, tours of duty in America inspired both officers and enlisted men in the French Army with Revolutionary ideals, which they promoted when they returned to France;[61] and three, French support of the United States opened the country to American ideas, which converted numbers to the cause of revolution. The difficulty, of course, is assessing the exact dimensions of the "impact" or "influence" of American ideas and experiences upon Frenchmen. This problem applies to areas like Latin America as well, where the personalities and ideas of the American Revolutionaries were known. On the basis of familiarity it is possible to assert, as Mario Rodriguez does, that the "movement in North America served as an inspiration for the emancipation of the Americas to the South,"[62] but what exactly does this mean in the face of massive evidence that the French Revolution was the model preferred by Latin leaders? And suppose a reformer like the Norwegian judge C.M. Falsen names his son, George Benjamin, after Washington and Franklin. What, if anything, does this indicate about the impact of the American Revolution in Scandinavia?

Given the difficulty of these questions and the failure of Professor Morris to produce new evidence that the American Revolution "provoked" the French, it seems more prudent to adhere to the conventional view that the American Revolution exerted "influence," however defined, on the French Revolution, but that it did not cause it. Robert R. Palmer's thesis that both upheavals were links in a chain of democratic revolutions that swept the Atlantic community in the late 18th century seems particularly appropriate.

Edmund Burke greeted the signing of the Treaty of Paris in these words:

A great revolution has happened—a revolution made...by the appearance of a new state, of a new species, in a new part of the globe. It has made as great a change in all relations, and balances, and gravitations of power, as the appearance of a new planet would in the system of the solar world.[63]

On this occasion Burke's enthusiasm got the better of his judgment. The United States did not immediately change the balances or system of international relations. It did not challenge the accepted method of conceptualizing international politics—the balance-of-power system—and it did not disrupt the maritime balance between Britain and France. On the continent of Europe its appearance as a newly recognized state had no effect whatsoever on the major trend of the 1780s, the growth of Russian power in the east.

The long-range impact of the Treaty of Paris is more difficult to assess. It is a subject, as has been said, that stretches the imagination of historians. And not merely of American historians. J.H. Plumb, for example, in relating how American independence shifted the focus of the British Empire to India, pointed out that the loss of Georgia produced the settlement of Australia, as a new "dumping ground for convicts." Warming to his subject, Plumb stated that "the possession of Australia naturally raised the strategic importance of the Malacca Straits, leading to the foundation of Singapore. Nor could the French in New Zealand be tolerated."[64] At this point he caught himself, perhaps heeding the admonition of Palmer that "the later the date the more difficult and unrealistic it becomes to try to identify any specific effects of the American Revolution."[65] Yet it is impossible to deny that over the long range the American Revolution had some influence in other parts of the world, by serving as an example for revolutions or, as in British India, by fostering geopolitical strategies. In this sense Burke was right to perceive the dynamic implications of the Treaty of Paris.

NOTES

1. Forrest McDonald, E Pluribus Unum (Boston, 1965), pp. 235-36.

2. Richard B. Morris, The Emerging Nations and the American Revolution (New York, 1970), pp. 181, 204, 217, 220.

3. Felix Gilbert, To the Farewell Address (Princeton, 1961), pp. 54, 56, 66, 85-89.

4. Morris, Emerging Nations, p. 48.

5. Samuel Flagg Bemis, The Diplomacy of the American Revolution (New York, 1935), p. 14.

6. Gilbert, Farewell Address, pp. 56-69.

7. Bailyn's thesis is most fully developed in The Ideological Origins of the American Revolution (Cambridge, 1967).

8. Montesquieu might be considered a philosophe, but of this there is considerable doubt. Stourzh claims that Montesquieu made early American foreign policy idealistic, but his description of Montesquieu's foreign-policy ideas makes it appear that the Frenchman considered trade a source of power, as did the mercantilists and other power politicians, at least as often as he did an instrument of international comity. Stourzh, Hamilton and Republican Government, pp. 140-48.

9. <u>Notes on Virginia</u>, in Adrienne Koch and William Peden, eds., <u>The Life and Selected Writings of Thomas Jefferson</u> (New York, 1944), p. 215.

10. Gilbert, <u>To the Farewell Address</u>, p. 49.

11. Adams to Benjamin Rush, September 30, 1805, in John A. Schutz and Douglass Adair, eds., <u>The Spur of Fame...</u> (San Marino, Calif., 1966), pp. 38-39.

12. Alexander Biddle, ed., <u>Old Family Letters</u> (Philadelphia, 1892), p.120; see also Adams to John Jay, February 26, 1786, Adams Papers, microfilm ed., reel 112. Edward Handler observed that before February 1778, the date Adams embarked on his first European diplomatic mission, the ideas of the French Enlightenment "exerted minimum influence, whether by attraction or repulsion, on his mind." <u>America and Europe in the Political Thought of John Adams</u> (Cambridge, 1964), p. 33. For substantiation of this point, see Zoltan Haraszti, <u>John Adams and the Prophets of Progress</u> (Cambridge, 1952), p. 19.

13. Adams to John Thaxter, April 8, 1777, Adams Papers, microfilm ed., reel 91.

14. See, for example, John Adams to James Sullivan, August 16, 1785; to John Hancock, September 2, 1785, Adams Papers, microfilm ed., reel 111.

15. Peterson, "Thomas Jefferson and Commercial Policy," p. 590.

16. Irving Brant, <u>James Madison: Father of the Constitution, 1787-1800</u> (Indianapolis, 1950), pp. 245-54.

17. To Kames, January 3, 1760, Smith, ed., <u>Writings of Franklin</u>, 3: 71.

18. John Dickinson, <u>The Late Regulations Respecting the British Colonies</u>, in Bernard Bailyn, ed., <u>Pamphlets of the American Revolution</u> (Cambridge, 1965), p. 687.

19. Butterfield et al., eds., <u>Diary and Autobiography of John Adams</u>, 2: 214.

20. Boyd, ed., <u>Papers of Thomas Jefferson</u>, 1: 219.

21. C.F. Adams, ed., <u>The Works of John Adams</u>, 7: 100.

22. To Silas Deane, December 20, 1776, transcript in editorial office of Letters to Delegates to Congress, Library of Congress.

23. To Silas Deane, March 3, 1776, Burnett, ed., <u>Letters</u>, 1: 376.

16

24. To van der Capellen, January 21, 1781; to Edm. Genet, May 9, 1780, in C.F. Adams, ed., The Works of John Adams, 7: 161, 357.

25. To Samuel Huntington, September 25, 1780, in Francis Wharton, ed., The Revolutionary Diplomatic Correspondence of the United States, 6 vols. (Washington, D.C., 1889), 4: 67-69; to Edmund Jenings, April 27, 1781, Adams Papers, microfilm ed., reel 354.

26. Adams to Jean de Neufville, March 24, 1781, ibid., reel 102.

27. Adams to Robert Livingston, June 23, 1783, Wharton, ed., Revolutionary Diplomatic Correspondence, 6: 500; Adams to Edmund Jenings, July 18, 1780, Adams Papers, microfilm ed., reel 352; Adams to the president of Congress, December 8, 1778, ibid., reel 93.

28. Burnett, ed., Letters, 1: 3.

29. Hutson, ed., A Decent Respect, p. 108.

30. Wendell to Franklin, October 30, 1777, quoted in Stinchcombe, The American Revolution and the French Alliance, p. 11.

31. Adams Papers, microfilm ed., reel 93.

32. Warren-Adams Letters, 2: 192.

33. To Landon Carter, April 14, 1776, transcript in editorial offices of Letters to Delegates to Congress, Library of Congress.

34. Butterfield et al., eds., Diary and Autobiography of John Adams, 3: 122.

35. Transcript in editorial offices of Letters of Delegates to Congress, Library of Congress.

36. To Jay, August 13, 1782, C.F. Adams, ed., Works of John Adams, 7: 610.

37. Quoted in Stourzh, Hamilton and Republican Government, p. 153.

38. Ibid., p. 255, n. 89.

39. Quoted in Stinchcombe, American Revolution and French Alliance, pp. 25-26. For John Adams's agreement on this point, see to Izard, September 25, 1778; to Jenings, June 11, 1780; to Franklin, April 16, May 24, 1782, Adams Papers, microfilm ed., reels 93, 107, 352.

40. Notes on Virginia, in Koch and Peden, eds., Life and Writings of Thomas Jefferson, p. 285.

41. To Jay, July 19, 1785; to R.H. Lee, December 24, 1785; to Jay, October 27, 1786, November 20, 1787, Adams Papers, microfilm ed., reels 111, 112.

42. To Samuel Huntington, June 16, 1780, ibid., reel 110; see also to John Heath, July 10, 1778; to C.W.F. Dumas, May 19, 1781, ibid., reels 93, 102; also Butterfield et al., eds., Diary and Autobiography of John Adams, 3: 61, 68.

43. Adams to Edmund Jenings, April 25, 1780; to R.H. Lee, December 24, 1785, Adams Papers, microfilm ed., reels 112, 351.

44. Adams to Jenings, July 18, 1780, ibid., reel 352.

45. To Robert Livingston, February 5, 1783, Wharton, ed., Revolutionary Diplomatic Correspondence, 6: 243; Butterfield et al., eds., Diary and Autobiography of John Adams, 3: 105, 115-16; Adams to Jenings, April 18, 1783, to Matthew Robinson, Adams Papers, microfilm ed., reels 108, 113.

46. Rush to Adams, August 14, September 21, 1805, Adair and Schultz, eds., Spur of Fame, pp. 32, 36.

47. Butterfield et al., eds., Diary and Autobiography of John Adams, 4: 337.

48. Orville Murphy, Charles Gravier Comte de Vergennes (Albany, 1982), p. 454.

49. Ibid., p. 399.

50. Charles Ritcheson, Aftermath of Revolution: British Policy Toward the United States (Dallas, 1969), p. 31.

51. Information in this paragraph is derived from Owen Dudley Edwards, "The Impact of the American Revolution in Ireland," in The Impact of the American Revolution Abroad (Library of Congress, Washington, D.C., 1976), pp. 135-44.

52. Silas Deane to John Jay, April 8, 1781, Deane Papers, New York Historical Society, Collections (1889), p. 299.

53. Notes on Virginia; to Elbridge Gerry, May 13, 1797, in Koch and Peden, eds., Life and Writings of Thomas Jefferson, pp. 285, 543; quoted in Gordon Wood, The Creation of the American Republic, 1776-1787 (Chapel Hill, 1969), p. 113.

54. Adams to Benjamin Rush, December 28, 1807, Biddle, ed., Old Family Letters, p. 176; Silas to Simeon Deane, May 16, 1781, Deane Papers, pp. 336, 341.

18

55. Wood, <u>Creation of the American Republic</u>, p. 110.

56. Quoted in Bernard Bailyn, <u>The Ideological Origins of the American Revolution</u> (Cambridge, 1967), p. 143.

57. Ibid., p. 87.

58. Elbridge Gerry to John Adams, November 23, 1783, Gerry Papers, Library of Congress; Report, December 20, 1783, in Julian P. Boyd, ed., <u>The Papers of Thomas Jefferson</u>, 19 vols. (Princeton, 1950-   ), 6: 397.

59. Morris, <u>Emerging Nations</u>, p. 153.

60. Ibid., pp. x, 39.

61. For recent reservations on this point, see Claude Fohlen, "The Impact of the American Revolution on France," in <u>The Impact of the American Revolution Abroad</u> (Library of Congress, Washington, D.C., 1976), pp. 25-28.

62. Mario Rodriguez, "The Impact of the American Revolution on the Spanish and Portuguese-Speaking Worlds," ibid., p. 117.

63. Morris, <u>Emerging Nations</u>, pp. 34-35.

64. J.H. Plumb, "The Impact of the American Revolution on Great Britain," in <u>The Impact of the American Revolution Abroad</u>, op. cit., p. 74.

65. Robert R. Palmer, "The Impact of the American Revolution Abroad," ibid., p. 6.

COMMENTARY

Jack P. Greene

James Hutson makes two principal points. First, he argues that the Treaty of Paris, the achievement of U.S. independence, and the diplomatic behavior of the new nation during its first few decades had very little influence on either the international state system or the conduct of diplomacy. Second, and <u>very</u> briefly in the conclusion, he contends that many scholars, especially Richard B. Morris, have overestimated the Revolution's long-range impact.

Within the narrow range of discussion set by Hutson, both contentions seem defensible. The United States and its emissaries <u>did not</u> change the way diplomacy was conducted, nor did they alter established patterns of international relations. Of course, this is precisely the conclusion reached by Felix Gilbert in his 1961 study <u>To the Farewell Address: Ideas of Early American Foreign Policy</u>, on which Hutson focuses so much of his criticism.

But Hutson's explanation for this lack of change in diplomatic patterns is somewhat less satisfying. In contrast to Gilbert, who argues that the Americans aspired to change existing patterns of diplomacy but failed because they lacked the necessary clout to alter behavior that was so deeply entrenched, Hutson suggests that Americans did not want to change traditional patterns of diplomacy. Why? Because "they accepted the international state system based on the balance of power and tried to manipulate it for their own benefit." Also, he says, they were persuaded that their revolution was not exportable, because "Europe...and the world at large were so corrupt that they could not sustain a republican revolution." Thus, "the virtuous American Revolution" would have to "remain at home, for it could not flourish in regions of vice."

But there are several problems with this explanation. First, Gilbert adduces a lot of persuasive evidence to show that when the Americans first entered the diplomatic game in 1776, they did indeed aspire to change existing diplomatic modes. But, as Gilbert shows, they were quickly disabused of such notions once they entered into diplomatic negotiations in France and elsewhere. Thereafter, as both Gilbert and Hutson agree, Americans knew that they could not change the existing system. So they worked within that system—except for a brief period right after the signing of the Treaty of Paris—trying to manipulate traditional balance-of-power considerations to their own advantage.

But there seems to be little evidence that their behavior in this regard was a matter of preference. Rather, as Gilbert seems to imply, it probably came from a realistic assessment of their own continuing vulnerability within the international state system and from a clear-headed perception of their national interests. Their inability to always manipulate the international situation to their own advantage no doubt frustrated American leaders and diplomats and may even have helped reinforce the notions of those few Americans who believed that foreign commerce was incompatible with republicanism. But American leaders knew that their polity consisted of societies whose inhabitants had always had a strong commercial orientation and were then becoming ever more heavily involved in international trade. American leaders had no choice but to operate within the system in order to pursue their vital commercial--that is, national--interests.

Hutson is more persuasive when he criticizes Gilbert for giving the philosophes too much credit for shaping American opinion. At the same time, however, it is important to point out that our whole conception of the Enlightenment has expanded enormously since Gilbert published his work in 1961. We now take in British thinkers from Locke and Newton forward to the Scottish common-sense philosophers, as well as to such Continental writers as Pufendorf, Burlamaqui, and Vattel, none of whom is, strictly speaking, a philosophe. If Gilbert revised his analysis in light of this expanded conception, he could probably argue convincingly that American thinking on diplomacy and the state system was profoundly influenced by Enlightenment thought. Vattel's Law of Nations, for example, published in 1758 and widely read in America and Europe, contained opinions on diplomatic and commercial relations that are astonishingly similar to those Hutson attributes to American leaders and diplomats. Like most American leaders, Vattel believed both that trade was "agreeable to human nature" and, because freedom was so "very favorable to commerce," that nations "should support trade as far as possible, instead of cramping" it "by unnecessary burdens or restrictions." An advocate of commercial treaties, he recognized also, like the Americans, that the extent to which any nation could support trade was limited by its obligations to itself, with considerations of its "own advantage or safety" always being, in Vattel's words, "paramount to" its "duties to others."

Similarly, there is an enormous amount of evidence to suggest that American leaders, contrary to Hutson's view, believed that the American Revolution was exportable. Not only passionate enthusiasts like Thomas Paine but sober and hard-headed realists like John Adams and James Madison heralded the Revolution's likely impact on the traditional political and social world. "The progress of society," said John Adams in a moment of almost millennial rhapsody, "will be accelerated by centuries by this revolution....Light spreads from the dayspring in the west, and may soon it shine more and more until the perfect day." America, said Madison's friend George Turberville, "may rejoice and plume herself in the idea of having made the Rent in the great curtain that withheld the light from human nature--by her exertions she has let the day and the Rights of Man become legible and intelligible to a Shackled World." "Nothing has excited more admiration in the world," crowed Madison, "than the manner in which free governments have been established in America, for it was the first instance, from the creation of the world--that free inhabitants have been seen deliberating on a form of government, and selecting such of their citizens as possess their confidence, to determine upon and give effect to it." "America's purpose," its larger mission, declared Dr. David Ramsay, the most perceptive contemporary historian of the Revolution, "is to prove the virtues of republicanism, to assert the Rights of Man, and to make society better." Henceforth, a great many of the Founding Fathers hoped, the United States would serve as a beacon light of freedom to the rest of mankind. Like their initial diplomatic goals, these hopes were quickly dampened by experience. But they never completely disappeared. "The flames kindled on the fourth of July 1776," Thomas Jefferson assured John Adams long after the Revolution, "have spread over too much of the globe to be extinguished by the feeble engines of despotism."

Americans were not alone, for radical British thinkers like Dr. Richard Price and a wide variety of observers on the Continent powerfully reinforced such sentiments. "All Europe is on our side of the question as far as applause and good wishes can carry them," Benjamin Franklin wrote from his ambassadorship in Paris in 1777. "'Tis a common observation here, that our Cause is the Cause of all Mankind, and that we are fighting for their Liberty in defending our own. 'Tis a glorious task assign'd us by Providence; which has, I trust, given us Spirit and Virtue equal to it, and will at last crown it with success."

It would be a serious mistake, of course, to suggest that the American Revolution made as much of a difference as American leaders and their transatlantic supporters had initially projected. Hutson is right: Americans never became active missionaries of revolution. With John Adams, they might have believed that "a Republican...Form of Government" was "the best, of which human Nature is capable." Thomas Paine excepted, however, they were not, in the words of Adams, such "enthusiast[s]" as to wish "to overturn [all existing] Empires and Monarchies, for the Sake of introducing Republican Forms of Government." They created no Third International. But the leading variable in this situation was not ideology, and not even their admittedly growing skepticism about the relevance of the American experience to other societies. Rather, it was the same sort of practical realism and the same sense of acute vulnerability that had long since reconciled them to functioning within the existing international state system.

Hutson is also right in emphasizing the limited character of the Revolution's immediate impact on the existing state system.

The Revolution certainly did not weaken Britain economically, as Britons, Americans, and Frenchmen had initially expected. On the contrary, it constituted demonstrable evidence of the accuracy of Dean Tucker and Adam Smith's earlier insight that economic hegemony does not require political control. It can be plausibly argued that the Revolution helped breathe new life into Anglo-Irish yearnings for greater home rule, but it did nothing of the sort for colonies that remained under British hegemony after 1783. The extreme economic and/or military dependence of both the Caribbean and Canadian colonies upon the metropolis, a dependence so vividly underlined for them during the Revolution by their total incapacity to follow the example of the rebellious colonies, contributed (at least in the Caribbean) to the creation of a psychology of passive dependence that would continue for some time.

But surely it is wrong to suggest that the creation of an independent American state had no impact on the international state system. Just as the Treaty of Utrecht in 1713 signified a "growing awareness" on the part of the European powers "of the importance of non-European parts of the globe," so the Treaty of Paris in 1783 served notice that these same areas might have independent aspirations of their own and, even more important, that imperial powers might be unable to prevent them from realizing those aspirations. Some historians, no doubt, have greatly exaggerated the influence of the American Revolution upon the French Revolution, although I think it was considerably more influential than does Hutson. As Peggy Liss demonstrates in Atlantic Empires, however, the Revolution was obviously an inspiration for much of the rest of the then-colonized world, particularly in Hispanic America. It thus had rather important and well-known effects upon both the foreign and the colonial policy of Spain, certainly one of the more important members of the international state system.

I have far fewer quibbles with Hutson's assessment of the Revolution's long-range impact. Its preeminence as an exemplar of revolution was extremely brief. After 1789, the French, not the American, Revolution became the model for most revolutionaries. Why? Perhaps because the American Revolution occurred in societies that were, by the standards of the day, both modern and well developed. For revolutionaries with a traditional order to overturn—and even for those who fought the many post-World War II colonial wars for self-determination—the American Revolutionary experience turned out to be irrelevant.

ADAM SMITH: THE DEMISE OF THE
COLONIAL RELATIONSHIP WITH AMERICA

Andrew S. Skinner

Adam Smith knew the Treaty of Paris was scarcely the inevitable outcome of late 18th-century debate and conflict. But he warned his contemporaries that the disturbances of the time carried with them the most profound implications for economic policy, for the constitutional structure of the state, and for Britain's future relationship with America.[1]

Smith's interest in the American question goes back to his time in Glasgow as student (1737-40) and professor (1751-64). He witnessed a particularly rapid rate of commercial development in and around the city, based largely on tobacco, which led in turn to major initiatives in manufacturing and banking.[2] Quite apart from his contacts with great merchants like Andrew Cochrane, founder of perhaps the first Political Economy Club, Smith could hardly help notice that Glasgow's emergence as a major commercial center was the result of the city's geographical position. This relationship of geography to commercial activity provided a classic modern example of the historical progression that is so dominant a feature of his treatment of the origins of "present establishments" in Europe.[3]

Smith's success as a professor brought him further important contact with the American question, in the generous shape of Charles Townshend. Townshend had married the widowed countess of Dalkeith in 1755 and was sufficiently impressed by Smith's Theory of Moral Sentiments (1759) that he made the author tutor to the young duke of Buccleugh. The post permitted Smith to travel in France between 1764 and 1766, and he was thus able to make contact with the French economists known as the Physiocrats.[4]

On Smith's return to London in 1766 he appears to have had at least two relevant exchanges in the increasingly fraught legislative environment. He was asked by Lord Shelburne for advice on the Roman colonial model, but was able to offer little comfort:

> Being in some measure little independent republics they natur- ally followed the interests which their peculiar Situation pointed out to them.[5]

During the same period, Smith annotated a document on the Sinking Fund, which had been prepared by Townshend,[6] and also may have

discussed the question of colonial taxation with him. What is clear
is that Smith approved of applying the main British taxes to the
colonies (land tax, stamp duties, customs, and excise), and this
may explain Arthur Lee's reference to him as "a Scotchman, and an
enemy to American rights."[7]

Finally, it should be observed that when Smith returned to
London in 1773 to finish work on Wealth of Nations, the delay in
finishing the book was attributed by some, notably David Hume, to
his growing preoccupation with the American problem. Hume wrote in
February 1776 to complain:

> By all Accounts, your Book has been printed long ago; yet it
> has never yet been so much as advertised. What is the Reason?
> If you wait till the Fate of America be decided, you may wait
> long.[8]

That Smith's interest in the American question caused the delay
is certainly plausible. The colonies are scarcely mentioned in the
lectures delivered in 1762-63, but feature in what is almost a
separate monograph in Wealth of Nations, in the form of the long,
three-part Chapter 7 of Book 4. In the latter, Smith reviewed the
options open to the British government during the mid-1770s. This
led Hugh Blair to complain that Smith had given the issues involved

> a representation etc. which I wish had been omitted, because
> it is too much like a publication for the present moment. In
> Subsequent editions when publick Measures come to be Settled,
> these pages will fall to be omitted or Altered.[9]

But as William Robertson noted with greater justice,[10] the major
part of the argument was addressed to longer-term issues. Smith
made use of the old colonial relationship (as defined by the Regulating Acts of Trade and Navigation) to demonstrate what he took to
be the fundamental inconsistencies of the mercantile system as a
whole. These inconsistencies clearly demonstrated the need for
changes in economic policy and constitutional practice, irrespective
of the outcome of the legal and political conflicts that were then
unfolding.

The Regulating Acts[11]

In describing the objectives of colonial policy, Smith concen-
trated mainly on their economic aspects and duly reported on the
extensive range of restrictions that Britain had imposed on trade
and manufacturing, domestic as well as American. To begin with,
the Regulating Acts of Navigation required that trade between the
colonies and Great Britain be conducted by British ships, and that
certain classes of commodities be confined initially to the market

of the mother country. These so-called enumerated goods were of two types: those produced in America or outside Britain, and those produced in Britain, but in quantities insufficient to meet domestic demand. Examples of the first type were molasses, coffee, and tobacco; of the second, naval stores, masts, pig iron, and copper. The first broad category of goods could not harm British industry. The object of policy here, as reported by Smith, was to ensure that British merchants would pay little for colonial goods, could supply other countries at higher prices, and at the same time could establish a useful carrying trade. In the second category, the objectives were to ensure essential supplies and, through the careful use of duties, to discourage imports from other countries "with whom the balance of trade was supposed to be unfavourable." Smith also took notice of another feature of British policy, namely, that the production of the more "advanced or more refined manufactures" was discouraged in the colonies.[12] Thus, woolen manufactures were forbidden there, and although they were encouraged to export pig iron, the colonists were prevented from erecting slit mills, which might have led ultimately to the development of manufactures competitive with those of Great Britain. There was a certain ingenuity in these arrangements (no doubt, as Smith suggested, as much the product of accident as design) in that the colonial relationship could be seen to benefit both parties, at least in the short run. The relationship with the colonies, as defined by the Regulating Acts, had the effect of creating a self-supporting economic unit whose main components provided complementary markets for each other's products, and in addition helped to minimize gold flows abroad.[13] By the same token, the colonial relationship gave Britain access to strategic materials, and thus contributed to national defense,[14] through the encouragement of the British mercantile marine.

The Sources of Economic Growth

The institutional environment established by the Regulating Acts of Trade and Navigation set the scene for Smith's discussion of economic growth, in which he laid particular emphasis on colonial performance. "There are no colonies," he wrote, "of which the progress has been more rapid than that of the English in North America."[15] He largely ascribed their progress to their distance from the central government, and said the American colonies were similar in this respect to those of ancient Greece:

Their situation has placed them less in the view and less in the power of their mother country. In pursuing their interest their own way, their conduct has, upon many occasions, been overlooked, either because not known or not understood in Europe; and upon some occasions it has been fairly suffered and submitted to, because their distance rendered it difficult to restrain it.[16]

There were other advantages, too, that were not merely a function of distance from Westminster. Smith drew attention to the absence in the colonies of both laws of primogeniture and entail and laws that prevented the "engrossing" of uncultivated land.[17] He pointed out in particular that the colonists enjoyed a high degree of personal liberty, secured by the rule of law and by the existence of "an assembly of the representatives of the people, who claim the sole right of imposing taxes for the support of the colony government."[18] In the colonies, Smith contended, there was nothing that corresponded to the House of Lords; if colonial institutions were not perfectly representative, he said, they were at least more representative than those in England:

> There is more equality...among the English-colonists than among the inhabitants of the mother country. Their manners are more republican, and their governments...have hitherto been more republican too.[19]

There were other more purely economic advantages. Colonial taxes, for example, were moderate, which Smith attributed partly to the lack of significant colonial contribution to the imperial obligation, and partly to the modesty of colonial administrative arrangements. Smith also contended that the colonists' "ecclesiastical government," unlike that of France and Spain, was "conducted upon a plan equally frugal,"[20] thereby freeing the colonists from tithes. Moreover, the colonies were undeveloped in a strictly economic sense:

> A new colony must always for some time be more under-stocked in proportion to the extent of its territory, and more under-peopled in proportion to the extent of its stock, than the greater part of other countries.[21]

This meant that the rates of both wages and profits were likely to be high, and that the level of economic activity would therefore be such that it prompted a "continual complaint of the scarcity of hands in North America. The demand for labourers, the funds destined for maintaining them, increase[s], it seems, still faster than they can find labourers to employ."[22] Elsewhere he noted that:

> The high wages of labour encourage population. The cheapness and plenty of good land encourage improvement, and enable the proprietors to pay...high wages....What encourages the progress of population and improvement, encourages that of real wealth and greatness.[23]

Finally, Smith argued that the legislative arrangements governing trade with the mother country had contributed most to colonial development, even though this had not always been their intent. Because "the most perfect freedom of trade is permitted between British colonies of America and the West Indies," he said, the colonies enjoyed a "great internal market" for their products.[24] In addition, the relative freedom of trade in nonenumerated commodities provided a further market for the colonies' primary products, while Britain also gave preferential treatment to American products that were confined to the British domestic market.

Also, Britain provided a large European market (albeit indirectly) for the enumerated items--goods like tobacco, for example, which were largely re-exported. The colonial policy had the effect of encouraging agriculture generally, which Smith called "the proper business of all new colonies; a business which the cheapness of land renders more advantageous than any other."[25] This point is of great importance, since for Smith agriculture was the most productive of all forms of investment, capable of generating a large surplus that could sustain further growth. He even argued that the restrictions imposed on colonial manufacturing had benefited the colonies by ensuring that they bought from the cheaper European markets and therefore avoided diverting any part of their available capital into less productive endeavors. He concluded:

> Unjust, however, as such prohibitions may be, they have not hitherto been very hurtful to the colonies. Land is still so cheap, and, consequently, labour so dear among them, that they can import from the mother country, almost all the more refined or more advanced manufactures cheaper than they could make them for themselves. Though they had not, therefore, been prohibited from establishing such manufactures, yet in their present state of improvement, a regard to their own interest would, probably, have prevented them from doing so.[26]

At the same time, Smith emphasized the benefits accruing to Great Britain. Together with its neighbors, Great Britain had acquired, through the control of the colonies, a "new and inexhaustible market" that had given rise to "new divisions of labour and improvements of art." Indeed, Smith's assertion of benefit accruing to Great Britain as a result of the colonial relationship simply reflects his own grasp of the gains to be made from trade.[27]

The Contradictions of the System

The relationship between mother country and colonies is thus represented as beneficial to both parties. It satisfied the politico-economic objectives of the Regulating Acts and stimulated economic growth. But Smith evidently believed at the same time that contradictions inherent in the colonial relationship would eventually manifest themselves. While Smith took pains to emphasize the great stimulus to the growth of the colonies, for example, he pointed out that their high and rapid rate of growth would ultimately come in conflict with the restrictions imposed on colonial trade and manufactures, restrictions that could be regarded as the "principal badge of their dependency,"[28] and as a "manifest violation of the most sacred rights of mankind." He also pointed out:

> In their present state of improvement, those prohibitions, per-
> haps, without cramping their industry, or restraining it from
> any employment to which it would have gone of its own accord,
> are only impertinent badges of slavery....In a more advanced
> state they might be really oppressive and insupportable.[29]

For this reason, Smith quite clearly believed that the colonial relationship would have to change, but he placed greater emphasis on Britain's more immediate problems.

Smith contended that, although the colony trade was "greatly beneficial" to Great Britain,[30] still the rate of growth was necessarily slower than it would have been in the absence of the Regu-
lating Acts. He asserted that "if the manufactures of Great Brit-
ain...have been advanced, as they certainly have, by the colony trade, it has not been by means of the monopoly of that trade, but in spite of the monopoly."[31] To support this contention, Smith suggested, first, that the monopoly of the colonial trade had inevitably increased the volume of business to be done by a rela-
tively limited amount of British capital and had, therefore, in-
creased the prevailing rate of profit. He argued that high rates of profit would affect the improvement of land,[32] and the frugality of the merchant classes,[33] while ensuring that available capital would be partly drawn, and partly driven, from those trades in which Britain lacked a monopoly. (That is, capital would be drawn by the higher profits available in the colony trade, and driven from them by a poorer competitive position.) But Smith especially emphasized that the pattern of British <u>trade</u> had been altered in such a way that her manufactures,

> instead of being suited, as before the act of navigation, to
> the neighbouring market of Europe, or to the more distant one
> of the countries which lie round the Mediterranean sea, have,
> the greater part of them, been accommodated to the still more
> distant one of the colonies.[34]

Smith added that alterations in her trade patterns made Great Britain unduly dependent on a single (though large) market:

> Her commerce, instead of running in a great number of small
> channels, has been taught to run principally in one great chan-
> nel. But the whole system of her industry and commerce has
> thereby been rendered less secure; the whole state of her body
> politick less healthful, than it otherwise would have been. In
> her present condition, Great Britain resembles one of those un-
> wholesome bodies in which some of the vital parts are over-
> grown, and which, upon that account, are liable to many danger-
> ous disorders scarce incident to those in which all the parts
> are more properly proportioned.[35]

Smith of course recognized that the dislocation caused by the "present disturbances" was not as great as this judgment taken by itself would seem to imply. He pointed out that a number of factors had cushioned the blow--including the high level of colonial demand for British products in the expectation of a "rupture," the requirements of the Spanish Flota, the needs of Turkey following on peace with Russia, and, most important in the long run, the increasing level of demand from Northern Europe.[36] Yet none of this qualified his view that the Regulating Acts caused a suboptimal rate of growth in Great Britain. "All the different regulations of the mercantile system," he wrote, "necessarily derange more or less the natural and most advantageous distribution of stock."[37] He added: "Every derangement of the natural distribution of stock is necessarily hurtful to the society in which it takes place."[38] "Though the wealth of Great Britain has increased very much since the establishment of the act of navigation," Smith concluded, "it certainly has not increased in the same proportion as that of the colonies."[39]

The Solution

Smith's account of the problem facing Great Britain was largely dominated by that of fiscal need. Britain's needs seemed to be growing more rapidly than its resources, and Smith noted in this connection that by January 1775 the national debt had reached the then-astronomical figure of ₤130 million (absorbing ₤4.5 million in interest charges), much of which was due to the acquisition of the colonial territories.[40]

This was a matter of some moment. It meant that a country whose rate of growth had been adversely affected by the colonial relationship had to face a large and probably growing tax burden, which would itself affect the rate of economic expansion and thereby compound the problem.

The mercantile approach to the colonial relationship was thus fundamentally flawed. In the long run, the colonies would have to confront the restraints imposed upon their manufactures, while at the same time Great Britain would have to confront the consequences of a suboptimal rate of growth.

Smith laid the blame for British policies of the period to the merchant groups:

We must not wonder, therefore, if, in the greater part of them, their interest has not been more considered than either that of the colonies or that of the mother country.[41]

As he remarked in one of the most famous passages of Wealth of Nations:

To found a great empire for the sole purpose of raising up a
people of customers, may at first sight appear a project fit
only for a nation of shopkeepers. It is, however, a project
altogether unfit for a nation of shopkeepers, but extremely fit
for a nation whose government is influenced by shopkeepers.[42]

As this implies, government, too, had fallen into a trap set by "the
groundless jealousy of the merchants and manufacturers of the mother
country,"[43] and compounded by the emotional considerations of national pride:

The rulers of Great Britain have, for more than a century past,
amused the people with the imagination that they possessed a
great empire on the west side of the Atlantic. This empire,
however, has hitherto existed in imagination only. It has
hitherto been, not an empire, but the project of an empire....
If the project cannot be compleated, it ought to be given up.
If any of the provinces of the British empire cannot be made
to contribute towards the support of the whole empire, it is
surely time that Great Britain should...endeavour to accommodate her future views and designs to the real mediocrity of
her circumstances.[44]

Yet Smith believed that the project of empire could be completed, and that the actual and potential tensions of the existing
colonial relationship could be resolved by the creation of an Atlantic Economic Community, which would establish "an immense internal market for every part of the produce of all its different provinces."[45]

Smith made three important points in this connection. First,
he argued that the colonies could and should be taxed:

It is not contrary to justice that both Ireland and America
should contribute towards the discharge of the publick debt of
Great Britain. That debt has been contracted in support of
the government established by the Revolution, a government to
which the protestants of Ireland owe, not only the whole authority which they at present enjoy in their own country, but
every security which they possess for their liberty, their
property, and their religion; a government to which several
of the colonies of America owe their present charters, and
consequently their present constitution, and to which all the
colonies of America owe the liberty, security, and property
which they have ever since enjoyed. That publick debt has
been contracted in the defence, not of Great Britain alone,
but of all the different provinces of the empire; the immense
debt contracted in the late war in particular, and a great
part of that contracted in the war before, were both properly
contracted in defence of America.[46]

Second, Smith noted that such a change of policy would require a form of union that would both give the colonies representation in the British Parliament and in effect create a single state. The extension of British taxes to the colonies

> could scarce, perhaps, be done, consistently with the princi-
> ples of the British constitution, without admitting into the
> British parliament, or if you will into the states-general
> of the British Empire, a fair and equal representation of all
> those different provinces, that of each province bearing the
> same proportion to the produce of its taxes, as the represen-
> tation of Great Britain might bear to the produce of the taxes
> levied upon Great Britain.[47]

Finally, Smith concluded:

> [T]here is not the least probability that the British consti-
> tution would be hurt by the union of Great Britain with her
> colonies. That constitution, on the contrary, would be com-
> pleted by it, and seems to be imperfect without it. The as-
> sembly which deliberates and decides concerning the affairs of
> every part of the empire, in order to be properly informed,
> ought certainly to have representatives from every part of
> it.[48]

In fact, the advantages of such an arrangement for America seem over-whelming, since in Smith's judgment America's progress "in wealth, population and improvement" had been so rapid that

> in the course of little more than a century, perhaps, the
> produce of American might exceed that of British taxation.
> The seat of the empire would then naturally remove itself
> to that part of the empire which contributed most to the
> general defence and support of the whole.[49]

The Short Term

Union--at least in the sense in which it has been discussed so far--represented for Smith the _logical_ solution to the economic and constitutional difficulties of mercantile policy. But union must be discussed in the context of options actually open to the British government at the time, on which Smith gave commentary in _Corres-pondence_ and _Wealth of Nations_. His views on the subject probably led Alexander Wedderburn, solicitor general in Lord North's admin-istration, to seek Smith's advice in the aftermath of Saratoga.[50] Wedderburn, it may be recalled, had been responsible for the hostile examination of Benjamin Franklin before the Privy Council in 1774, an exchange that moved Hume to remark in a letter to Smith that Wedderburn's treatment of the distinguished colonist had been "most cruel."[51]

One of the possible and practicable solutions in Smith's view was consistent with his general position, namely, union. But he was careful to remind his readers of the background to the case:

> The persons who now govern the resolutions of what they call their continental congress, feel in themselves at this moment a degree of importance which, perhaps, the greatest subjects in Europe scarcely feel. From shopkeepers, tradesmen, and attornies, they are become statesmen and legislators, and are employed in contriving a new form of government for an extensive empire which, they flatter themselves, will become, and which indeed, seems very likely to become, one of the greatest and most formidable that ever was in the world.[52]

It followed that the colonists would need an adequate inducement to abandon this initiative, and at one stage Smith believed that an incorporating union with colonial representation at Westminster might suffice:

> Instead of piddling for the little prizes which are to be found in what may be called the paltry raffle of colony faction; they might then hope, from the presumption which men naturally have in their own ability and good fortune, to draw some of the great prizes which sometimes come from the wheel of the great state lottery of British politicks.[53]

He added that union would also deliver the colonists "from those rancourous and virulent factions which are inseparable from small democracies...[and] which have so frequently divided the affections of their people, and disturbed the tranquility of their governments, in their form so nearly democratical."[54] Union was an option that Franklin considered in the 1750s, and it is interesting to recall that the First Continental Congress debated Joseph Galloway's plan for union as late as 1774. But by the time Smith published Wealth of Nations the opportunity had been lost: "We, on this side of the water, are afraid lest the multitude of American representatives should overturn the balance of the constitution,"[55] he wrote, while those "on the other side of the water are afraid lest their distance from the seat of government might expose them to many oppressions."[56] His tone had hardened further in his Memorandum on the American War in 1778: "[I]n their present elevation of spirits," he advised Wedderburn, "the ulcerated minds of the Americans are not likely to consent to any union even upon terms the most advantageous to themselves."[57] In Britain, he wrote, the plan of union "seems not to be agreeable to any considerable party of men."[58] He thus concluded:

> The plan which, if it could be executed, would certainly tend most to the prosperity, to the splendour, and to the duration of the empire, if you except here and there a solitary philosopher like myself, seems scarce to have a single advocate.[59]

A second possible solution was military victory and the restitution of existing institutional arrangements. But as Smith wryly pointed out, the difficulty in such a solution "arises altogether from the resistance of America."[60] Having little confidence in a military solution, Smith wrote to William Strahan in June 1776:

> The American campaign has begun awkwardly. I hope, I cannot say that I expect, it will end better. England, tho' in the present times it breeds men of great professional abilities in all different ways, great lawyers, great watch makers and Clockmakers, etc. etc., seems to breed neither Statesmen nor Generals.[61]

Perhaps Smith was even more insightful on this point in Wealth of Nations, where he noted that, while a professional standing army like Great Britain's was always likely to be the superior of a militia, experience suggested that this was not always true when the latter was long in the field:

> Should the war in America drag out through another campaign, the American militia may become in every respect a match for that standing army, of which the valour appeared, in the last war, at least not inferior to that of the hardiest veterans of France and Spain.[62]

Yet even if victory were possible, the outcome, he advised, would still be basically unworkable. A military government, he wrote, "is what of all others, the Americans hate and dread the most. While they are able to keep the field, they will never submit to it; and if, in spite of their utmost resistance, it should be established, they will, for more than a century to come, be at all times ready to take arms in order to overturn it."[63] He went on:

> After so complete a victory...after having, not only felt their own strength, but made us feel it, they would be ten times more ungovernable than ever; factious, mutinous and discontented subjects in time of peace; at all times, upon the slightest disobligation, disposed to rebel; and, in the case of a French or Spanish war, certainly rebelling.[64]

Besides, he concluded:

> By our dominion over a country, which submitted so unwillingly to our authority, we could gain scarce anything but the disgrace of being supposed to oppress a people whom we have long talked of, not only as our fellow subjects, but as of our brethren and even as of our children.[65]

A third option open to the British government was simplicity itself--voluntary withdrawal from the conflict and recognition of America as a separate state. The advantages of such a bold course

Barry University Library
Miami, Fla 33161

were, in Smith's opinion, immense. At one stroke, Britain would be
free of the crushing burden of expenditure needed to defend the
colonies and could avoid further conflict with France and Spain, at
least in the New World. As Smith wrote in Wealth of Nations:

> By thus parting good friends, the natural affection of the col-
> onies to the mother country, which, perhaps, our late dissen-
> sions have well nigh extinguished, would quickly revive.[66]

Even if the two countries were to part with some evidence of bad
feeling, he advised Wedderburn, "the similarity of language and manners would in most cases dispose the Americans to prefer our alliance to that of any other nation."[67]

Yet withdrawal from the conflict was unlikely:

> Such sacrifices, though they might frequently be agreeable to
> the interest, are always mortifying to the pride of every na-
> tion, and what is perhaps of still greater consequence, they
> are always contrary to the private interest of the governing
> part of it.[68]

He further elaborated this point in his Memorandum on the American
War in 1778:

> [T]ho' this termination of the war might be really advanta-
> geous, it would not, in the eyes of Europe, appear honourable
> to Great Britain; and when her empire was so much curtailed,
> her power and dignity would be supposed to be proportionably
> diminished. What is of still greater importance, it could
> scarce fail to discredit the government in the eyes of our own
> people, who would probably impute to mal-administration what
> might, perhaps, be no more than the unavoidable effect of the
> natural and necessary course of things.[69]

Smith was not above a little Machiavellian intrigue in the popular sense of that term. He suggested, for example, that Britain
might restore Canada to France and Florida to Spain and thus "render
our colonies the natural enemies of those two monarchies and consequently the natural allies of Great Britain."

> Those splendid, but unprofitable acquisitions of the late war,
> left our colonies no other enemies to quarrel with but their
> mother country. By restoring those acquisitions to the [an-
> cient] masters, we should certainly revive old enmities, and
> probably old friendships.[70]

Smith also suggested a policy of misleading the British people by
making an agreement with the Americans that would eventually lead to
dismemberment--"the former mistaking, and the latter understanding
the meaning of the scheme."[71]

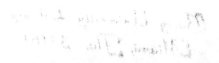

But for Smith the most likely outcome was also the most expensive: partial military defeat, he said, would mean the loss of all or some of the "thirteen united colonies" and the retention of Canada. The Memorandum must have made bleak reading for the solicitor general, but it would have seemed bleaker still had he known how accurately Smith had forecasted the events of 1783.

Conclusions

The narrative as just set forth is of value as a record of the views held by one of the key authors of the doctrine of economic liberalism. But there are other reasons for suggesting that Smith's writings should still command attention.

To the student of Smith, the form of the argument is of some significance. Smith began his account by offering a statement about the legislative environment before showing the ways in which economic development would manifest itself in both Britain and America. His argument prompts the conclusion that the quantitative development of productive forces must impinge upon the legislative environment itself. This turns out to be the classic pattern of philosophical history as manifested, for example, in Smith's essay on astronomy and in his treatment of the origins of the "present establishments" in Europe.

But the content of the analysis is also noteworthy. Smith's analysis of the long-run causes of change in the nature of the imperial relationship, for example, appears to rest on two trends: the relatively slow rate of growth attained by Britain in the face of self-imposed costs and restrictions, and the relatively high rate attained in America, which, at least in part, had resulted from those restrictions. It is also evident that Smith's explanation of British economic performance at the time rests very heavily on his thesis of the natural progress of opulence and on the consequent belief that any derangement of the natural balance of industry would slow the rate of growth. Yet there is remarkably little here by way of empirical verification, a point that moved Governor Pownall to remark that Smith was using theses established in one part of his book as proven principles in another.[72] The governor recognized the central importance of Smith's views on the productivity of investment, but noted: "In that part, however, which explains the different effect of different employments of capital...I will beg to arrest your steps for a moment, while we examine the ground whereon we tread: and the more so, as I find these propositions used in the second part of your work as data; whence you endeavour to prove, that the monopoly of the colony trade is a disadvantageous commercial institution."[73]

But the governor's rejection of Smith's formal explanation for the phenomenon of differential rates of growth refutes neither the factual statement that the rates of growth were different, nor the argument that this phenomenon must lead to a change in the nature of the relationship between the colonies and the mother country. This is the burden of the major part of Smith's treatment, which wisely places the Regulating Acts at center stage, even though the colonists never gave them that status. Britain's commercial (as distinct from imperial) policy did not figure in such key documents as the Declaration of Colonial Rights and Grievances (1774), the Olive Branch Petition (1775), or even the Declaration of Independence (1776), which contained a comprehensive indictment of Britain's performance.[74] Even if the contemporary crisis had been resolved, Smith seems to suggest, the major problem of the colonial relationship would remain to be addressed. As we have seen, the preferred solution to long-term problems was an incorporating union of the kind introduced by the Act of 1707 and later extended (as Smith suggested) to Ireland. But this was union with a difference, since it envisaged the eventual transfer of the imperial Parliament from London to the American capital. Smith clearly accepted the kind of assessment offered by Franklin in a letter addressed to Lord Kames:

> Scotland and Ireland are differently circumstanced. Confined by the sea, they can scarcely increase in numbers, wealth and strength, so as to overbalance England. But America, an immense territory, favoured by Nature with all advantages of climate, soil, great navigable rivers, and lakes, etc. must become a great country, populous and mighty; and will, in less time than is generally conceived, be able to shake off any shackles that may be imposed on her, and perhaps place them on the imposers.[75]

Smith's treatment of the options open to the British government is also notable for the coolness of its tone, for the broad accuracy of his predictions, and for the attention given to the constraints under which that government labored. Smith's interest in the origins of the modern British state made him peculiarly aware of the role of economic forces in changing the balance of political power. The Revolution Settlement of the late 17th century--and the superior position of the Commons--helped at once to explain the bases of English liberties, and so expose the importance of the Commons as a focus for sectional interests. As we have seen, Smith felt that contemporary policy toward the colonies was the product of mercantile interests; legislative proposals coming from such sources, he said,

> ought always to be listened to with great precaution, and ought never to be adopted till after having been long and carefully examined, not only with the most scrupulous, but with the most suspicious attention.[76]

The legislative process was, in Smith's eyes, further complicated by the nature of political activity--essentially competitive, and motivated in part by the desire for status. "Men desire to have some share in the management of publick affairs," he noted, "chiefly on account of the importance which it gives them." As for "the leading men of America,"

> [they], like those of other countries, desire to preserve their own importance. They feel, or imagine, that if their assemblies, which they are fond of calling parliaments, and of considering as equal in authority to the parliament of Great Britain, should be so far degraded as to become the humble ministers and executive officers of that parliament, the greater part of their importance would be at an end.

Smith concluded that Americans "have rejected therefore, the proposals of being taxed by parliamentary requisition, and like other ambitious and high-spirited men, have rather chosen to draw the sword in defence of their own importance."[77]

Status may obscure the interests of countries as well, observed Smith,[78] who added a variant of the point in drawing attention to the importance of domestic and international opinion. The most rational choice open to the British government was withdrawal from the conflict; the real constraints were represented by loss of face in Europe and at home:

> A government which, in times of the most profound peace, of the highest public prosperity, when the people had scarce even the pretext of a single grievance to complain of, has not always been able to make itself respected by them; would have everything to fear from their rage and indignation at the public disgrace and calamity, for such they would suppose it to be, of thus dismembering the empire.[79]

But Smith's realism was also a source of some comfort. When Sir John Sinclair of Ulster complained of Britain's lack of progress in the colonial war and exclaimed that "if we go on at this rate, the nation must be ruined," Smith could dryly reply: "Be assured, my young friend, that there is a great deal of ruin in a nation."[80] His grasp of economic reality also permitted him to assure William Eden that there was little to fear in the long run from the temporary loss of American commerce.[81] In the same vein, he looked forward to a special relationship with America based on a "similarity of language and manners."[82]

But in Glasgow, a city whose street names (Jamaica, Tobago, Glassford, Cochrane, and Buchanan, to name but a few) still recall a colonial age, and where in a sense this story began, the outcome of what was essentially a civil war was treated less philosophically. The atmosphere is beautifully caught by Alistair Phillips:[83]

> During the middle days of January 1783, while the Powers of Versailles were putting the finishing touches to the document

that would give the revolted colonies their official independence, in Glasgow John Mennons, a printer but lately come to Glasgow from Edinburgh to seek, or rather to improve, his fortune, was laying out the first edition of the newspaper he intended to launch upon the commercial capital of the West. But he was not yet quite ready to lock up the last forme. He still lacked his lead story. It was, however, worth waiting for, and might reasonably be identified as the weightiest newspaper scoop of the succeeding two hundred years. It came on the eve of publication, when the Lord Provost sent round to him a copy of a personal letter he had just received—no doubt by fast horseman—from Lord Grantham, the Foreign Secretary. The message read:

My Lord,

I have the satisfaction to acquaint your Lordship that a messenger is just arrived from Paris with the preliminary Articles between Great Britain and France and between Great Britain and Spain were (sic) signed at Versailles by Mr Fitzherbert his Majesty's Minister Plenipotentiary and the Ministers Plenipotentiary of the aforesaid Courts. The preliminaries with Holland are not yet signed, but a Cessation of Hostilities is agreed upon.

I send your Lordship immediate notice of this important event, that it may be made public in the City without loss of time.

                                        Grantham

But this was the Glasgow of the Tobacco Barons and for them this was no joyous coincidence. To quote from "Senex," a venerable contributor in the paper in a later generation:

Well do I remember the melancholy and dejected countenance of every person in our city at the sad news of the loss of America; and the circumstance is still fresh in my memory of my father, almost with tears in his eyes, reading to us all the first number of the Glasgow Advertiser published by Mennons in which at full length were recorded the preliminaries of peace between Great Britain and the United States.

There were no rejoicing here at this peace, no illuminations, no bonfires, no squibs or crackers, no firing of guns or ringing of bells—all was silence and sorrow.

NOTES

1. This paper is based upon materials collected in the course of preparing the Glasgow edition of Wealth of Nations (Oxford, 1976). I first published a version of Smith's treatment of the American question in the Journal of the History of Ideas (1976) and reprinted as "Mercantilist Policy: The American Colonies" in A System of Social Sciences: Papers Relating to Adam Smith (Oxford, 1979). While the present version follows the argument of the original in secs. 2 and 3, the purpose differs. This paper is simply designed to provide a statement of the contradictions inherent in mercantile policy and to review the options open to the British government in the late 1770s as seen by Adam Smith.

2. See, for example, R.H. Campbell and A.S. Skinner, Adam Smith (1982), chap. 6.

3. The role of the city is emphasized in Wealth of Nations, bk. 3, chap. 3. Subsequent references to Smith's works are to the Glasgow edition and employ the abbreviations there used, viz.:

WN = Wealth of Nations, ed. R.H. Campbell, A.S. Skinner, and W.B. Todd (1976).

TMS = Theory of Moral Sentiments, ed. D.D. Raphael and A.L. Macfie (1976).

Corr. = The Correspondence of Adam Smith, ed. E.C. Mossner and I.S. Ross (1977).

Essays = Essays on Adam Smith, ed. A.S. Skinner and T. Wilson (1975).

4. The classic account of Physiocratic doctrine is provided by R.L. Meek in The Economics of Physiocracy (1962).

5. Corr., p. 124. Letter 101, February 12, 1767.

6. Corr., pp. 328ff. Letter 302, October/December 1766.

7. Essays, p. 214.

8. Corr., p. 185. Letter 149, February 8, 1776.

9. Corr., p. 188. Letter 151, April 3, 1776.

10. Letter 153.

11. Recent references to Smith's treatment include: R. Koebner, _Empire_ (1961); D. Winch, _Classical Political Economy and the Colonies_ (1965); D. Stevens, "Adam Smith and the Colonial Disturbance," in _Essays_, above cited. There is also W.D. Grampp, "Adam Smith and the American Revolutionist," in _History of Political Economy_, II (1979).

12. WN, 2: 581.

13. WN, 2: 647.

14. WN, 1: 484.

15. WN, 2: 571.

16. WN, 2: 567.

17. WN, 2: 572.

18. WN, 2: 585.

19. WN, 2: 585.

20. WN, 2: 574.

21. WN, 1: 109.

22. WN, 1: 88.

23. WN, 2: 566.

24. WN, 2: 580.

25. WN, 2: 609.

26. WN, 2: 582.

27. WN, 1: 446.

28. WN, 2: 615.

29. WN, 2: 582.

30. WN, 2: 608.

31. WN, 2: 610.

32. WN, 2: 611.

33. WN, 2: 612.

34. WN, 2: 596-97.

35. WN, 2: 604.

36. WN, 2: 606-7.

37. WN, 2: 630.

38. WN, 2: 632.

39. WN, 2: 596.

40. WN, 2: 923.

41. WN, 2: 584.

42. WN, 2: 613.

43. WN, 2: 582.

44. WN, 2: 946-47.

45. WN, 2: 935.

46. WN, 2: 944.

47. WN, 2: 933.

48. WN, 2: 624.

49. WN, 2: 625-26.

50. The memorandum, edited by G.H. Guttridge, was first published in the American Historical Review 38 (1932/3). It appears
in a new edition, prepared by David Stevens, in Corr., app. B. All
references are to this edition.

51. Letter 140, February 13, 1774.

52. WN, 2: 623.

53. WN, 2: 622-23.

54. WN, 2: 945.

55. WN, 2: 625.

56. WN, 2: 625.

57. Corr., p. 381.

58. Corr., p. 382.

59. Corr., p. 382.

60. Corr., p. 381.

61. Corr., pp. 196-97.

62. WN, 2: 701.

63. Corr., p. 381.

64. Corr., p. 383.

65. Corr., p. 381.

66. WN, 2: 617.

67. Corr., p. 333.

68. WN, 2: 617.

69. Corr., p. 383.

70. Corr., p. 383.

71. Corr., p. 384.

72. A Letter from Governor Pownall to Adam Smith (1776), in Corr., app. A. My 1976 article, above cited, suggests that Smith's treatment of the American issue in WN was essentially an essay in persuasion.

73. Corr., p. 354.

74. The distinction between a mercantile and an imperial policy is brought out by a number of authors. See, for example, C.M. Andrews, The Colonial Background of the American Revolution (1924), and O. Dickerson, The Navigation Acts and the American Revolution (1951). See also M. Beloof, The Debate on the American Revolution, 1761-1783, 2d ed. (1960). The problems inherent in the British application of the doctrine of parliamentary sovereignty, brought out by Beloff, find an interesting if more modern echo in G. Marshall's Parliamentary Sovereignty and the Commonwealth (1957).

75. In I.S. Ross, Lord Kames and the Scotland of His Day (1972), pp. 340-41.

76. WN, 1: 267.

77. WN, 2: 622.

78. See generally TMS, "The Origin of Ambition and of the Distinction of Ranks."

79. Corr., p. 383.

80. Corr., p. 282n.

81. Corr., p. 271.

82. Corr., p. 383.

83. A. Phillips, Glasgow's Herald (1983), pp. 11-12. I am
grateful to Mr. Phillips for permission to reproduce these passages.

II

The European Response: Do We Return to the Status Quo?

BRITISH POLITICS IN THE WAKE OF
THE AMERICAN REVOLUTION

Alison G. Olson

British responses to the Treaty of Paris have been studied
from a number of angles.[1] What has not yet been attempted, however,
is an analysis of how the removal of the Americans from the Anglo-
American political community of the earlier 18th century affected
English politics. Several excellent studies, beginning with Richard
Pares's George III and the Politicians and coming down to John Connor's edition of essays in The Whig Ascendancy, suggest general
changes in British politics over the reign of George III without
attempting to link any of them to American independence.

There are, I think, at least two reasons for this. One is the
inherent difficulty of the attempt. It is far easier to look at
politics at the beginning and end of a period and spot the changes
than it is to locate the reasons for change. Further, while historians generally agree about the direction of change in George
III's reign--we talk, for example, about the growing importance of
parliamentary legislation and the "waning of the influence of the
crown," about the growth of political parties and the increasing
recognition of the need for various reforms--it is difficult to
get any agreement on the importance of American independence or,
more specifically, to distinguish the rather direct effects of
losing a war from the indirect effects of losing the United States.

Another reason is that we have tended to look upon American
colonial issues as questions of trade and administration. Having
discovered that English trade with the Americans returned to its
old channels with astonishing speed after the war, we tend to look
on the political effects of independence as little more than the
loss of a secretaryship of state and the temporary abolition of the
Board of Trade.

Recently, however, a small but growing number of historians
have begun looking at the American colonies not as subordinate
administrative units but as parts of an Anglo-American community,
functioning in many ways like the contemporary provinces in England.
We can thus ask how--if at all--their departure from the community
affected politics in the English part that remained.

There are two discrete factors to be considered here. One is
the removal of American colonial issues from British political debate; the other is the removal of American colonial administration
from the structure of British politics. Before the accession of

George III, the American colonies had generally been a stabilizing element in British politics. American issues, always potentially volatile, rarely came before Parliament and even more rarely came before the British public. American administration, providing patronage and favors helpful for holding vital British political interests in line, served generally to reinforce ministerial stability. After 1760, however, the reverse had become true. American administration became a less important part of British politics, while divisive American issues increasingly came before Parliament and the British public. This shift would have been destabilizing in any period, but it was particularly so in the 1760s and early 1770s because it aggravated other sources of instability that were also developing in British politics. The question that confronted British leaders in 1783, then, was whether the removal of volatile American issues would allow British politics to reverse the changes and return to the pattern that prevailed before the turbulent opening years of George III's reign.

We can see their concern more fully if we begin by looking at the reasons for political stability as George III came to the throne, and then examine how the American colonies contributed to that stability. One of the reasons for the longevity of ministries from the 1720s to the 1750s was that they could count on support from a number of sources that were unavailable to the opposition. The core of their support, as we have long known, included their own dependents, court officeholders, Scottish peers, bishops of the Church of England, friendly Whig magnates, and "moneyed men" of the City of London, directors of large chartered companies whose loyalty to almost any government was assured by their ownership of government bonds.[2]

Beyond these were a number of groups whose support had to be worked for continuously, interest groups whose goodwill depended not upon their settled position in English politics, but on what the ministers did for them. Lesser merchants in London and the outposts composed one such group. Processors of imported raw materials --tobacco manufacturers, cotton printers, and sugar refiners, for example--were another. Charitable associations and educational groups like the Society for the Propagation of Christian Knowledge or societies for the reformation of manners constituted another category. And among the most important of all were the church groups, both lesser Anglicans who did not have the good fortune to be appointed bishops, and Dissenters, especially Baptists, Presbyterians, Congregationalists, and, quite distant from the rest, Quakers. These groups were largely on the fringes of politics, and, except for the Anglicans, they did not have many of their own members in Parliament. But they did have pockets of electoral influence, and they also had specialized information the ministers needed in framing and administering particular policies.

While some of the groups were purely local in orientation, others were part of larger networks of communication that took in the British Isles and parts of the empire, especially the American colonies. In these networks, Americans functioned very much like other provincials in some of the loose interest-group networks that ministers had to keep mollified. The various yearly meetings of American Quakers, for example, corresponded with the London Yearly Meeting, and American Quakers in need of political favors (like exemptions from local church rates) looked to the London Meeting for Sufferings to get them.[3] Dissenting groups in the colonies corresponded with the Dissenting Deputies (a committee of representatives of Presbyterians, Congregationalists, and Baptists in and around London), asking their help in obtaining the appointment of a sympathetic governor, for example, or licensing their itinerant ministers.[4] Chesapeake tobacco growers wrote to the London merchants with whom they traded when they wanted a lighthouse built, or when they wanted parliamentary legislation to limit Scottish tobacco smuggling.[5]

These networks had varying degrees of cohesion, but however tight or loose their organization, the networks centered in London. On matters of common concern, the Londoners, who were generally richer, better organized, better informed, and able to act faster than their provincial colleagues, usually did the political lobbying for all the groups in the network. It was London leaders who passed on to ministers or the appropriate government boards their provincial colleagues' requests for help. Londoners got the prestige of associating comfortably, even clubbily, with ministers; provincials were happy enough to defer to men who did their lobbying for them.

Londoners thus served as intermediaries between ministers and provincial interests, and ministers were wise to take account of them, to give them sufficient favors to keep them from going over to the opposition. George II's leading ministers had been masters of the art. They had understood well that politics required the knack of balancing the conflicting demands of active politicians in Parliament, and with consummate tact had doled out patronage to the interests, given some of them generous contributions from the civil list, appointed sympathetic officials to handle local problems, met requests for legislation with assurances that such legislation would certainly be considered at an "appropriate time," and managed the parliamentary agenda so the time never seemed appropriate and their intentions never could be tested.

Faced by the rather awesome combination of parliamentary groups that would normally support a ministry anyway and fringe interests that could be kept quiet by favors, parliamentary opponents of the government were at a considerable disadvantage. They might get the support of the independent country gentlemen and metropolitan shopkeepers, but this was unlikely, since the country gentlemen believed that England was a homogeneous agrarian society in which everyone shared--or ought to share--ideas about the common good. There was no room in their thinking for diverse interests, and no opposition leader could have convinced these Anglican gentlemen to enter any long-run combinations with groups as different from themselves as the Dissenters or the small urban shopkeepers.[6]

Thus, the opposition ordinarily had to wait until a key issue --like the Excise Crisis, the troubles over Jenkins' Ear in 1739, or the wartime crises of the mid-1750s--temporarily aroused public opinion, embarrassed ministers in Parliament, and undermined the government's ability to keep relevant interest groups happy. On these occasions, opposition leaders could block a policy, as they did with Walpole's plan for a tobacco excise in 1733, or effect a change in the ministry, as they did in 1742 and 1756. But these key issues rarely came up, mostly because Parliament didn't legislate very much. As a result, opposition activity was necessarily episodic. It succeeded only in crises, especially over foreign policy. It was never able to build up a coalition of supporters on domestic policy. And so it stood for very little except politicians seeking office.[7]

The configuration of English politics gives us some explanation for the stability of mid-18th-century politics, and it is important to note that the configuration contained some American elements that contributed significantly to this stability. Least important was the fairly continuous membership of a handful of Americans in Parliament, men who generally voted with the ministry. Far more important, colonial administration contributed handsomely to the patronage available to ministers. From colonial councillorships to customs offices to governorships, to membership on the Board of Trade and even to the secretaryship of state, there were American jobs available--over 150 of them--for friends and relatives of active members of Parliament. But perhaps most important was American participation in interest networks, for American favors could be used by ministers to obtain the support of English groups. The favors American groups demanded were the kind it was easy for government to give without antagonizing other groups in England. Occasionally American interests needed parliamentary legislation-- or needed to block legislation that was proposed--but the most common favors they sought were the appointment of sympathetic governors and the vetoing of discriminatory colonial laws, neither of which attracted much attention from rival groups in England. American favors were thus "cheaper" than domestic ones for ministers to give, and ministers distributed them adeptly.[8]

When ministers in 1748 raised the tobacco duties for London merchants trading to Virginia, for example, they were nevertheless able to demonstrate their continued goodwill to the merchants by sending a tobacco merchant to Virginia as governor, by asking the merchants' advice about the location of Chesapeake Bay lighthouses, and by showing them copies of Virginia laws sent over for review.[9] Virginia merchants were quietly loyal to the ministries of the

1750s. As a further example, English Dissenters above all wanted the repeal of the Test and Corporation Acts, which limited their political rights. But Anglican opposition to this was so strong that ministers dared not suggest it, choosing instead to fob off Dissenters with excuses about the time being inappropriate. But the Dissenters were not left empty-handed. They were appointed to minor office and let off nuisance charges in England;[10] equally important, they were appointed to some key colonial governorships and, through pressure the ministers applied on colonial governors, were both exempted from paying taxes to established Anglican churches in the colonies and promised that Anglican bishops would not be sent to America. This, despite the continuation of the Test and Corporation Acts, was enough to assure Dissenters of the ministers' goodwill, and it inspired them to call the duke of Newcastle "the bulwark of our religion and liberties" and to "suitably prize the blessings we have of Protestant Religion and legal government and resolve to stand fast in defense of them as they are."[11]

In general, before 1760, American interests acted as a stabilizing factor in English politics, allowing ministers to develop support among some groups they might not have otherwise attracted. Occasionally the opposite happened; American questions came before Parliament only episodically before the 1760s, but when they did-- as with the Excise Crisis of 1733 (prompted by Sir Robert Walpole's proposal for an excise on tobacco), the Spanish quarrel over the Carolina/Georgia boundary, and the Seven Years' War (over defense of the Ohio territory)--they were capable of arousing public concern and unsettling the government's relations with important interests.[12] When the equilibrium was thus upset, the opposition made the most of it to create a political crisis.

In the configuration of British politics that existed when George III took the throne, therefore, American issues were occasionally disruptive, but normally they reinforced the resources by which ministers maintained a stable government. Shortly after the king's accession, however, the configuration began to shift and so, accordingly, did the American role in it. The first indication of such a shift came as early as 1763, when the duke of Newcastle, who had served for over 40 years in various ministerial capacities, was dismissed, creating among the solid core of traditional government supporters considerable confusion about whether their primary loyalty to him had been to the man or to his office. One such group was the bishops, and Newcastle took half of them with him into opposition; another was the "moneyed men," and the duke took a few of these. Along with the bishops and the financiers went some of the American merchants (like William Baker), who were becoming linked to one or another of the growing opposition factions in increasing numbers toward the end of the 1760s.[13]

Some other groups that had usually supported the government became disenchanted when the various ministries of George III's early years gave up some of the American favors by which they had courted the support of English interests. After 1765, the Board of Trade heard no English interests speaking on behalf of American requests; they reviewed colonial laws only with respect to their conformity to parliamentary law, not their effect on local interests. They took up no issues affecting religion in the colonies; when they took up questions of trade, they did not consult the merchants. No London merchant trading to America appeared at the Board of Trade after 1765. The ministers were, in effect, giving up their claims to be responsive to the demands of English interests with American connections, and hence giving up a fairly costless way of gaining their support.[14]

The defection of hitherto loyal government supporters and the loss of favors to keep loyalties from wavering were mere straws in the wind in the 1760s. They suggested on a small scale that ministers might be losing some of the resources they had used to dominate politics and remain unchallenged for long periods of time. A more important sign of change was Parliament's taking up new issues affecting all or several American mainland colonies at once; between 1763 and 1767, in fact, Parliament took up nine such issues. This was important in two ways. First, it anticipated both a general increase in the volume and importance of parliamentary legislation during the reign of George III and an enhancement of the power of Parliament vis-à-vis the king.[15] Second, it meant that interest groups that might be affected by parliamentary legislation would need to strengthen and broaden their organization. To lobby on the new American issues, a committee of London merchants was set up, representing for the first time all the London merchants trading to America and intensifying coordination with merchants in the English outposts.[16] Even the merchants found the innovation controversial.

Even more controversial was the emergence of the first public-opinion lobby, introduced in 1769 in the Bill of Rights Society and organized to fight John Wilkes's repeated expulsions from Parliament. Not only did the new lobby appeal to the general public beyond the confines of any particular interest groups, it also became so hostile to ministers that traditional "favors" could never placate it.[17] The merchants divided sharply over whether the new lobby should serve as a model for them. Some could not stomach the idea; others argued that an appeal to public opinion was the only way to defeat the American measure, and that there was no point anyway in cooperating with ministers whose policies threatened the very existence of their trade.[18] In their newly radicalized approach, they were joined by some Dissenters, who were themselves working on an appeal to Parliament for relief from political disabilities and identifying the American "cause" strongly with their own. By the eve of the Revolution, some British economic and religious interests with American connections were both fragmented and partly radicalized. They were incapable for the moment of playing a role supportive of the government.

By the time Parliament took up the Treaty of Paris, therefore, there was considerable uncertainty about the direction of British politics. Would Parliament continue to take up increasingly important issues, or had the conjunction of the Wilkerte and American issues simply created a typical episodic crisis that would quickly disappear? If Parliament continued to expand its legislative activity and ministries continued to lose the backing of both core supporters and interests, would this offer an opportunity for the opposition to pick up support and function continuously? Would it also require a long-run restructuring of interest groups affected by parliamentary legislation, so they could lobby on a larger scale and act more independently of ministers, or even in opposition to them? Would these changes, combined with the reduction in resources available to the government, ultimately create a truer balance of power between ministers and their parliamentary opponents? In short, once the Revolution was over, would the controversial innovations of 1760 to 1775 cease to be innovations at all and become instead the basis for a new configuration of politics?

If contemporaries looked to the handling of the Treaty of Paris for answers to these questions, they might well have concluded that no new configuration was likely to emerge. For the treaty was handled almost classically in the fashion of mid-18th-century politics. The active politicians were divided into three factions, the followers of Charles James Fox, Lord North, and the prime minister, Lord Shelburne. Shelburne could count on the House of Lords; in the Commons he had the support of 140 active politicians, nearly two-thirds of the independents, and the few moneyed men who remained after an earlier act prohibiting government contractors from sitting in the House of Commons.[19] His greatest weakness was among the professional officeholders: he lost some when his American patronage was cut off, though the impact of this was not felt immediately, since American officeholders were hopeful of getting other jobs. He lost still more (40 percent) because North, like Newcastle earlier, took a number of officeholders with him into opposition. Had Shelburne more actively sought a coalition with North or Fox he might have made it work; had he done so his parliamentary strength would have been unassailable.[20]

The actual negotiations for the treaty were handled very much as Newcastle would have handled them a generation earlier. Shelburne's chief negotiator at Paris, James Oswald, was adept at handling pressures from English interests who saw themselves affected by the treaty; between negotiating sessions he consulted with them. He also worked with the prewar American merchants of London who wanted a guarantee that the debt owed them by American correspondents would be repaid; "Upon the whole," wrote Oswald, "those Gentlemen seemed to be pretty well, if not perfectly Satisfied—So that if the Settlement on the subject of Debts is objected to in Parliament it won't probably be at their desire."[21] Similarly, another member of Shelburne's Cabinet, Henry Dundas, negotiated with the prewar merchants of Glasgow.[22]   Shelburne's chancellor of the exchequer, William Pitt, met with a committee of merchants (different from the prewar merchants) who desired to open up trade with the United States after the war.[23]   The secretary of state defended the treaty's cessions in India on grounds that "they were made under the cognizance and with the consent of the Court of Directors of the East India Company who certainly know their best interest."[24]

If the negotiation and ratification of the treaty were handled in quite traditional ways, so, too, were the treaty's two stipulations affecting British interests, which the Americans consistently failed to carry out. One was the Loyalist question (Article V stipulated that Congress would "earnestly" recommend to the states to restore their property and Article VI provided that they suffer no further persecution). A second was the payment of prewar debts owed to British creditors (Article IV provided that states would remove all legal impediments to their collection). On both issues, committees of Londoners, occasionally joined by provincials, lobbied the prime minister and secretary of state--calling on them, sending properly phrased memorials (and always receiving in return assurances of the ministers' goodwill), getting what favors the minister could easily give (like the nomination of consuls to America), but never getting substantial concessions. The Loyalists actually got their case before Parliament, but nothing came of it; the merchants considered going to Parliament in 1786 and then decided not to because it would raise too much "clamour."[25] A decade after the treaty both groups continued to observe a comfortable if not very productive relationship with ministers. There was little else for them to do.

That the Treaty of Paris and the issues coming from it were handled exactly as such issues had been handled a generation earlier could not have surprised contemporaries, since the first and most obvious effect of American independence on British politics was that the American questions were moved from the area of colonial policy, which was increasingly handled by Parliament, to the area of foreign policy, which was still largely the preserve of the king and his ministers. What probably did surprise them was that the younger William Pitt made it clear upon becoming prime minister in 1784 that he intended to handle all issues as they had been handled a generation before.[26] Time and again he made clear his distaste for dealing formally with broadly based lobbies like the Wilkertes and the pre-Revolutionary American movements, viewing them as deliberative assemblies and hence as rivals to Parliament. When he was considering measures to open trade with France, Pitt sent his chief economic adviser to consult separately with manufacturers of various towns, rather than recognize the manufacturers' efforts to establish a broadly based formal "Chamber of Manufacturers."[27] Pitt met informally with the London leader of the Dissenting Deputies, the Dissenters' organization, but he refused to recognize the Deputies when they created an official committee to apply for repeal of the

Test and Corporation Acts.[28] At one point, when he thought the pre-war London-American merchants might be going too far in organizing cooperative efforts with outpost merchants, Pitt sought out four individual merchant firms for consultation on American debts.[29]

Pitt expected to maintain the comfortable informal relationships with London lobbyists just as earlier ministers had done; he also expected that he could, as a general rule, count on placating interests exactly as his predecessors had also done--compromising, reconciling, granting minor favors when he could not grant major ones, and always keeping interests assured he had their wishes at heart. Observing his approach to politics, contemporaries would have concluded that removing American issues from British politics returned those politics to the pattern that had existed before 1760.

But this reaction, which could be described as an immediate British "response" to the treaty and independence, faded over the decade after 1783 as some of the indirect effects of American independence became clear. First, the Revolution eliminated the American patronage that the Crown had distributed to line up parliamentary support. It also ended the chance for Americans, who had in the past tended to support the ministry, to sit in Parliament. Second, the Revolution brought an end to the costless American favors the Crown had used to keep important interest groups in line.

Third, the Revolution contributed to a long-run increase in the importance (and volume--44 acts per year in George II's reign compared with 116 per year in George III's[30]--) of parliamentary legislation. Acts on American trade, for example, were more numerous during the 1780s than they had been in any decade before. Early in the spring of 1783, for example, Parliament considered an American Intercourse Bill. In the winter of 1784 it considered a temporary bill to allow the importation of American foodstuffs into Newfoundland. From time to time it considered customs duties on American products. And at the end of the 1780s it passed a comprehensive American-trade act embodying an earlier order-in-council that prohibited Americans from trading with the West Indies in non-British ships.

More important, the Revolution spun off several other parliamentary issues as important to British politics as American taxation had been--issues so difficult to settle that they were before the legislature for a generation or more.[31] The removal of the Americans from imperial commerce, for example, encouraged a rethinking of the basic assumptions of English commercial policy. The younger William Pitt proposed mutual tariff reductions with America, Ireland, and France between 1783 and 1786; his only success came on the French proposals, but the issues of free trade became endemic in parliamentary politics for over a century after that.[32]

A second issue, for which the Revolution was at least indirectly responsible, was the abolition of the slave trade. The Revolution split in two the old slaveholding part of the British Empire, leaving the West Indians without the support of the southern American mainland colonies; moreover, the new American constitution that went into effect in 1789 provided for the abolition of the American slave trade in 20 years. More vulnerable to attacks on slavery than they had ever been, the West Indian interests fell prey to the Abolitionist Society, one of the best-organized British lobbies in the half-century after the Revolution. In 1790, William Wilberforce introduced the first of his parliamentary motions to abolish slavery in the British colonies. From then until his ultimate success in 1833, Wilberforce's proposals for abolition were chronically before the house.[33]

Third, the combination of the departure of the American colonies from the empire and the addition of new colonies meant that the empire was no longer mainly a settlers' empire. This in turn meant that Parliament could no longer assume that most colonies should have governments modeled on the home government, with Parliament's responsibility being mainly to regulate both their commercial relationships with the home country and their contribution to imperial finance. Rather, each colony was to be governed separately with distinctive institutions, which meant Parliament had to undertake an entirely new type of imperial legislation.

Finally, the strong identification of English dissent and American Revolutionary ideas--independent American states could now serve as models to English reformers, something they could not do when their politics were shaped by British officials and restricted by British disallowances--encouraged English Dissenters to press for the abolition of their religious disabilities. Virginia's act promoting religious toleration, for example, proved to be a useful model. In 1787, 1789, and 1790, Parliament debated the first three postwar proposals for repeal of the Test and Corporation Acts; the debates were to continue until the acts were finally repealed in 1828.[34] Thus, inasmuch as free trade, the abolition of slavery, the remodeling of the empire, and the repeal of the Test and Corporation Acts were four of the most important questions to come before Parliament in the generation after 1783, the Revolution must rank as a major contributor to the growing importance of Parliament in British politics.

The corollary of parliamentary growth was the expansion of interest groups that lobbied for and against legislation. Lobbying could no longer be left to a handful of well-placed London leaders informally bartering their information and electoral support for ministerial concessions to themselves and their colleagues in the provinces. Instead, the interests were forced to develop widespread popular support so that members of Parliament would feel the pressure from great numbers of constituencies. To handle the job adequately, the men in London needed local organizers to circulate pamphlets and petitions. They needed a paid staff to keep records, copy petitions, circulate letters, and prepare articles for the press. They needed offices in which to meet people and keep files. Londoners alone did not have the resources for this: they had to call in provincial colleagues for both manpower and money.

Here they found that the American Revolution had contributed to yet another contemporary change--the growth of provincial self-consciousness. The Revolutionary period was one in which English provincial towns were growing with unprecedented speed. By the 1780s, the population and wealth of a number of them were growing faster than London's; the largest of them had their own newspapers that carried national as well as local news. New roads and canals linked these towns with London and brought them its newspapers; an evolving network of financial credit made London loans available to them and also gave them an interest in the doings of that city's financial world. No longer were the provincials isolated and pre-occupied with local affairs; no longer were they so far behind London in national news that they could not organize quickly enough to influence national affairs.[35]

Provincial leaders were thus increasingly likely to resist continued dependence upon and deference to their self-appointed spokesmen among the London lobbies. To provincials, the American Revolution represented simply the most extreme--and most successful --example of provincial rejection of London authority. When London interests sought their cooperation, the provincials were unwilling to give it unless the loose London-provincial networks gave way to more structured organizations in which provincial townsmen had adequate representation.

Here they were influenced in three further ways by the Revolution. First, the networks tying together London and the provincial interests had necessarily been loose as long as American groups were accommodated within them; the American departure left the groups free to organize along national lines. Second, the Committees of Correspondence, established by the Americans to organize public support for the Revolution, provided a model for the new lobbies. Committees of Correspondence, American style, were introduced to English politics through the Yorkshire Association beginning in 1779; Westminster and Gloucester Committees adopted the American title shortly after that.[36] When the war was over, London and provincial wig makers, hat manufacturers, calico printers, and other groups adopted the American model.[37] Third, provincial interests within the new organizations began demanding adequate "representation," by which they meant representation in national councils or meetings where strategy and demands were hammered out.[38] No longer were provincials content to let London interests serve as go-betweens, filtering their demands to ministers and the ministers' concessions back to them. Witness the tea dealers of "The Cities of London, Westminster, Borough of Southwark, the Liberty of Tower Hamlets, park adjacent, and every other dealer in town & Co," who held a mass meeting protesting that "a few individuals...have obtained an audience of the Right Honourable Chancellor of the Exchequer" and resolving "that any individuals forming private meetings or committees do not speak the sense of the trade at large."[39]

Londoners were understandably wary of demands that implicitly challenged their own leadership, made their relations with ministers more formal and less prestigious, and occasionally even threatened to take away all their flexibility in negotiations. Yet, if they were to carry weight with the government and use provincial resources, they would have to work out more ways of cooperating with the provincials. They did so largely by trial and error. Among those who experimented along these lines were the tobacco manufacturers, the General Chamber of Manufacturers, and the prewar North American merchants.

The strongest efforts--those that also reveal most clearly the difficulties of attempting to build a national organization--were made by the Dissenters. Like the Committee of American Merchants, the London Dissenters had to be prodded to work with provincial groups, in part because they were used to working with the ministry by themselves. In 1787, London's Dissenting Deputies set up a committee under Edward Jeffreys to conduct an application to Parliament for repeal of the Test and Corporation Acts. Recognizing the need for provincial support, they sent copies of their minutes to leading dissenting ministers in the provinces and called themselves "delegates from the country" rather than from London. Provincial Dissenters were not impressed: they offered virtually no help in the campaign for repeal in 1787. A year later, the Deputies made the gesture of adding five provincial members to the committee, but this was scarcely enough to convince provincials of their claim that "as a common interest must dictate similar feelings, we are confident that in general we express your sentiments whenever we declare our own."[40] So the following year, the Deputies brought six more county members to the committee and urged provincial Dissenters to set up regional boards of deputies to correspond with the London Deputies.[41] Still this was not enough. Once established, the regional committees of deputies in Birmingham and Nottingham proposed a national union of Protestant Dissenters; the Londoners had to acquiesce in the establishment of a new standing committee consisting of the 21 original Londoners and 42 new provincials with a minister from Northampton as chair.[42] The original Jeffreys committee was ultimately dissolved and the new national committee described itself as "an assembly of delegates; responsible to members in both London and the Provinces." Only when it was clear that a national union, rather than a London committee, was in charge of another application in 1790 did the provincials back up the Londoners by petitioning and by campaigning for sympathetic candidates in the parliamentary elections of that year.

Thus, American independence created new, significant, and long-sustained parliamentary issues, and the departure of the Americans from imperial interest-group networks allowed (and American examples encouraged) the development of more cohesive national lobbies. But there was yet another change in British politics to which American independence contributed—the beginning of coalitions among rival British interests incapable of uniting as long as the Americans were part of the empire. Merchants trading to the American mainland, for example, had chronically been at odds with West India planters and merchants over questions like the duties paid by the Americans on foreign sugar. Once the Americans were independent, this was no longer a British issue and therefore no longer a source of contention between the two groups of merchants, so they immediately combined to oppose the prohibition of American shipping to the West Indies. Merchants who imported American raw materials and manufacturers who processed them had long been at odds over the handling of duties on the raw materials when they were reexported. Once the Americans could no longer be required to reexport goods through Britain, the rivalry between manufacturers and merchants abated, and hat makers and fur importers and snuff makers were able to form coalitions to lobby for lower import duties. A clear example of merchants seeking coalitions is provided in the report of a committee of Glasgow tobacco merchants sent to London to lobby for the repayment of prewar American debts. In the course of their visit they wrote that "they were called upon to assist and attend the English manufacturers at the Secretary of State's office to solicit a removal of sundry obstructions that at present shut out the printed goods and other British manufacturers from Spain....They have likewise assisted in the progress of the measures now adopting for improving British fisheries and in the plan proposed for commuting the duty of salt and coals to Scotland."[43]

The American departure from the empire added slightly--though only slightly--to the development of interest-group coalitions on ad hoc issues. As this happened, the parliamentary opposition, under Charles James Fox, hesitantly began to think of putting together a coalition of interests to broaden its political base. During the 1780s, Fox may have been moving toward the creation of a pluralist opposition party. He and his friends revealed such familiarity with interest-group deliberations in some parliamentary debates that they must have enjoyed close connections with those interests. When the treaty of peace was discussed in 1783, both ministers and the opposition knew about the views of the directors of the East India Company.[44] This was perhaps not surprising, since a number of the MPs were members of the company. A far more striking example presented itself in 1785, when Fox told Parliament of the substance of the West India Committee's debates on Irish trade. Fox's supporter Alderman Newenham reported that the merchants were deterred from petitioning because they were afraid Pitt would be vindictive.[45] Two years later, Henry Beaufoy, supporting Fox on the repeal of the Test and Corporation Acts, quoted in Parliament from the minutes of two Assemblies of Dissenting Delegates.[46] Two years after that, William Brinsley Sheridan, next to Fox the leading opposition debater in Parliament, repeated firsthand there the views of tobacco manufacturers on the Tobacco Excise Bill, confessing that "he was not present at [their] meeting but he spoke upon their authority."[47]

With opposition leaders beginning to court their support, interest groups in the 1780s had new options to explore. But they, too, moved hesitantly. Since Fox's party was a parliamentary minority lacking the resources of government, it could not hope to defeat the government on issues affecting interests, unless the interests themselves mounted an extensive campaign in the press, in provincial meetings, and in Parliament itself, where they had to provide both petitions and public testimony. Interests, in other words, had to drum up popular support on particular issues in the hope that a combination of opposition MPs and those MPs whose votes were swayed by pressure from constituents would be sufficient to defeat the government forces.

Sometimes it worked. Burke exulted that the opposition was strong enough (in 1789) "to keep a majority in considerable awe,"[48] and a year later Sheridan spoke with considerable pride of the changes that the opposition had been able to effect in legislation.[49] But the support required of the interests was expensive, time consuming, and often futile; when a particular campaign was over the interests were likely to feel that they had been used by the opposition, rather than profiting from the association.

As the decade wore on and Pitt's political views began to take clearer shape, the various interests found themselves having to decide, largely by trial and error, whether they were better off continuing to support the ministry, or thinking the hitherto unthinkable and attaching themselves to the opposition. The experiences of four of them—the Old American merchants, the General Chamber of Manufacturers, the tobacco manufacturers, and the Dissenting Deputies—indicate four different ways in which interests approached the decisions and four different results.

By 1785 the Committee of American Merchants had become concerned that, despite their memorials, addresses, and interviews and their initial success in getting the question of debts included in the peace treaty, the prime minister was not working very hard to get their American debts back. Fifty-four merchants that year made a rather remarkable decision to bypass Pitt and go directly to Virginia, notifying the Assembly there that they were willing to accept repayment of their debts in seven annual installments. When the Virginia Assembly not only failed to help them but left in place a law that no debt due a British merchant could be recovered in the state,[50] the merchants pursued three other options. They prepared another memorial to the secretary of state, they "took measures to apply to Parliament," and they met more or less secretly with John Adams, the newly arrived American minister to the Court of Saint James, and with Adams's chief aide.[51] For nearly a year, from June 1785 to early April 1786, the merchants kept all their options open. But in April 1786 one option closed when the merchants decided they should no longer count on Adams for help;[52] thereafter, the question was whether they should continue to rely on ministers or pursue their own approach to Parliament. A majority of the leaders seem to have favored the latter, but they gave up on it after a year because they could not get unanimity (some merchants, like Patrick Colquhoun, secretary of the Glasgow Chamber of Commerce, opposed the application on the grounds it would "raise too much clamour")[53] and because they apparently could not arouse the interest of Fox without first inspiring public interest. So they were driven back to the prime minister, and since the matter had not come before Parliament after the debates on the peace treaty, Pitt never had to commit himself to any procedure in the public debate, and was free to string the merchants along in the best Walpolean tradition, always assuring them of his personal goodwill, but never doing very much for them. The last we hear of the merchants working as a group was in 1794, when they successfully appealed for recognition of their claims in the Jay Treaty. But it was almost a decade later, after the group had apparently broken up, that some of them got a small fraction of their debts back.[54]

Though the prewar American merchants never had a chance to work with the opposition, the tobacco manufacturers did have such a chance, and their experience showed rather clearly how indecisive both opposition MPs and interest-group leaders could be about cooperating with each other. When Pitt first proposed an excise on tobacco in 1788, they fought it by themselves, lest "by throwing themselves into the army of opposition they should bring upon themselves the ill will of government,"[55] that is, provoke harassment by the excise commissioners. The following year, however, they had changed their mind: when they sought repeal of the excise they "determined to apply to parliament through the medium of opposition wishing that their case should come before that house, and the public."[56] This time it was Fox who could not decide what to do. Lamenting that he lacked the strength to assist them effectively, he exploded that "surely gentlemen had no right to expect on every occasion, when the interests of their constituents, or some personal matter to themselves induced them to wish the measure of the minister opposed, that he, and those who acted with him, would be at their command, and ready to act as perpetual adversaries of the minister and his measures whether those measures would appear to them to be well or ill founded."[57] But one year after that, when the manufacturers tried again for repeal, Fox came around to their support, and his supporter Sheridan, speaking warmly in the manufacturers' favor, turned Fox's words somewhat more favorably to party and criticized the widely held assumption that "measures proposed by a minister were opposed of course by his political adversaries." Fox opposed the excise not because it was Pitt's measure, but because it was wrong.[58] The opposition failed, and the excise stayed on the books, but the tobacco manufacturers were moving into Fox's camp.

If the tobacco merchants and the tobacco manufacturers ended up in two different camps, the General Chamber of Manufacturers ended up dividing over Fox's attempt to bring it under his partisan banner. Early in 1785, Pitt brought in a bill establishing reciprocal trade agreements with Ireland. Several committees representing English manufacturers in various regions asked Pitt if they might speak against the bill. When Pitt refused, the committees called a general meeting and established the General Committee of Manufacturers, issuing a Declaration of Principles making clear their intention to develop political influence. They immediately petitioned Pitt to postpone the Irish bill, but Pitt refused to receive the petition on the grounds that the General Chamber was not a legitimate organization.

The manufacturers were now in a dilemma. Samuel Garbett, the Birmingham leader, was deeply offended by Pitt's response, but still felt it was improper to oppose him. Josiah Wedgwood, however, the other Midlands leader, went into open opposition and published a violent attack on Pitt in the newspapers. He also worked with Fox's associate William Eden to elicit petitions against the bill from committees of manufacturers, giving Fox the opportunity to argue that "so large a number of petitions never were presented from the manufacturers on any former occasion" and to add pointedly that "Mr. Wedgewood...and the other great manufacturers...have received from the right hon. gentleman (Pitt) every species of ill treatment that the lower or most degraded characters could receive."[59]

The combined forces of Fox's parliamentary opposition and some of the manufacturers forced Pitt to make so many changes in his Irish trade bill that the Irish Parliament refused to accept its provision. But the victory did not bring Fox the alliance with the General Chamber he had hoped for, because Wedgwood had begun to suspect that Fox had used him. Wedgwood was soon describing himself as "a man who despises party." He added that "great pains have been taken by little minded men to clothe the manufacturers with party colored robes,"[60] but that these were not their true colors. In the following year, when Pitt brought in a measure for opening up reciprocal trade arrangements with France, the older London manufacturers backed Fox in opposition to the measure because they needed protection against French competition. But Wedgwood and the Midlands manufacturers supported Pitt, so the General Chamber split over the issue, leaving manufacturers no national organization and Fox disillusioned at the failure of his first search for a base of national support.[61]

Like the other groups, the Dissenting Deputies supported Pitt when he first came to office. Fox had earlier held office in a coalition with Lord North, the Dissenters' arch enemy, while Pitt was widely thought to be liberal in his religious views. When dissenting laymen and ministers (represented in the Dissenting Deputies and the Ministers of the Three Denominations) met to discuss the best way to get Dissenters included in a law for registering births in 1785, they agreed that "the most prudent mode of conducting this Business would be to consult the persons in power, without attracting any public observation," and Pitt had complied with their wishes.[62]

When the Dissenters decided to press for repeal of the Test and Corporation Acts in 1787, they went routinely to Pitt, having reason until the actual debate to expect that he would support them and Fox would not.[63] When Pitt was forced in debate to reveal his opposition to repeal of the acts, the Dissenters, like the manufacturers earlier, divided over whether they should appeal to Fox for help. Some claimed pointedly that they should not seek "to avail themselves of party division." Edward Jeffreys, chairman of the Dissenters Aggregate Committee, wrote "this is no party business... with Administration or opposition in question the Dissenters have nothing to do."[64]

To growing numbers of Dissenters, however, Fox seemed the only hope. In 1788, Jeffreys's own committee drafted letters in favor of repeal and sent them to opposition newspapers. Jeffreys himself was sent by the Deputies to wait upon Fox and thank him for "his late and obliging intimation of his continued good wishes and proposed support in favour of the Protestant Dissenters in their application." Whereupon Fox wrote, "I have no objection to the Dissenters applying to me in any manner and I shall certainly do what they ask."[65] In December 1789, after the motion for repeal had been defeated a second time, a dissenting lawyer asked William Adam, Fox's party manager, to use the Whig organization in favor of repeal; the following month, Jeffreys, in a circular letter, announced that "the Dissenters have...resolved to pay a marked attention (in the upcoming election to those candidates who shall already have voted in their favor)."[66] (About two-thirds of their supporters were Foxite Whigs; only one or two were closely associated with the prime minister.) Pitt accused them of going further and imposing a test upon all candidates, new as well as incumbent.[67] The Deputies' association with Fox was revealed even more clearly when Fox appeared on the platform with Jeffreys at a Dissenters' rally and received nine huzzahs from the crowd before going on himself to move repeal of the Test and Corporation Acts.[68]

Fox's appearance before an interest-group rally may well have marked the most open identification of interests with parties in the 18th century. Certainly his conviction that "party could provide its members with a system of beliefs wiser than any person could singly evolve for himself" implied that one of the functions

of party was to overlap and reconcile a variety of interests.[69] By
the early 1790s, Fox was taking the first tentative steps toward
building up such a party, bringing together liberal Anglicans and
some London manufacturers and shopkeepers (particularly tobacco manufacturers)--interests that saw no hope of working with the government and some slight advantage from the publicity and parliamentary
support they got from the opposition. Pitt for his part had retained the support of the pre-1776 merchants trading to America,
the West Indian interests, most of the Anglicans, and the provincial
manufacturers--groups who thought it essential to maintain traditional relations with the minister, because their concerns were
likely to be handled by ministers rather than Parliament, because
their affairs were not popular enough to attract opposition support, because they needed ministerial patronage, or simply because
they agreed with the ministers' views. Commercial and industrial
groups, having developed at uneven rates, divided among themselves
over the merits of Pitt's economic policies. Among religious groups
the divisions were much more consistent. Religion thus became the
strongest base for party as the 19th century began.[70]

By the last decade of the 18th century, therefore, new national
interests were emerging--structured, politically specialized, and
often willing to work with political parties, occasionally even in
opposition. The permanence and pervasiveness of the parliamentary
opposition should not be exaggerated, however. At its strongest,
the party could count on only 115 consistent members (over the
1790s, it _lost_ support); thus the rivalry between the parties of
Pitt and Fox can hardly be considered on a continuum with the two-
party "system" that flourished in Victorian England. Moreover,
the "waning of the influence of the crown," the dominance of Parliament, the burgeoning influence of the provinces, the large-
scale organization of interest groups and their continuous identification with political parties--all were barely visible in the
decade after the American Revolution.

Nevertheless, it was beginning to be clear in the 1780s that
political alignments would not return to their mid-century configuration. The days were fast disappearing when active politicians,
whoever they were, all stood for more or less the same thing, and
when ministers, whoever _they_ were, could always count on support
from dependents, officeholders, bishops, financiers, a section of
the Whig aristocracy, and London interests won over by royal favors
without ever having to commit themselves on controversial parliamentary legislation. So were the days when parliamentary opponents
could be effective only during periods of crisis. A new pattern
was developing, in which ministers had fewer favors to give and little chance of avoiding parliamentary stands that cost them support
from one interest or another; both ministerial and opposition parties were becoming umbrellas for interest groups increasingly national in their orientation. Probably this would have happened
without the American Revolution. But the new parliamentary issues

raised by American independence, the provincial consciousness the
American complaints raised, and the American resources the ministers lost certainly speeded the changes along.

NOTES

1. The events immediately surrounding the negotiation and
ratification of the treaty and Parliament's response to them were
covered in a number of able papers presented at a March 1982 conference in Washington, D.C. ("Peace and the Peacemakers: The Treaty
of 1783"). The imperial response—the effect of the treaty
on British attitudes toward empire—has been covered in detail in
Vincent Hurlow's Founding of the Second British Empire, a 30-year-
old classic that hasn't yet been superseded. The domestic response,
particularly British handling of problems left unsettled by one
treaty or caused by the inability of the weak American government
to carry out parts of the treaty, is the subject of Charles Ritcheson's Aftermath of Revolution.

2. "Monarchy and The Party System," in Personalities and
Powers (London, 1955), pp. 13-38, esp. pp. 21-38; Richard Pares,
King George III and the Politicians (Oxford, 1954), p. 41; Lucy S.
Sutherland, The East India Company in Eighteenth-Century Politics
(Oxford, 1952), pp. 21-22.

3. Copies of letters exchanged between English and American
Quakers at mid-century are in the London Yearly Meeting records,
"Epistles Received," vol. 3; "Epistles Sent," vols. 3-4; and Minutes,
vols. 28-33, Friends Library, London.

4. See Alison Gilbert Olson, "Parliament, the London Lobbies,
and Provincial Interests in England and America," Historical Reflections 6 (Winter 1979): 387-96. For the New England Congregationalists, see Benjamin Colman to Samuel Holden, May 30, 1734,
Colman Mss., Mass. Hist. Soc. Presbyterian Itinerants are discussed
in Minutes of the Dissenting Deputies, February 27 and November 27,
1754 and January 29, 1755, Guildhall Ms. 2083/1, ff. 370, 380, 381,
Guildhall Library, London; Board of Trade to President of Virginia
Council, September 1, 1750, C. O 5/1366, ff. 457-62; and George
William Pilcher and Samuel Davies, Apostle of Dissent in Colonial
Virginia (Knoxville, Tenn., 1971), pp. 125-27. Carl Bridenbaugh,
Mitre and Sceptre, Transatlantic Factors, Ideas, Personalities,
1689-1775 (New York, 1962), pp. 104-5, discusses local taxation of
religious minorities.

5. Robert Cary to William Dawkins, May 25, 1728, Robert Cary
Letter Book, Va. Hist. Soc. "The Humble Petition of Several

Merchants trading to Virginia and Maryland in behalf of themselves and others," November 13, 1722, Great Britain, P.R.O., T(reasury) 1/240, f. 369.

6.   For the country gentlemen see Sir Lewis Namier, "Country Gentlemen in Parliament," in Personalities and Powers, pp. 59-77. For the country ideology and the difficulty in developing a workable idea of party, see J.G.A. Pocock, The Machiavellian Moment (Princeton, N.J., 1975), esp. pp. 483-84.

7.   Pares, King George III and the Politicians, pp. 4-5.

8.   Alison Gilbert Olson, "The Board of Trade and London—American Interest Groups in the Eighteenth Century," Journal of Imperial and Commonwealth Studies 8 (January 1980): 33-50.

9.   James Abercrombie to Gov. Fauquier, December 28, 1758, Abercrombie to J. Blair, May 3, 1759 and March 5, 1758, Abercrombie Letterbook, 1746-1773, Va. Hist. Soc.; Board of Trade to Privy Council, June 27, 1754, Board of Trade to George II, July 12, 1758 and January 18, 1759, GB, PRO CO 5/1367, ff. 45, 332-41, 346-49; Jas Buchanan, John Hanbury, and William Anderson to William Pitt, January 5, 1757, PRO 30/8/95, f. 158-59; Joseph Albert Ernst, Money and Politics in America, 1755-1775 (Chapel Hill, N.C., 1973), pp. 51-53; Alison G. Olson, "The Virginia Merchants of London: A Study in Eighteenth-Century Interest Group Politics," William and Mary Quarterly, 3d ser. 15 (July 1983).

10.   Charles F. Mullett, "The Legal Position of English Protestant Dissenters, 1689-1767," Virginia Law Review 23 (February 1937): 400;   Samuel Stenett to Duke of Newcastle, December 17, 1766, B.M. Add. Ms. 32, 978, f. 386; Benjamin Avery to Newcastle, November 16, 1749, Add. Ms. 32, 719, f. 296.

11.   Minutes of the Dissenting Deputies, May 5, 1749, London, Guildhall Ms. 3081, p. 315; Joseph Stenett to Newcastle, November 7, 1757, Add. Ms. 50, 447, f. 454; John Hodge, A Sermon Preached at Little St. Helens, London, 1751, pp. 21-22; quoted in Richard Burgess Barlow, "Citizenship and Conscience, A Study in the Theory and Practice of Religious Toleration in England during the Eighteenth Century" (Ph.D. thesis, University of Pennsylvania, 1951).   During the ministerial crisis of 1756, the Baptist leader Joseph Stenett lamented the "spirit of political madness...throughout this country...dividing the people, & if possible destroying the Administration," in Stenett to Newcastle, September 5, 1756, Add. Ms. 32, 867, f. 244.   For the appointment of a Dissenter to a key governorship, see Jonathan Belcher's thank-you letter to Lord Hardwich for the governorship of New Jersey, July 16, 1746, Add. Ms. 35, 909, f. 103, and W. Harris's letters to Benjamin Colman congratulating him on Belcher's original appointment to Massachusetts in 1730, April 29, 1730, Colman Correspondence, Mass. Hist. Soc.

12.   Arthur Pierce Middleton, Tobacco Coast: A Maritime History of Chesapeake Bay in the Colonial Era (Newport News, Va., 1953), p. 130; Paul Langford, The Excise Crisis, Society and Politics in the Age of Walpole (Oxford, 1975), pp. 28-31, 36, 45, 61, 64; Parliamentary Debate, March 9, 1738/39 (Commons), Leon Francis Stock, ed., Proceedings and Debates of the British Parliaments Respecting North America, vol. 4 (Washington, D.C., 1937), pp. 781-97, Cabinet Minutes, November 12, 1739, Add. Ms. 35, 909, ff. 82-83; King's Speech and Debate in Lords, November 13, 1755, Commons Debate, November 13, 1755, in R.C. Simmons and P.D.G. Thomas, eds., Proceedings and Debates of the British Parliaments Respecting North America, 1754-1783, vol. 1 (London, 1982), pp. 80-87.

13.   L. Stuart Sutherland, "Edmund Burke and the First Rockingham Ministry," English Historical Review 46 (1932): 46-72, and L. Stuart Sutherland, "The City of London in Eighteenth Century Politics," in Essays Presented to Sir Lewis Namier, ed. A.J.P. Taylor and Richard Pares (London, 1956), pp. 68-69. For the growing alienation of the Dissenters, see Bartholomew Schiavo, "The Dissenter Connection: English Dissent and Massachusetts Political Culture, 1630 to 1774" (Ph.D. thesis, Brandeis University, 1976), p. 17.

14.   Alison Gilbert Olson, "Parliament, Empire, and Parliamentary Law, 1776," in Three British Revolutions: 1641, 1688, 1776, ed. J.G.A. Pocock (Princeton, N.J., 1980), pp. 301-3.

15.   Parliament increased its output from an average of 44 public laws a year in George II's reign to an average of 112 public laws per year in George III's reign. John Brewer, "English Radicalism in the Age of George III," in Three British Revolutions, p. 340.

16.   "Letters of John Hancock," Proceedings of the Massachusetts Historical Society 55 (February 1922): 217-23; American Archives, 6 vols. (Washington, D.C., 1837-46), 1: 1086.

17.   Robert E. Tooney, Liberty and Empire: British Radical Solutions to the American Problem, 1774-1776 (Lexington, Ky., 1968), p. 10; John A. Sainsbury, "The Pro-American Movement in London, 1769-1782: Extra-Parliamentary Opposition to the Government's American Policy" (Ph.D. thesis, McGill University, 1975), p. 60; John Brewer, Party Ideology and Popular Politics at the Accession of George III (Cambridge, England, 1976), pp. 201-16.

18.   William Molleson to Lord Dartmouth, n.a., Dartmouth Ms. D (W) 1778/11, f. 1037, and Molleson to Dartmouth, October 11 and February 28, 1776, ibid., ff. 1560, 1663; American Archives, ed. Force, 1: 1086-87, 1107, 1219-21; London Evening Post, December 31, 1774-January 3, 1775, January 3-5, 1775; Jack M. Sosin, Agents and Merchants: British Colonial Policy and the Origins of the American Revolution (Lincoln, Neb., 1965), p. 196; The Parliamentary History of England from the Earliest Period to the year 1803, ed. William Cobbett, 36 vols. (London, 1803-36), 18: 187, 17: 195, 186-88.

19. John Norris, Shelburne and Reform (London, 1963), pp. 249-69.

20. For attempts at coalition, and their difficulties, see Shelburne and Reform, pp. 246-49. See also John Brooke, King George III (New York, 1972), p. 233.

21. Oswald's "Several observations on ye American Treaty," February 6, 1783, P.R.O. 30/8/343, ff. 37-42. The merchants memorialized Shelburne on April 18 and August 1, 1782, sent representatives to Secretary Townshend November 23 and 28, 1782, and memorialized Fox in May 1783. Duncan Campbell, William Molleson, and Jon Nutt, "A Brief State of the British Merchants and Traders for Compensation for their Losses and Sufferings by the American War," February 5, 1791, P.R.O. 30/8/343, ff. 171-74.

22. Dundas's speech, February 17, 1783, in William Cobbett, Parliamentary History of England, 25: 472. The ministry originally had been prepared to waive the rights of the merchants' creditors but changed its mind after receiving the merchants' demands: See T.M. Devine, The Tobacco Lords, A Study of the Tobacco Merchants of Glasgow and Their Trading Activities, ca. 1740 to 1790 (Edinburgh, 1965), p. 54; and Katharine A. Kellock, "London Merchants and the pre-1776 American Debts," Guildhall Studies in London History 1 (October 1974): 112.

23. "Observations of London Merchants on American Trade, 1783," ed. Edmund C. Burnett, American Historical Review 18 (1912-13): 659-80.

24. Secretary Townshend, February 17, 1783, in Cobbett, Parl. Hist. Engl., 25: 463.

25. Adams to John Jay, June 6, 1785, Adams Letter Book, Ms. 3, ff. 17-20.

26. Pitt became prime minister in large part because, as Secretary Dundas noted, "There is scarce any other political character of consideration in the country to whom many people...will not have objection." (He was not tarred with either the military defeat or the peace treaty.) See R.K. Webb, Modern England from the Eighteenth Century to the Present (New York, 1968), pp. 97-98.

27. Pitt to William Eden, December 16, 1785, Journal and Correspondence of William Lord Auckland, vol. 1 (1861), pp. 90-91. Significantly, Wedgwood had just asked Eden to do the opposite, i.e., if separate applications came from "particular places or individuals, to signify...your expectation or approbation of such applications coming from the Chamber," December 13, 1785, in The Selected Letters of Josiah Wedgwood, ed. Ann Finer and George Savage (London, 1965), pp. 289-90. See also John Ehrman, The British Government and Commercial Negotiations with Europe, 1783 to 1693 (Cambridge, England, 1962), p. 45, and Ehrman's

The Younger Pitt, pp. 206-25. Norris's Samuel Garbett, Econ. Hist. Rev., 2d ser. 10: 45, also discusses the negotiations.

28. March 8, 1787, in Parl. Hist. Engl., 26: 818-19.

29. John Adams to Rufus King, December 23, 1785, Adams Family Letters, film reel 11B.

30. John Brewer, "English Radicalism in the Age of George III," in Three British Revolutions, p. 340.

31. For a discussion of the "fresh outlook" on parliamentary activity that emerged in the wake of the Revolution, see Norman Baker, "Changing Attitudes towards Government in Eighteenth Century Britain," Statesman, Scholars and Merchants, Essays in Eighteenth Century History presented to Dame Lucy Sutherland, ed. Anne Whiteman, J.S. Bromley, and P.G.M. Dickson (Oxford, 1973), pp. 202-19, esp. 214-19.

32. For early negotiations on trade, see Charles R. Ritcheson, Aftermath of Revolution: British Policy Toward the United States, 1783-1795 (Dallas, 1969), chaps. 1, 2.

33. Patricia Hollis, ed., Pressure from Without in Early Victorian England (London, 1974), p. 27.

34. Colin Bonwick, English Radicals and the American Revolution (Chapel Hill, N.C., 1977), chap. 7.

35. Donald Read, The English Provinces 1760 to 1960, A Study in Influence, (London, 1964), chap. 1. John Money, in Experience and Identity, Birmingham and the West Midlands, 1760 to 1800 (Montreal, 1977), p. 33, points out that by the 1780s the reactions of the West Midlands were faster than those in the capital. More and more provincial businessmen were getting credit from London sources and hence were interested in the London money market. See John Brewer and J.H. Plumb, The Birth of a Consumer Society: The Commercialization of Eighteenth Century England (Bloomington, Ind., 1982), p. 229; and John Brewer, "English Radicalism in the Age of George III," in Three British Revolutions, pp. 335-37.

36. Bonurch, English Radicals, p. 141.

37. Morning Chronicle, July 8 and 28, 1784.

38. This was, of course, by no means the only definition of representation current. Dissenters sought representation in local government, Quakers and Catholics sought it in national politics, and they thought of "representation" as the right to hold office free of any disability. Opponents of parliamentary reform argued that major interests ought to be—and already were—represented in Parliament. See J.R. Pole, Political Representation in England and

the Origins of the American Republic (London, 1966), p. 443.

39.   London Chronicle and London Advertiser, July 3, 7, and 12, 1784.

40.   Bernard Lord Manning, The Protestant Dissenting Deputies, ed. Omerod Greenwod (Cambridge, 1952), p. 32.

41.   Lincoln, Political Ideas of Dissent, p. 243, 246-47, 259-60.   Differences between Londoners and provincials are discussed in Ursula Henriques, Religious Toleration in England, 1787-1833 (London, 1961), pp. 58-62.

42.   Barlow, Citizenship and Conscience, pp. 256, 272, 274-75.

43.   "American Debts," Report of Patrick Colquhoun and Alexander Brown, 1785, Minutes of Glasgow Chamber of Commerce, University of Strathclyde, Glasgow.

44.   Lucy S. Sutherland, The East India Company in Eighteenth Century Politics (Oxford, 1952), p. 409.

45.   March 28, 1787, in Cobbett, Parl. Hist. Engl., vol. 26. In the debates on the commercial treaty with Ireland in 1785, Alderman Newenham, a supporter of Fox, said that great objections to the bill existed among merchants and manufacturers "as was evident from the language held at various meetings in the City of London by men of both descriptions," March 11, 1785, in Parl. Hist. Engl., 25: 360-62.

46.   Barlow, Citizenship and Conscience, p. 232; March 28, 1787, in Parl. Hist. Engl., 26: 786.

47.   March 8, 1790, in The Speeches of the Right Honourable Richard Brinsley Sheridan, ed. "A Constitutional Friend," 3 vols., vol. 1 (London, 1842), p. 524.   Pitt told Sheridan that "if he really wished for information, to attend the Committee in his place; instead of going about the town to converse with traders he could in a more regular manner converse with them when at the bar of the House," London Chronicle, June 23-25, 1789, p. 607.

48.   Burke to William Windham, June 24, 1789, in Furber, ed., Burke Correspondence, 5: 441.

49.   April 16, 1790, in Parl. Hist. Engl., 28: 651-53. The achievements of the opposition are discussed in Archibald S. Foord, His Majesty's Opposition, 1714-1830 (Oxford, 1964), pp. 403-14.   It was fairly common for interests to meet—often at London's Half-Moon Tavern—and draw up resolutions or petitions on government measures affecting them that had recently been brought up in Parliament.   But if they did not go beyond this and cultivate further support within and without Parliament, they were not likely

to get very far. See, for example, notices of the meeting of the Cotton and Callico Printing Trade, Hat Manufacturers and Vendors of Hats, The Building Trades, Peruke Makers, and Silk Merchants and Manufacturers, Morning Chronicle and London Advertiser, July 2, 3, 8, 28, and 31, 1784.

50. Devine, Tobacco Lords, pp. 156-57.

51. Adams to John Jay, January 4, 1786, Adams Family Papers, John Adams Letterbook, film reel 112.

52. Charles R. Ritcheson, Aftermath of Revolution, p. 429. Jefferson, then in London, described a meeting of himself, Adams, and Duncan Campbell that seems to have broken up over the subject of wartime interest payments. Jefferson noted that Campbell did not come back for further discussions. See Jefferson to John Jay, April 23, 1786, in Julian Boyd, ed., The Papers of Thomas Jefferson, vol. 9 (Princeton, 1954), pp. 403-5.

53. Adams to John Jay, June 6, 1785, Adams Letterbook, Ms. 3, ff. 17-20.

54. For their continued applications to the ministry, see the letter of Molleson and Nutt to Pitt, August 29, 1792, P.R.O. 30/8/160. Their reliance on Dundas is shown by several letters in the Melville Papers, William L. Clements Library. See esp. Nutt to Dundas, March 27, 1787, Nutt and Molleson to Dundas, August 31, 1791, Milleson to Dundas, August 18, 1792, Molleson and Nutt to Dundas, August 30, 1792, and Nutt, Milleson, and Campbell to Dundas, November 30, 1791. The last letter I have found, mainly on Jay's treaty, is from Nutt and Molleson to Lord Grenville, September 17, 1794, P.R.O. 30/8/344, ff. 64-65.

55. Sheridan speech, April 16, 1790, in Cobbett, Parl. Hist. Engl., 27: 526-27.

56. They also took the unusual step of refusing information to Pitt, preferring to give it to "representatives of the people," Sheridan's speech, March 8, 1790, Parliamentary Debates, 27: 483. Their petition to the Lords, July 20, 1789, is in the House of Lords Ms.

57. Fox's speech, July 15, 1789, in Parl. Hist. Engl., 28: 245-46. Also quoted in J.A.W. Gunn, Factions no More: Attitudes to Party in Government and Opposition in Eighteenth Century England (London, 1972), pp. 235-36.

58. April 16, 1790, in Cobbett, Parl. Hist. Engl., 32: 651-54. See also Sheridan's speech of March 8, 1790, The Speeches of the Right Honourable Richard Brinsley Sheridan, ed. "A Constitutional Friend," vol. 1 (London, 1842), pp. 521-25.

59. May 12, 1785, in T.C. Hansard, The Parliamentary History of England from the Earliest Period to the Year 1803 (London, 1815), 25: 622-23.

60. Wedgwood to William Eden, June 16, 1787, in Auckland Journal, 1: 92-93.

61. The debate over the French treaty, which clearly revealed the divisions among manufacturers despite opposition attempts to paper it over, occurred on February 5, 12, 15, and 21, 1787. It is covered in Cobbett, Parl. Hist. Engl., 26: 350-59, 377-92, 432-35, 480.
An excellent analysis of the manufacturers' dilemmas, with emphasis on Garbett's position, is in John Money, Experience and Identity: Birmingham and the West Midlands, 1760-1800 (Montreal, 1977), pp. 33-49. See also J.M. Norris's fine article, "Samuel Garbett and the Early Development of Industrial Lobbying in Great Britain," Econ. Hist. Rev., 2d ser. 10 (1957): 450-60. Wedgwood's change of heart is revealed in The Selected Letters of Josiah Wedgewood, ed. Ann Finer and George Savage (London, 1965), esp. pp. 280-94.
For good general analyses of the General Chamber, politics, and Pitt's commercial policy, see W.O. Henderson, "The Anglo-French Commercial Treaty of 1786," Econ. Hist. Rev. 10 (1957-58): 104-12; Will Bowden, Industrial Society in England towards the End of the Eighteenth Century (New York, 1925), pp. 165-92; and Bowden, "The Influence of the Manufacturers on Some of the Early Politics of William Pitt," A.H.R. 19 (July 1924): 655-74. See also Vincent Harlow, The Founding of the Second British Empire, 1763-1793, vol. 1 (London, 1952), pp. 601-9, and John Ehrman, The Younger Pitt (London, 1969), pp. 206-8, 225, 253, 456, 491-92.

62. February 9 and August 4, 1785, Minute Books of the Three Denominations of Dissenters in London (Dr. William's Library), 2: 250-51, 262.

63. Ursula Henriques, Religious Toleration in England, 1787 to 1833 (London, 1961), p. 57. Just how late the Dissenters remained ignorant of Pitt's views is unclear. Sir John Trevelyan wrote March 1, 1787 that "I hear that the Presbyterians intend to propose in the House of Commons the repeal of the Test Act, with the object of distressing ministry. The opposition will adopt it to a man as a party question and many members are returned by a majority of such interest who will not dare to oppose it." Quoted in Sir Lewis Namier and John Brooke, The House of Commons 1754-1790, vol. 1 (London, 1964), p. 114.

63. The Dissenters' abhorrence of party division was claimed by Beaufoy in the debate on the motion for Repeal of the Test and Corporation Acts, May 8, 1789, in Parl. Hist. Engl., 27: 2. Jeffreys's denial of association with the opposition is in Odgers Ms. 94H (Dr. William's Library, London), and is quoted in G.M. Ditchfield, "The Parliamentary Struggle over the Repeal of the Test

and Corporation Acts, 1767-1790," Eng. Hist. Rev. 89 (1974): 559. Ditchfield notes the existence of a dissenting interest in Parliament, a majority of whose members supported Fox on the Regency bill. Fox's statement that he did not object to Dissenters' applying to him was made in a November 13, 1789 letter to Lord Fitzwilliam, quoted by Ditchfield, p. 561.

64. Fox to Fitzwilliam, November 13, 1789, quoted in G.M. Ditchfield, "The Parliamentary Struggle over the Repeal of the Test and Corporation Acts, 1787-1790," Eng. Hist. Rev. 89 (1974): 551-77.

65. G.M. Ditchfield, "The Parliamentary Struggle over the Repeal of the Test and Corporation Acts, 1787 to 1790," Eng. Hist. Rev. 89 (1974): 572-73.

66. March 2, 1790, in Parl. Hist. Engl., 28: 408.

67. Henriques, Religious Tolerance, p. 62; Loren Reid, Charles James Fox, A Man for the People (Columbia, Mo., 1966), pp. 260-61.

68. Reid, Fox, p. 443.

69. See E.R. Taylor, Methodism and Politics, 1791-1851 (New York, 1933), pp. 1-2.

THE TREATY OF PARIS AND IRELAND

A.P.W. Malcomson

In August 1782, the new British prime minister, Lord Shelburne, spoke to one of the American peace commissioners, Henry Laurens, with a loftiness of tone and of view that was characteristic of the man but perhaps unbecoming of a defeated and humbled power. "The constitution of Great Britain is sufficient to pervade the whole world," said Shelburne, who derived from this the hope that the 13 American states would "be content to be upon the same footing with Ireland." "Surely not," retorted Laurens: "The respective cases differ very widely" because Great Britain made to Ireland the timely concessions denied to America.[1] Edmund Burke, an eloquent but conservative protagonist of both Irish and American rights, dated the difference in the two cases from 1778, when he told his Bristol constituents: "I oppose the American measures upon the very same principle on which I support those that relate to Ireland. God forbid that our conduct should demonstrate to the world that Great Britain can in no instance whatever be brought to a sense of rational and equitable policy, but by coercion and force of arms."[2] Privately, Shelburne would have concurred with Burke and Laurens that the difference was wide. Like Burke, he had been most reluctant to concede to Ireland the so-called Constitution of 1782, and his employment of it in conversation with Laurens later in the year as a precedent for an autonomous United States still within the empire was a diplomatic gambit pure and simple. In December 1782, he showed how different he really regarded the cases of Ireland and America by declining to extend to autonomous Ireland the magnanimous "empire of trade" concept he had formulated for independent America. Shelburne's formula for Ireland was a commercial treaty that would provide for "a proportionable contribution to be paid by Ireland for the general protection of the Empire"--thus, a foreshadowing of Pitt's Commercial Propositions of 1785, not an echo of Shelburne's American policy of 1782-83.[3]

Prior to the late 1770s and early 1780s, the difference between the Irish and the American cases had seemed less wide. In 1770, the Dublin radical and agitator Dr. Charles Lucas was sufficiently well known, at least in New England, to be included among the British notables who were sent a copy of the Boston Town Meeting's pamphlet on the Boston Massacre.[4] In 1773, speaking of a new edition of The case of Ireland's being bound by acts of parliament in England stated (first published in Dublin in 1698 by the Anglo-Irishman William Molyneux), Benjamin Franklin commented to an American correspondent on the "new preface, shrewdly written. Our part is warmly taken by the Irish in general, there being in many points a similarity in our cases."[5] Molyneux, indeed, was of a symbolic significance that transcended the substance of his writings. Because of his pen-friendship with Locke, and the latter's incorrectly assumed approbation of The case of Ireland's being bound, Molyneux was useful in lulling the intellectual doubts of American pamphleteers, who in general "were far less worried about drifting away from George III than they were about finding themselves in opposition to...Locke." Partly because he was treated as a symbol rather than a source, Molyneux and his commentators were less effective in stating the Irish case and establishing the Irish analogy than the letters of "Novanglus," published in the Boston Gazette in 1775 by John Adams. Adams has been called "the statesman and political thinker who of all 18th-century Americans came to know the Irish constitutional problem best, occupied himself with it most and proved to have the soundest grasp of the complexities involved."[6] His conclusion was simple: The American colonies deserved the same liberties as Ireland, particularly the freedom to legislate on all matters not imperial in scope.[7]

The special relationship between America and Ireland reached its apogee with Congress's celebrated Address...to the people of Ireland. Promulgated on July 28, 1775, it was to a greater or lesser extent Adams's handiwork. Though it assigned no special role to the people of Ireland--other than the mediating role expected of all well-disposed "fellow-subjects beyond the Atlantic"--the very fact that they were the recipients of this most important official statement of the American position between the outbreak of hostilities and the Declaration of Independence "reveals the degree to which Ireland was seen as the nation most nearly sharing the American experience, and hence as that which could be addressed with the greatest confidence in a common frame of reference."[8] At about the same time, Franklin presented to Congress a visionary scheme for a legislative union of the American and West Indian colonies and Ireland, one that would operate under the British Crown but be independent of the British Parliament. What is perhaps most interesting about this nonstarter is the share of the representation accorded to Ireland--30 members in an 80-member House of Commons (the American colonies would have 41), and 10 in a 20-member House of Lords (the other 10 still had to be made peers by the Crown).[9] This was not a generous arrangement--the respective populations of Ireland and America at this time were 3.7 million and 2.4 million, with only four-fifths of the latter white and free.[10] But in light of Franklin's natural predilection for America, and of his first-hand knowledge of how unrepresentative the Irish representatives could only be, it speaks much for the specialness of the Irish-American relationship. More to the point, Congress tried to recognize the relationship in terms that would confer some benefit on

Ireland: whereas Ireland had, after some congressional soul search-
ing, been included in the August 1774 nonintercourse measures directed primarily at Great Britain, Congress in July 1775 excluded
Irish shipping from the legitimate war aims of American privateers.
(In practice, men like John Paul Jones paid little heed to this ex-
clusion.)[11] Not surprisingly, the friends of America in Ireland
responded with becoming warmth to these manifestations of goodwill
and with a sense of common cause. When the Irish parliamentary
session opened in the autumn, George Ogle, MP for County Wexford,
spoke for them all when he declaimed: "If you vote the Americans
to be rebels for resisting a taxation where they are not represented,
what can you say when the English will tax you?"[12]

Yet even in this earlier period, differences between the American and the Irish cases had plainly appeared. It was inherent in
the imperial situation that there should be colonial nationalisms,
but no one colonial nationalism. The sainted Molyneux himself had
indignantly disclaimed any resemblance between Ireland and the American colonies (admittedly poorer things in his day than they were by
the 1770s): "Do not the kings of England bear the style of Ireland among the rest of their kingdoms? Is this agreeable to the
nature of a colony? Do they use the title of kings of Virginia [the
oldest of the colonies], New England or Maryland?" American pamphleteers were also quick to disclaim the resemblance. James Otis,
Jr., who in 1764 wrote the most celebrated pamphlet against the
Stamp Act (The rights of the British colonies asserted and proved,
described as "the first notable example of citation of the Irish
case in support of American demands for redress"), pointed out that
Ireland, unlike America, was a conquered country, and then went on
to observe condescendingly that conquered peoples should nevertheless be treated as liberally as others "upon submission and good
behaviour."[13] This wounding contrast was also drawn by three
others: John Dickinson in his famous Letters from a farmer in
Pennsylvania (reprinted in Dublin in 1768, the year it first appeared in Philadelphia), the Scotsman James Wilson in his Considerations on the nature and extent of the legislative authority of the
British Parliament (Philadelphia, 1774), and finally the benign
"Novanglus."[14] This, of course, was an argument that could be
turned inside out, particularly in the cases of New York and New
Jersey; or applied equally to the displacement of the aboriginal
inhabitants of both countries--the native Irish and the American
Indians; or applied roundly, as Blackstone did, to the two countries as a whole.[15] Whatever the emphasis, it was a divisive line
of argument.

So, ultimately, was the propaganda of Irish "Patriots," including George Ogle's scare mongering about the British Parliament's
alleged intention of following up taxation of America with taxation
of Ireland. "No attempt to tax Ireland without the consent of its
own parliament was in fact made in the time of Molyneux or of his
18th-century successors, and in the period leading up to the Ameri-

can Revolution, this distinction between Ireland and the colonies was recognized."[16]   Indeed, an English pamphlet of 1778, reprinted in Dublin, advocated using the Irish precedent as a basis for ending the war, conciliating the colonies, and revamping the first British Empire:

> Ought they [the colonies] not...to contribute to the burdens of the state?...I would wish to know if we might not safely trust that such contribution would be cheerfully granted by their own assemblies, as is done by the parliament of Ireland. ...It has been said, however, that such a mode...[might make] the crown...independent of the British Parliament. But this objection, which applies equally to the case of Ireland,... could easily be obviated...by passing an act which would bind his Majesty that all acts of assembly or of the Irish Parliament containing grants of money to the crown and not appropriated to special purposes in the colony should, before they are read the third time in America or Ireland, be communicated to both Houses of the British Parliament and receive the approbation of each....[17]

Irish Patriot myth making about the Irish Parliament, its rights, privileges, and antiquity—serviceable though it was in juxtaposition to the claims of British-appointed viceroys and the British Parliament—tended only to accentuate the contrast between Ireland and the colonies. Henry Flood, for example, the principal figure in the Irish parliamentary opposition between 1760 and 1775, a man whose ancestor had come to Ireland with Cromwell, persisted in asserting the Anglo-Norman origins of his class and their Parliament.[18] Burke argued complacently in his 1775 pamphlet On conciliation with America: "Ireland has ever had from the beginning a separate, but not an independent, legislature, which, far from distracting, promoted the union of the whole. Everything was sweetly and harmoniously disposed through both islands for the conservation of English dominion and the communication of English liberties."[19] And in 1776, Burke's friend, the Irish Patriot MP Sir Hercules Langrishe, denied "that doctrines which may be applicable to [the American colonies] are applicable to Ireland, an ancient kingdom, great in its own growth, entrenched behind an ancient constitution, co-equal and coeval with England."[20]

The cases of Ireland and America were not always stated with an eye to point scoring of this kind. But at the best of times, they differed sufficiently in their ideological and constitutional background to preclude common articulation, and to arouse the suspicion that Ireland took up the American case either unthinkingly or for tactical reasons.

> The Irish had good reason to think in less radical terms [than the Americans]....By comparison, the Americans had no such wealth of precedent [as did the Irish] and so, perhaps, relied

more heavily on abstract theories of consent, contract and
Revolution principles in general....The logic of Irish ideology
therefore pointed to establishing a semi-autonomous kingdom:
American thinkers had no such clear-cut alternative....Repub-
licanism may thus have required less of a leap for the coloni-
als than for the Irish, among whom the notion hardly took hold
even during the French Revolution.[21]

Another facet of these different thought processes was

> that constitutional theory...did not overshadow other consid-
> erations [with Irish], as it did with American, thought....
> The first and inescapable problem for the Irish was to win
> control of their parliament: the subject of imperial represen-
> tation and the relationship of Ireland's domestic legislature
> to the empire was secondary....[The Americans] found themselves
> impelled into the field of imperial relationships by their
> desire to preserve the power already acquired by their local
> representative bodies.[22]

Given the Irish Parliament's preoccupation with, and success in,
establishing control over supply in the period after 1692, and the
recent renewal of controversy over the constitutional niceties of
this control (1753, 1761, and 1769), it is not surprising that "No
Taxation without Representation" was a maxim that caught the imagination of Irishmen."[23] But what is more significant is that the
only practical effect given to the maxim was the successful campaign
of 1774-75 waged by the Northern Presbyterians against the Vestry
Act of 1774, under one clause of which they were disabled from sitting and voting on parish vestries when money was being raised for
the repair of Church of Ireland churches. This campaign coincided
with the crisis in American affairs and came from that part of Ireland most responsive to American influence, the same area that had
been so responsive to the earlier lure of emigration to the New
World.[24] But it was a campaign against an act of the Irish Parliament, not the British Parliament, a parochial issue (quite literally), one bearing only nominal resemblance to the imperial issue of
"No Taxation without Representation."

Two general points are worth noting about Irish expressions of
sympathy with the American cause. First, they were "rhetorical" in
all senses of the word, made by men "under no compulsion to take
any immediate action, and so...[free to] express themselves with
the exuberance that often accompanies a lack of responsibility."[25]
Second, the utterances of many Irish politicians were directed more
at "embarrassing Dublin Castle and the British government" than
at "giving moral support to the Americans." In the striking case
of the radical opposition newspaper Freeman's Journal, "editorial
denunciations of the tyranny of George III suddenly gave way to rejoicing over the news of British victories" when Ireland's own immediate demands were satisfied with the granting of a "Free Trade"

in December 1779.[26] Cynically, but with substantial truth, Mr. Owen
Dudley Edwards has warned that "any analysis of the [Irish] pamphlet
literature of the period invites a strong line of distinction to be
drawn between the American events which helped bring about Irish
constitutional independence, and its alleged American ideological
origins. America had not shown...[Ireland] what freedom meant beyond a rhetorical expression; she had shown that Britain was weak
and could be forced to make concessions at a moment of adversity."[27]
Elsewhere, the same writer concludes: "Irish publicists were much
more concerned to use the Revolution for their own ends than to
respond to it." Perhaps this is an unkind way of endorsing Professor Palmer's aphorism that "people are influenced in ways to which
they are already susceptible."[28]

The ideological and constitutional differences between the
cases of Ireland and America were compounded by conflicting and
often inverted differences in the political realities of their situations. Depite all the Hibernian hyperbole to the contrary, the
Irish Parliament had always been "wholly dependent for its existence
on English power." And, since its character and compositon had been
crucially altered in the 17th century, and its last constituency
actually enfranchised as late as 1683, it was not so very much more
venerable than the assemblies of the American colonies, all but one
of which (Georgia's, founded in 1732) were of 17th-century foundation.[29] That there were 13 colonial assemblies and only one Irish
Parliament gave some practical preeminence to Ireland, as did the
fact that the Irish Parliament was made up of the traditional English components of king, Lords, and Commons. In the Declaratory
Acts of 1720 and 1766 (the latter modeled on the former), Great
Britain had asserted its right to legislate for Ireland and America,
respectively. Of some 250 British acts passed between 1720 and
1782 and in some way or other binding on Ireland, however, "only
about a dozen...can be regarded as new, special legislation imposed
on Ireland in the interests of Britain, while in America's case the
right enunciated in the 1766 Declaratory Act was put to more purposeful imperial use. Moreover, even so purposeful an imperialist (and
mercantilist) as Charles Jenkinson, first earl of Liverpool, admit-
ted that "the establishment of a parliament in Ireland precluded
Great Britain from taking that kingdom," while the 1766 Declaratory
Act demonstrably included the right to tax America.[30] With the
short-lived exception of Virginia in the late 1670s and early 1680s,
there existed in the constitutions of the American assemblies no
equivalent of the celebrated "Poynings' Law" passed by the Irish
Parliament in 1494; but by the 1770s, Poynings' Law no longer
amounted to any significant curb on the calling of that parliament
or on its legislative initiative (though it still greatly circum-
scribed the House of Commons', and especially the House of Lords',
freedom to amend legislation). It was also a more flexible agency
of imperial control than the colonial governors and the British
Privy Council's powers to veto and disallow measures of the colonial
assemblies.[31]

As for the tripartite relationship between parliament/assembly, privy council/council, and viceroy/governor, however, Irish constitutional arrangements were (in the opinion of Francis Bernard, governor of Massachusetts, 1760-70) so much more conducive to imperial control than American ones that they were a "perfect model" for what the government of Massachusetts ought to become.

> When compared to Ireland's lord lieutenant, the governor of Massachusetts was almost powerless....The lord lieutenant of Ireland had to answer to the British cabinet; the governor of Massachusetts had to answer to the local council...[which] was not appointed by the governor....Rather, it was elected each year by the lower house of the assembly [the council itself constituting the upper], which in turn was elected by the people...in town meeting....Through election of the council [the assembly] exercised much control over the executive, while the Irish Parliament had none...[and until 1768 was] subject to no septennial act [and to no place act until 1793]....

In the sphere of law enforcement, imperial authority in Massachusetts was on an even more disadvantageous footing than in Ireland:

> The governor could not appoint...[or] remove without the consent of the council any judge or justice of the peace, even for neglect of duty...[whereas both held office during pleasure in Ireland, and the former were often non-Irishmen]. Without the councillors, the justices of the peace and the grand jurors, the rioters who made Boston famous might have stayed off the streets....To act against crowds, the army needed directions from a civilian officer, or [it] could not act at all: the colonial governor would not do....[Under the Irish Whiteboy Act of 1765], a single Irish magistrate, acting on his own suspicion, was invested with more arbitrary power than was possessed by the entire government of Massachusetts Bay.[32]

Massachusetts was not colonial America. But it was not altogether untypical. Virginia, an equally important colony in the making of the American Revolution, possessed similarities. The governorships of Connecticut and Rhode Island were actually elective. And in other colonies where the constitutional and theoretical powers of the governors were autocratic, politics were characterized by "a radical reduction of the actual power...exercised by the executive, a reduction accounted for by the weakness of the so-called 'influence' by which the crown and its ministers in England actually managed politics in that country."[33] Though the situation varied from colony to colony, it is fair to conclude that "the colonial governors lacked either coercive powers or the patronage to build strong bases of local support," and "often found their tenure dependent on alliances" with local interest groups. "Before 1776, the Americans had become almost completely self-governing."[34]

If this was the reality, it was not the reality perceived at the center of imperial power, the British government and Parliament. Herein lay a difference between Ireland and America far more important than ideology, constitutions, and even the practical basis of power: Ireland was so close to the mother country that British governing circles had more knowledge of its circumstances and respect for its sensitivities than they did for America's. Dublin, the second city of the empire, meant something--and might even be known to--members of the British government, at a time when large parts of England itself were terra incognita. Many influential Englishmen were linked to Ireland by family connections and land-ownership, and, together with Anglo-Irishmen constantly or partly resident in England, constituted an effective "Irish lobby" at Westminister. America "simply did not have an absentee elite resident in London," with one or two exceptions like the sixth Lord Baltimore and the third Viscount Weymouth. Baltimore, the absentee proprietor of Maryland, though resident in England, was without influence there, thanks to the disreputability of his character. Weymouth, the last of the aristocratic English proprietors of North and South Carolina (the rest having sold out to the Crown in 1744), was a member of the British Cabinet when he inherited his million American acres in 1776, by which time it was too late.[35] Moreover, the species of English politician that held high office in Ireland was much more influential than that in America; after their Irish term of office was over they had a natural bias toward crying up the difficulties of the Irish situation to magnify their own achievements or excuse their shortcomings.

The very fact that many high political, administrative, and judicial offices in America, including some governorships, were held by Americans--and that no Anglican episcopate was ever set up there --meant that the British ruling class had a smaller vested interest in America's prosperity (and above all tranquillity) than it did in Ireland's. Not even the duke of Newcastle in the period 1724-39 contrived or sought to exploit American patronage for political ends. Undoubtedly, the British ruling class's vested interest in America was increasing as the 18th century wore on, but not by the leaps and bounds of the vested interest in Ireland. The period 1714-c.1775 saw the maximum infiltration of Englishmen (and some Scots) into Ireland's civil and ecclesiastical patronage. In peacetime, most of the officers of the British Army were quartered, if not actually in Ireland, at least on the Irish establishment. At all times, there were more absentee placemen and pensioners on the civil establishment of Ireland than on that of America, partly because the medieval origins of the Irish administration afforded greater scope for modern sinecurehood, and partly because the American bureaucracy, though on the increase, also had an increasing range and volume of responsibilities to discharge.[36] Thus, when a retirement provision had to be found for Governor Bernard of Massachusetts, it was on the Irish, not the American, revenue establishment that he was placed. John Dickinson in his Letters from a farmer had warned his fellow Americans of the "pensions...purloined out of the national treasure of Ireland under the mask of salaries annexed to public offices useless to the nation, newly invented for the purposes of corruption"; and the 19th-century Irish historian W.E.H. Lecky pointed out: "The example of Ireland, with its 'hereditary revenue, the scandalous pension list, the monstrous abuses of patronage,' was always before...[the Americans'] eyes,' and they were quite resolved not to suffer similar abuses in America."[37] Irish eyes were hardly smiling at the prospect either. But with hindsight it is possible to view these English incursions into the patronage of Ireland as a form of insurance.

At the level of high politics, too, British and Irish affairs were considerably intertwined: the reign of a lord lieutenant was likely to be terminated by the fall of the British government that had appointed him. This was especially true during the political struggle that went on in Ireland in the period 1753-56, because different factions in Ireland were supported (or were supposed to be supported) by different components of the British government. British and American factions, too, had made common cause and proved capable of concerted action during the whole period 1689-1714 and, illusorily, in 1732-33 and the first half of the 1750s. But such concert was largely a thing of the past, and in any case had never quite paralleled the Irish situation of 1755-56, when the lord lieutenancy was held by the fourth duke of Devonshire, a major figure in British political terms, whose success or failure in Ireland had major implications for the balance of power back home.[38] In essence, Irish politics were seen in Britain as an extension of home politics, not just as the politics of Britain's closest colony. American politics had ceased to possess—if they had ever possessed —this dimension.

It was also important for the future that the Irish Parliament had successfully shown its teeth in 1753-56 on the eve of "the Great War for the Empire": from 1764 to 1774, when the dominant imperial issue was how to pay for the defense and administration of the new parts of the empire acquired in that war, Ireland was treated with a degree of conciliation and cajolery that was not vouchsafed to North America.[39] With Ireland, like the rest of the empire, such moves to tighten imperial control derived not from long-range government policy, but from the reactions and initiatives of individuals (in Ireland's case, the fourth Viscount Townshend, lord lieutenant, 1767-72, and elder brother of Charles Townshend of "Townshend Duties" fame). Ireland, however, seems to have been exempted from a subtler trend of imperial administration—the increasingly legalistic, standardizing, even Anglicizing approach Britain was adopting toward the rest of the empire, the same approach that as early as the 1730s and 1740s had inclined some Americans "to think of parliament as an English institution rather than an imperial one," and had started in some of the American colonies "a shift in orientation from the imperial centre to the local electorate."[40]

Ireland thus enjoyed a unique combination of advantages in its relations with the mother country. On the one hand, it possessed its own Westminster-style parliament, near enough and "restive" enough to command attention; on the other, it was "virtually represented" at Westminster itself by an Anglo-Irish, absentee-landowning lobby at least as effective as the East and West Indian lobbies, and much more effective than the North American lobby in the crucial period 1764-74.[41] The Irish lobby was of course liable to be overborne by one still nearer home, the English merchants, and precisely this happened in 1778 over the first batch of commercial concessions held out to Ireland by Lord North. But it is the comparison with other colonial lobbies that counts, and in this connection it is significant that the Rockingham Whigs, who formed the core of both the agitation against the proposed 1773 tax on the rents of Irish absentee landowners and the opposition to the American war, were successful in the former and unsuccessful in the latter.[42] It is also significant that the first secretary of state for the colonies, Lord Hillsborough, himself a member of the Anglo-Irish colonial elite (though peripatetic rather than absentee, and certainly not a Rockingham Whig), took a West British not a colonial view of Ireland, and was obsessive in his advocacy of a legislative union between the two kingdoms. Amusingly, his disregard of whatever parallel there was between Ireland and America gave Franklin a chance to score conversation points on him when they met during Franklin's Irish tour in 1771.[43]

The other major difference between Ireland and America was that Ireland possessed a colonial elite, a small, socially and denominationally exclusive Anglo-Irish ascendancy; yet America, with the marked exception of New York and Virginia, was a "relatively classless" society. In the late colonial period, some parts of America--"the cities and long-settled coastal areas--were becoming old societies, their demographic and social patterns now bringing them nearer to [the] Old World," and "the long-term tendency seems to have been toward greater inequality, with more marked class distinction...." But "the effect of the Revolution was to reverse these trends, at least temporarily," with the result that one distinctive feature of federal America in the 1790s was that it "simply lacked a national governing class, that is, one that had intermarried across state boundaries."[44] This governing class was one of the few things Ireland did not lack. To Franklin, apostle of the "happy mediocrity" (by which he meant middle class) of Pennsylvania, the striking feature of the social structure of Ireland (and Scotland) was the absence of such a middle class, the extremes of wealth and poverty, and the small proportion of the population in enjoyment of the former:

In those countries, a small part of society are landlords, great noblemen and gentlemen, extremely opulent, living in the highest affluence and magnificence; the bulk of the people tenants, living in the most sordid wretchedness in dirty hovels

of mud and straw and clothed only in rags. I often thought of
the happiness of New England, where every man is a freeholder,
has a vote in public affairs, lives in a tidy, warm house, has
plenty of good food and fuel....I assure you that in the possession and enjoyment of the various comforts of life, compared
to these people [the peasantry of Ireland and Scotland] every
Indian is a gentleman....[45]

Modern research has softened the bleakness of this picture in some
respects. It has suggested that, even for the Irish peasantry,
there were glimmers of prosperity in the second half of the 18th century, though these were subsequently dimmed by population explosion
and by the post-1815 agricultural depression.[46] It has shown that
the Irish practice of perpetuity leasing somewhat obscured the distinction between landlord and tenant, and that middlemen, tradition-
ally the carpet-bagging villains of the agrarian piece, sometimes
fulfilled the function of a healthy yeomanry.[47] Above all, it has
suggested that the Anglo-Irish ruling elite included men of intelligence and constructive ideas (Gaelic revivalists as well as agricultural improvers) who do not suffer by comparison with the scions of
other European aristocracies; that as a class it was fit for more
than carrying claret to a chamber pot, being composed in general of
men who were better intentioned, though with less freedom of economic action, than has hitherto been appreciated; and that it was
not a hermetic elite, but was penetrated in this period by a number
of arrivistes, two of whom owed some or all of their fortunes to
the American war. The first was William Hare, a Cork provisions
merchant who purchased, among other landed properties, the Kerry
estate of Lord Shelburne's cousin (third earl of Kerry) and who
died earl of Listowel; the second was Henry Bruen, a suspected em-
bezzler of public money "who as deputy-quarter-master-general in
America...amassed ₤400,000" and who subsequently acquired large
estates and considerable political influence in Ireland, as an insurance against prosecution in Great Britain.[48]

If the Anglo-Irish elite was rather more broadly based, however, and a good deal more able and more amiable than used to be
thought, these attributes served only to make the class all the
more effective as a brake upon Irish revolution in the American
Revolutionary era. This seems to have occurred even to the enthusiastic and overoptimistic Lafayette. Writing to Franklin at the
beginning of November 1779--that heady time when the Irish Parliament was clearly out of control and the Volunteers of Ireland,
formed in localized units as a police force or home guard to support
the regular army in the event of French invasion, had turned to
politics and were stiffening the resistance of Parliament--Lafayette
still had the sense to observe: "I am not very found [sic] of seeing dukes and other lords at the head of the business. Nobility is
but an insignificant kind of people for revolutions. They have no
notions of equality between men; they want to govern; they have too
much to loose [sic]. Good Prebiterian [sic] farmers would go on
with more spirit than all the noblemen of Ireland."[49]

86

The "Prebiterian farmers" were not ripe for revolution in 1779, but it still required a high degree of flexibility (and some dissimulation) on the part of the noblemen to superimpose their position of hereditary leadership on an ostensibly democratic organization like the Volunteers.[50] In this respect, the temporary political eclipse of the less flexible or the stupider among the elite speaks volumes for the achievement of the rest.[51] This achievement consisted in extorting from the hard-pressed British government those concessions that benefited the elite--first, Free Trade in 1779-80, which opened to Ireland hitherto closed branches of trade with foreign countries and the British Empire; second, the Constitution of 1782, which made the Irish Parliament legislatively and judicially independent of the British and left the disapproval of the king, exercised on the advice of his British ministers, as the only restraint on its legislative freedom. In 1783-84, when measures were mooted that would not have redounded to their advantage (parliamentary reform, for one, and a crude protectionism that would have brought British economic reprisals), the elite disassociated itself from or helped to "perplex" this more popular, or middle-class, aspiration.[52] Perhaps Dr. David Doyle is too charitable when he describes their attitude and the contrast between it and that of the "relative conservatives" in the American Revolution:

> The Patriots realised, like their American counterparts, that some form of nationalism was vital to securing their position amongst an aroused people, as to pressing their claims against Britain; but it was a nationalism to be defined from the top down, a strangely artificial though not insincere product. Instead of reconciling fastidious gentlemen to the rising place of their plainer fellow-countrymen in politics, as did the nationalism of Washington and [John] Jay, it sought to reconcile ordinary men to the idea that they should gracefully withdraw from politics, and leave it to the gentry who knew what was best for the nation.[53]

The elite maintained their position--at best paternalistic, at worst monopolistic--not just because of their own adroitness, but also because "Ireland...was...a society whose central characteristic was sectarian conflict such that we should speak of a caste system between Protestant episcopalians, Presbyterians and Catholics."[54] At a superficial level, the religious question stood on similar footing in America and Ireland in the 1760s and early 1770s: "The American colonists found the danger from French Canada removed just about the time the Irish Protestants were ceasing to fear a Catholic rising."[55] But this very analogy both makes and misses the essential point, that "popery" for the Americans had been an external threat--gone except for its utility as a stick with which to belabor the British government or native whipping-boys like Thomas Hutchinson--while in Ireland it remained for all Protestant Irishmen an immediate and potent domestic enemy. Within America, "Maryland was the only colony with a substantial majority of Catholics"; and, though it is now clear that many Irish Catholics (perhaps as many as 120,000) emigrated to America before 1776, they did not tend to retain a separate Irish and Catholic identity, and were therefore not regarded as a sinister infiltration.[56]

Within Ireland, Catholics constituted well over three-quarters of the population. They were, not surprisingly, a far from homogeneous body. Their social leaders--the surviving gentry, the middle-class merchants and graziers, and the churchmen--professed and probably felt loyalty to the established order in Ireland (the British government and its representatives in Dublin Castle rather than the Irish Parliament). The gentry in particular took the lead in staging demonstrations of loyalty and in much-publicized attempts to raise soldiers to fight against the Americans. Both efforts contributed materially to obtaining the Catholic Relief Act of 1778.[57] The motivation of the great mass of Catholics is harder to fathom, though they were probably not as apolitical as many have thought. It is obvious that the activities of the Catholic leadership could not but arouse both fear and resentment in most Protestants; and it has recently been suggested that "Protestants probably had a better understanding of...the sub-culture [of the Catholic rank and file] than they are usually credited with...."[58]

Whether from prescience or paranoia, Protestants could not view the American Revolution in anything but the refracted light in which Catholics saw it. The Northern Presbyterians did not number religious toleration among their virtues (as their Scotch-Irish brethren showed when they gained control of the state government of Pennsylvania between 1776 and 1790);[59] and in their propaganda against the Quebec Act of 1774 and the subsequent (illegal) recruitment of Irish Catholics to fight in America, they had expressed themselves not just as pro-American but against popery and its alleged concomitant of arbitrary government.[60] They saw the same combination in the Catholic Relief Bill of 1778, and opposed it in the Irish Parliament through their usual Church of Ireland spokesmen (Hercules Langford Rowley, MP for County Meath; James Stewart, MP for County Tyrone; and James Willson, MP for County Antrim).[61] Later in 1778, when the Americans succumbed to popery and arbitrary government by allying with France (and John Paul Jones made his celebrated descent on Belfast Lough), the Northern Presbyterians flocked to join the Volunteers, who continued to draw their inspiration and a disproportionate amount of their numerical support from the North and who remained (apart from a flurry of Catholic participation in 1779) overwhelmingly Protestant until the days of their decline, beginning in 1783. This coincidence of pro-American and anti-Catholic sentiment is also to be found among the Patriots in Parliament, including Henry Grattan himself, who emerged as the leader of the group and one of the opponents of the Catholic Relief Bill of 1778. A much more prominent opponent, however, was Sir Edward Newenham, MP for County Dublin, a regular correspondent of Washington's (whose villa outside Dublin contained an "American room" or shrine

that gave "much satisfaction" to the widow of General Richard Montgomery when she visited Newenham in 1789).[62] The 1778 bill, though
it related nominally only to the Catholics' position as tenants and
landholders, actually raised a major political issue: if the Catholics were to be permitted to hold land in freehold, they would be
given, ipso facto, indirect electoral influence through the votes
of the Protestant freeholders on their properties. It was politically sensitive on other counts as well. It followed immediately
on Sir George Savile's act for the relief of the English Catholics,
and was therefore liable to the objection that the denominational
demography of Ireland was too unalike for English precedent to be
appropriate. Moreover, it was carried only because the British
Privy Council made full and provocative use of its powers under the
Poynings' Law, deleting an Irish amendment benefiting the Presbyterians and inserting an English amendment allowing the Catholics
to hold land in freehold. In view of this almost direct challenge
by the British government to the political monopoly of the Anglo-
Irish elite, it is at least plausible that an aristocratic Protestant backlash was responsible for winning the Constitution of 1782.

Seen in this perspective, the noblemen of Ireland were not so
much "an insignificant kind of people for revolution," nor a brake
on a revolution that might have occurred anyway. They were the
engineers of a small, successful, conservative revolution of their
very own. Their mistake was in keeping it to themselves; indeed,
their only concession to the Northern Presbyterians and other Protestant Dissenters in 1780 (a concession aborted by the British
Privy Council in 1778 and withheld from English Dissenters until
1828) was the repeal of the Sacramental Test formally excluding
them from holding offices of trust or profit under the Crown.[63] In
the short term, the mutual animosities of Dissenters and Catholics
made it possible for the Anglo-Irish elite to disregard both, and
these and other internal animosities split the Irish parliamentary
reform movement in 1783-84, rendering it harmless.[64] In the longer
term, however (as John Adams, in spite of remoteness from Irish
events, may dimly have understood),[65] the permanence of the new
constitution could not be guaranteed without letting Dissenters,
Catholics, or both share in its advantages. In particular, it might
have been foreseen that the British government would be less disposed to regard the Anglo-Irish elite as West Britons--as "one
description of Irishmen"--and would renew their overture of 1778
to another description of Irishmen, the Catholics, the more so when
prompted by the precedent of representative institutions granted
to French Catholic Lower Canada under the Canada Act of 1791.[66]
As is well known, "the loss of the American colonies...clarified
and stimulated the transfer of British interest and effort to the
Far East, a process already noticeable for some two decades before
the war."[67] There may have been a psychological, as well as an economic, impulse behind this transfer, however. "India was the imperial problem most successfully confronted by parliament: no British settlement was involved, and all authority was ultimately vested

in London. Britain failed disastrously in America and Ireland, where permanently resident populations of British origin could claim in their countries of settlement the liberties which they attributed to the mother country."[68] From the point of view of the British population of Ireland, or at least the Anglo-Irish elite, the effects of the American Revolution were twofold and short-lived. They got the opportunity to extort from the British government a constitution to their liking. And they got a little time to enjoy it, at least until the British government recovered its nerve,[69] or, as it turned out in 1792-93, found that confrontation with the elite was less scary than the danger inherent in the status quo.

The processes of waging war and making peace only accentuated the existing differences between Ireland and America, particularly (as far as Ireland was concerned) after America entered into alliance with France in 1778 and (technically) into cobelligerence with Spain in 1779. As Thomas Day, an English pamphleteer who believed Great Britain should recognize the inevitability of American independence and thus end the war, pointed out in 1782:

> It must appear evident that no conclusion whatever can be admitted from the situation of the Irish to that of the Americans, excepting that a weak and oppressive government will produce similar effects in every part of its dominions. The Irish have obtained everything they demanded..., and they now declare themselves, as they have every reason to be, contented with the concessions of government. They have never voted themselves independent, never entered into foreign alliances, never seen their country ravaged or themselves proscribed under the pretence of restoring constitutional liberty and happiness. There can be little doubt that the half of these concessions offered to the Americans when they petitioned in the year 1775 would have preserved their union with this country inviolate....[70]

For the Americans, concern for Irish affairs had always been understandably self-interested:

> [Americans]...saw that events in Ireland could influence British and European Ministers in their attitudes to the British colonies in America, or that those events might divert British energies from whole-hearted absorption in the American struggle....If only because the root causes of American disaffection from Britain were in many respects provincial, it was to the Americans' moral advantage to appear as citizens of the world....It was not enough to cite Ireland: the Americans demonstrated an anxiety to surpass British mastery of Irish questions....[71]

By 1783, neither strategy nor a sense of provincial inferiority was a consideration that carried much weight on the scale of American attitudes toward Ireland. Americans had some reason to accuse the Irish of "too much of a disposition to be satisfied," as Alexander Hamilton sourly commented in May 1780 on the effusiveness of Irish gratitude for Free Trade.[72] The failure--under circumstances of suspected perfidy, proven bribery, and farce--of Lord Carlisle's peace proposals to America in 1778 contrasted sharply with the acceptance, or rather the extortion, of a broadly similar scheme of legislative autonomy by Ireland in 1782.[73]

By then, of course, not many Americans would have been sufficiently interested in Ireland to have drawn the disparaging conclusion that Ireland had grasped at what America had disdained, though some leading figures--Owen Dudley Edwards suggests John Adams, John Dickinson, Franklin, and Washington--retained an interest in and regard for Ireland for its own sake. In Washington's case, this seems to have been tempered by a growing appreciation that the Irish nation for which his correspondent Newenham spoke was one from which Catholics and (though this was not for want of trying by Newenham) Protestant Dissenters were still effectively excluded. It was a nation contrasting strikingly with post-Revolutionary America, which had witnessed "the first comprehensive enhancement of the status of Irish Presbyterians and of Irish Catholics within the English-speaking world...."[74] Certainly, if numbers alone are decisive of such things, the Irish in America ought to have had great sway in the councils of the new republic; at the end of the Revolutionary period they numbered between 350,000 and 450,000 out of a total white population of some 3 million, a considerably higher proportion than was to be attained in the 19th or 20th century. In fact, their influence was small in proportion to their numbers. Many of them had been raised by service in the armies of the Revolution to respectability, but hardly to influence. In general, the military contribution of the Scotch-Irish has been exaggerated (mainly because of the propaganda or wishful thinking of the contemporary British authorities), and the contribution of the Catholic Irish, like their contribution to the manpower of Britain's own Army and Navy, must have been economically rather than ideologically motivated.[75] Moreover, many Irish Americans fought against the Revolution. Witness the prowess of the Volunteers of Ireland, a Loyalist provincial corps that was raised by Lord Rawdon (himself the heir to an Irish peerage and estate) and was more familiar to Americans than the organization of the same name back in Ireland. Witness the number of Loyalist claimants for compensation after the war who mentioned their country of origin. Almost a quarter said Ireland.[76] (This last consideration enhanced John Adams and Benjamin Franklin's argument that America's treatment of the Loyalists was justified because Irish Catholics who had backed the losing side in the 1640s and the late 1680s had been similarly dispossessed.[77]

In any case, even if the Irish Americans had been far more influential during and after the Revolution than now seems to have been the case, it would still have been contrary to the whole tenor of U.S. relations with European powers in the post-1783 period for that influence to be reflected in American foreign policy. This was partly because American standing in Europe was very low between the Treaty of Paris and the establishment of the federal government in 1789. As a French sympathizer warned in 1784, this was bound to remain so "till you order your Confederation better, till you take measures in common to pay debts which you contracted in common, till you have a form of government and a political influence."[78] It was also partly because most Americans had been only too happy to pocket their independence and run from the further pollutions of European politics. This process is both particularly visible and particularly striking in Franklin's case. Until 1775, Franklin had been distinguished among Americans for the breadth of his imperial vision. Of all prominent Americans, he might reasonably have been expected to be most active and enduring in his sympathy for Ireland. After all, he was one of the few to know Ireland at first hand and to appreciate the social dimension of the Irish question. As late as October 1778, in An address to the good people of Ireland on behalf of America, whose main object was to serve the strategic objectives of the moment and to discourage a premature uprising in Ireland, Franklin took the time to express "the cordial concern that Congress takes in everything that relates to the happiness of Ireland." Yet by 1782, Franklin, for all his internationalism and alleged Francophile sympathies, was eager to extricate the United States from European alliances after it won independence, and he proved single-minded and none too scrupulous in playing European politics for the particular national advantage of the United States.[79] Franklin's crowning achievement on behalf of his country, the French alliance, had not only exorcised the ghost of the old empire and alienated Protestant Ireland from America; it had also made it difficult for Americans to continue to advertise their revolution as a model for export. "Strident calls for the overthrow of monarchy were, to say the least, inappropriate when French arms and men were sustaining the bid for American independence." In any case, exporting revolution was inconsistent with American convictions of being a chosen people, their country an asylum for the less fortunate. One American preacher, in a discourse inspired by the Treaty of Paris, "spoke of the successful rebellion as 'a principal link' in a larger 'grand chain of providence....'" But, insofar as its external influence was considered at all, the more usual claim was that it had "'softened the rigours of tyranny [in Europe], and taught even kings to revere the great laws of justice and equity.'"[80] The Constitution of 1782 was one such softening of the rigors of tyranny. Franklin himself was typical of this new emphasis in that his Irish pamphlets of the 1780s were exhortations to emigrate to--not emulate--the United States.[81]

America's comparative indifference to Ireland, at least on the
political level, was more than reciprocated. As has been seen, Ireland accomplished its elitist revolution (embodied in the concession
of free trade in the winter of 1779-80 and the Constitution of 1782
in the spring of that year) before the signing of the preliminary
articles of peace in January 1783 and the definitive treaties that
September; further, it had shown "too much of a disposition to be
satisfied" with both. At one point, the progress of the negotiations in Paris crucially affected the direction of British policy
toward Ireland. In November 1782, the lord lieutenant of Ireland,
the second Earl Temple, urged a dissolution of the Irish Parliament
and a general election. This, he hoped, would liberate Parliament's
members from Volunteer influence and detach the "aristocracy" from
the "middling and lower orders" (in effect, the same result the parliamentary reform issue was soon to produce almost without effort
on the government's part). The prime minister, Lord Shelburne,
while not approving this specific measure, thought a tougher line
should be taken, and could with safety, as soon as news of the conclusion of peace arrived from Paris. "Such an event would throw
the Volunteers upon their backs," he said, "would bring back the
army to that country and to this, and also would bring the fleet
into the Channel." Bad news from nearer home preceded the anticipated good news from Paris, however. The result was not gunboat
politics but a further concession to Irish demands, this time the
safely nominal concession in April 1783 of the so-called Renunciation Act.[82] When news of the signing of the preliminaries reached
Dublin, there was reportedly rejoicing. But it was not of a politically fraternal nature. It derived from economic expectation—notably about the resumption of exports of linen and other manufactures
to America; and the prospect of importing from there "an immediate
and abundant supply of bread, corn and flour...[that] will, by the
month of of April next, reduce the staff of life at least 50%, to
the great and seasonable relief of the poor, and the just punishment
of the hoarders of corn, who by their avaricious monopolies have
added to the distress of the nation from the scantiness of the harvest."[83] The preliminaries were published in pamphlet form in Dublin; but because the publisher also sponsored the London edition,
his remarks sound like commercial speculation, not Irish popular
sentiment.[84]

The Irish Parliament was out of session in January 1783, and
it did not reconvene until mid-October, after the signing of the
definitive treaties, by which time the issues had been debated ex-
haustively in the British Parliament and press and Ireland had un-
dergone the heat and distraction of a general election. Nevertheless, the address from the throne, and the address-in-reply, referred with surprising brevity to the restoration of "the blessings
of peace" and of "the public tranquillity," again mentioning them
in a commercial, not a political, context.[85] Before gaining legislative independence, the Irish Parliament had been more responsive
than this to matters of foreign policy—particularly the Peace of
Paris in 1763 and the American war in 1775. On subsequent occasions

Grattan's Parliament, too, was to be more responsive--over the Anglo-French commercial treaty in 1787, the Nootka Sound dispute with Spain in 1790, the war with France in 1793, and the breakdown of the negotiations at Lille in 1797. On all but one of these occasions, diplomatic papers were formally laid before it. On all of these occasions, however, the British government actively sought the support of the Irish Parliament or felt it necessary to justify its measures in that parliament's eyes; whereas in 1783, it was so concerned about the lengths to which the newly granted legislative independence might be carried that it feared "the utmost confusion" might ensue if it encouraged Irish parliamentary interest "in matters affecting war and peace."[86] While this explains the British government's silence, it does not explain the silence of the Irish Parliament. Alone among members of that parliament in 1783, Sir Edward Newenham raised the question of Ireland's inclusion in the treaties being forged in Paris. But his concern was with a possible commercial treaty with the United States, and it may well be that he was really acting on behalf of his American friends, who by this stage had come to appreciate the weak U.S. bargaining position vis-à-vis Great Britain.[87] Certainly, it would have been more to the point to raise the question of Ireland's inclusion in the commercial treaties Britain was encouraged to conclude with the European (though not the American) belligerents.[88] If Newenham was playing American rather than Irish politics, it was an isolated echo of the old special relationship. During 1784--despite much economic distress, particularly in Dublin, and a good deal of nonimportation and tarring and feathering--newspaper references to pre-Revolutionary America were rare. One such was a headline in the Volunteer Journal of Dublin that read "Lexington redivivus"; in fact, this report related to nothing more sinister or significant than a drunken brawl in which certain "frolicsome" viceregal aides-de-camp had become involved in a public house on Ormond Quay.[89]

Two principal reasons explain the absence of Irish political reaction to the Treaty of Paris. The first was that the question of Ireland's inclusion in British treaties had already arisen in more striking form in the case of Portugal. Portugal joined the Armed Neutrality against Britain in July 1782, but well before then it was regarded as having "deserted" its ancient ally.[90] Early in 1781, the Portuguese government advanced the argument that the Free Trade granted to Ireland in 1779-80 represented a unilateral adjustment by Britain in the terms of the Methuen Treaty of 1703, and that, in spite of Ireland's new freedom to export woolens to European countries (prohibited in 1703), Portugal was not bound to regard Irish woolens as British within the meaning of the treaty. Representations and counterrepresentations passed between London and Lisbon on the subject, giving rise early in 1782 to some troublesome debates for the government in the Irish Parliament.[91] It was principally due to the implications of these negotiations with Portugal that Lord Temple insisted in December 1782 that the British commissioners in Paris act on behalf of Ireland as well as Great Britain, and should "establish [the] principle that every compact made respecting the trade, manufactures or commerce of Great Britain doth and shall of course comprehend Ireland."[92] Newenham, too, in his isolated intervention in October 1783, had mentioned the effect on the "perfidious Portuguese" of establishing this principle. It seems reasonable to conclude that the newly fledged Irish Parliament did not spread its sovereign wings in discussion of the Treaty of Paris, because it already knew that much of Ireland's prosperity depended on Ireland's continuing to be deemed British in treaties with foreign powers. After all, it was at precisely this time that the Americans "were learning the hard facts of life in the cold world of sovereign nations."[93] Earlier in the year, just after the signing of the preliminaries, Lord Temple had observed: "We say very little on...[Britain's] peace, for in truth no one understands it; and I believe as long as we have the same trade security as England, we shall look little further...."[94]

The other reason for the lack of political response to the Treaty of Paris was that the signing of the preliminaries and of the definitive treaties coincided with Irish absorption in two successive political issues of a peculiarly Irish character--"Renunciation" and parliamentary reform. Renunciation was the demand of the major, or at any rate the most vociferous, part of the Volunteers, headed by Henry Flood, that the British government, in addition to repealing the Irish Declaratory Act of 1720, should renounce the principle on which it had been based. Since the American Declaratory Act of 1766 had not been repealed (although the British Parliament in 1778 had declared its intention of never again taxing the North American colonies for revenue), there was no direct American analogy. A general sense of American loss weighed heavily on the ministers who had to deal with this new phase of Irish agitation, however. W.W. Grenville, chief secretary for Ireland and Lord Temple's younger brother, lamented in November 1782 that Shelburne was not prepared to renounce the power of "external legislation" over Ireland, which Grenville reckoned could never be exercised and would therefore "become, like the tea duty, a ground for contest and ill-blood, without the possibility of advantage." But when pressed on this point, Shelburne blamed the distinction between internal and external legislation on his political opponent, Charles James Fox, "who took it from Lord Chatham, by whom it had been adopted, for want of a better expression, in the case of America"; all Shelburne wanted to ensure, he protested, was that the opportunity to secure a unified Anglo-Irish foreign and commercial policy, by means of a formal compact between the two countries, should not be cut off by a Renunciation Act.[95] It is interesting that Grenville and Temple, the sons of George Grenville of sugar-duty and Stamp Act fame, and Shelburne, Lord Chatham's leading disciple, should have cast off their natural or political progenitors in their anxiety to avoid a repetition of errors in earlier American policy. In the end, the Renunciation Act--which received the royal assent in mid-April 1783 after Shelburne's fall--accommodated both viewpoints, since it was actually a recognition act. Instead of renouncing rights formerly exercised by Britain, it recognized "the rights claimed by Ireland" under the Constitution of 1782.[96] Matters were thus left very much on their former footing, and an ugly agitation that had dominated Irish politics since the summer of 1782 was laid to rest.

Renunciation was succeeded by parliamentary reform, an issue, like so many others, that subtly became transformed in the context of Ireland. In Great Britain, Professor Plumb has argued,

> the first strong movement..was sired by the American Revolution. Before the 1770s and 1780s, the discussion of parliament had centred on the position of placemen and pensioners or on the duration of parliaments, not the reform of the representative system as a whole. But during those decades the question of franchise and of the redistribution of representation came to the fore. This reform movement also gained from America's success, which strengthened the argument that the British Parliament was not responsive to the nation's will or even competent to carry out a policy, no matter how wrongheaded....The unrepresentative nature of the House of Commons was scarcely questioned in the 18th century until the issue was raised by Wilkes and by Americans.[97]

In Ireland, the timing and stimulus of the parliamentary reform movement were quite different. In effect, there was no such movement there until 1783, and the external stimulus to it did not come from America.[98] It is truly remarkable that in 1775-76, when Irish sympathy for the Americans was at its precarious peak and the Irish electorate was about to have a second chance to show its octennial teeth, only isolated and passing mention was made by pamphleteers and polemicists of the unsatisfactory state of the Irish representative system.[99] Such external stimulus as there was to the Irish parliamentary reform movement came later and from England. By 1782, a number of prominent English parliamentary reformers had come to recognize that the cause of reform in Ireland enjoyed the unique advantage of Volunteer backing and, thus supported, might achieve results that could not fail to create a vital precedent for Great Britain. But the principal stimulus was purely internal: the desire, genuine or feigned, to prevent the Irish Parliament from selling those rights the British Parliament had surrendered in 1782 and supposedly renounced in 1783; the contest between Henry Flood and Henry Grattan for popular preeminence, a contest that had first manifested itself in the early stages of the Renunciation agitation; and the failure of the Irish Parliament to ameliorate Ireland's economic distress. Insofar as the Treaty of Paris was at all relevant to the Irish parliamentary reform movement, it was as a factor in the economic distress, mainly because "the American War and the [Irish] non-importation agreement of 1779 had helped mask" the fact that the Dublin textile industry was "increasingly uncompetitive in the face of the mechanization of the emerging industrial revolution [in Great Britain]."[100]

The expectation had of course been--and most of the Irish interest in the Treaty of Paris was founded on this expectation--that the cessation of hostilities and the resumption of trade with America and its European associates, as with the West Indies (the seat of much of the war), would prove an economic panacea. Lord Temple himself participated in the widespread optimism, mainly because it was hard even for officialdom to calculate the effects of peace, particularly in the period of uncertainty between the signing of the preliminaries and of the definitive treaties. Temple wrote in February 1783: "The war has prevented us from judging of the nature or extent of the Irish foreign trade, except to the old [though only newly legalized] markets of France, Spain, Portugal and the Streights. But I am clear that the benefit will rapidly increase."[101] He may or may not have counted the United States among the new, "foreign" markets, because, until the signing of the definitive treaties, it was uncertain whether the United States was legally foreign, though the law officers of the Crown in Ireland ruled at the end of May that year that they were.[102] The "foreignness" of America had important implications for Ireland, because of

> the duties imposed in consequence of the British act which opened to Ireland the colony trade [i.e., the Free Trade of 1779-80] upon terms of equal duties with those which their trade with Great Britain is subject to....As to such of them as are laid upon import or export from or to those parts of North America which form the United States, I suppose the British act will not be considered to extend to them, they having in effect ceased to be colonies, though the definitive treaty confirming their independence is not yet signed.[103]

Thus, before Ireland had had a chance (because of the war and the dispute with Portugal) to derive much, if any, practical advantage from Free Trade, its terms became subject to drastic readjustment.

In some quarters, notably among the Irish tobacco importers, it was hoped that Ireland would take advantage of the uncertainty and steal a march on Great Britain. If the United States were now a foreign country, they argued, Ireland was not bound to raise its import duty on American tobacco to the British level, and consequently could hope to undercut the British importer in Britain's home market. "The general system" adopted, however, was "to follow Great Britain."[104] At the end of 1783, after the definitive treaties had been signed, the Irish Parliament passed, with minimal opposition from the tobacco interest, both an act for facilitating and promoting commercial intercourse with the United States and a tobacco act. Both measures were renewed annually, mutatis mutandis, for several years to come, and kept Irish trade with America on the

same footing as British trade, which was broadly the old, preferential, colonial footing and which suited the Irish economy well, at
least as far as imports were concerned (there were "few articles
which the interests of this kingdom cannot allow to be imported
from thence").[105] In 1785, the British prime minister, William
Pitt, sought by his celebrated Commercial Propositions to effect a
customs union with Ireland;[106] and the 16th of these propositions,
introduced at Westminster in May 1785, related to Irish trade with
America and was designed to render Ireland's following of Great
Britain automatic.[107] But this and other components of the propositions outraged the constitutional sensitivities of Grattan's Parliament to such an extent that the whole scheme had to be abandoned
and the pari passu legislative approach of 1783-85 resumed. Actually, the spectacular failure of the Commercial Propositions conceals
a high level of practical achievement, on the pari passu basis, in
harmonizing British and Irish commercial interests. This is true
not only with respect to the American trade but to incorporating
both Irish shipping in the new British Navigation System of 1786
and Ireland in the terms and benefits of the 1786 commercial treaty
with France (the only one to emerge out of the permissive provisions of the treaties with the European belligerents).[108]

It was not, therefore, because of legal or constitutional difficulties—serious though these were—that Irish expectations of
great economic gains were dashed following the restoration of peace.
Rather, it was because of the operation of market forces and a general reorientation of the British and Irish economies. In some
sectors, notably exports of linen to the United States, Irish optimism proved to be justified: these increased almost sixfold, from
632,100 yards in 1783 to 3,540,000 yards in 1784.[109] Moreover, the
fear expressed in August 1783 by John Foster, chancellor of the
Irish Exchequer and a hyperactive protector of the linen industry,
that "the infinite detriment which this kingdom will probably receive in its staple manufacture...if the American States shall...
be allowed a free intercourse of trade with the West Indies" went
unrealized. American trade with the British West Indies, except
in British ships, was prohibited.[110] Nevertheless, the buoyancy
of transatlantic exports of linen failed to compensate for depression in most other sectors of the economy.

> The end of the war, in spring 1783, brought a short-lived im-
> provement in economic life, but there was no post-war boom....
> Conditions deteriorated appreciably in the autumn of 1783 and
> winter of 1784:...the provisions trade had a disastrous season,
> failing to recapture its peacetime markets in the West Indies
> in the face of competition from North America....The legacy of
> the crisis was evident in the changes which it brought in the
> nature of the Irish economy, especially in the shift from de-
> pendence on trans-Atlantic markets in favour of British....[111]

98

Moreover, in the resumed and greatly increasing trade between Great
Britain and its former North American colonies (basically a trade
in manufactures from Britain and unmanufactured goods from the
United States),[112] Ireland, due to the nature of its economy, was
more likely to become a competitor with America for the British
market than a cobeneficiary with Britain of the American market.
This in fact became reality by the end of the decade. By then America had established itself as the principal corn exporter to the
British West Indies and Canada, and had threatened Irish predomi-
nance in this commodity in the British market as well.[113] It is
difficult and perhaps pointless to assess the contribution of either the Treaty of Paris or the American war to these developments.
All would presumably have come to pass--perhaps with even more of
a vengeance--had the first British Empire and the old Navigation
System survived.

The one clear and almost immediate effect of the Treaty of
Paris on Ireland, also in the economic sphere, was the resumption of emigration from Ireland to the newly independent United
States.[114] The combined influences of a bad harvest in 1782,
the attraction of cheap provisions in America, and the tradition
of emigration (interrupted since 1775) gave the movement its
special impetus. By February 1783, within days of the cessation
of hostilities and the reopening of trade between America and
Ireland, the first ships had arrived in Belfast and were ready to
transport passengers to Philadelphia.[115] Two months later an
estimated 500 people had already left the country, and, as prices
rose in the summer, so, too, did the number of vessels advertising
for passengers and the number of people willing to make the journey.[116] Because transatlantic shipping was relatively disorganized
throughout 1783 and emigrating was so expensive, those who left
that year were hardly the impoverished and unemployed industrial
workers of Dublin or the landless agrarian laborers of the country-
side who were hardest hit by price rises at home. The overwhelming
majority of them were manufacturers, tradesmen, artisans, "warm,
comfortable" farmers, many of whom could not only pay the high fare
with ease, but also possessed the £300-£700 with which to make a
start in the New World.[117] The available evidence suggests that
at least 5,000 people emigrated in 1783, and that a great many
more were prevented from doing so only by the low shipping levels
and the high cost.[118] The rate of emigration rapidly increased
in 1784. As in the previous year, a blow to the economic security
of the population, occasioned this time by the unusually harsh winter of 1783-84, played a major role.[119] Moreover, there was by
then no shortage of transport--witness the dramatic increase in
Irish linen exports to the United States. With increased traffic,
the cost of passage became unmistakably more competitive: 10
guineas, a decline of 66 percent over 1783, was the maximum price
charged. This reopened the prospect of emigration to a wider
social sphere, though the fare was still far above the prewar
average.[120]

The emigration of 1783-84 was, however, more than just a resumption of the prewar phenomenon. There was a greater broadening of the geographical catchment area and a marked correction of the denominational imbalance that had characterized earlier emigration. In 1784, there was for the first time an exodus from the southern counties of Ireland, one that compared with levels hitherto reached only in the province of Ulster. The strong Roman Catholic complement in the emigration of 1784, from Ulster as well as from the other three provinces, was sufficiently unprecedented to elicit the surprised comments of contemporaries. Robert Stephenson, inspector general of the linen industry in Munster, reported from there in June that "the migrations [have] become alarming at Cork, at Waterford and all the ports on these coasts, as well as in Leinster and Ulster, a circumstance not much known before the present time."[121] Indeed, there is some evidence to suggest that of the four counties where the rate of emigration was reputedly highest in 1784, three were outside Ulster.[122] The total number of emigrants from Ireland to the United States in 1784 is very difficult to estimate. What is certain is that virtually every ship involved in the Atlantic trade carried passengers--from 100 or so on a small vessel to some 500 on the larger ships that regularly plied the route after May 1784. The number of ports involved in the passenger trade, the great number of vessels (some of which did not advertise), and the fact that emigrants could travel via Liverpool, make the calculation particularly hazardous. But estimates of the period are close to modern estimates that the number leaving was greater in 1784 than in any single year in the 1770s (12,000, according to R.J. Dickson's calculation, had left in 1773).[123] A figure of 30,000 is not impossible; 20,000, or double the number hitherto suggested, is more likely. After 1784, the level declined to an average of about 5,000 annually in the years before Waterloo. Outside Ulster the rate of decline was sharper: the early high levels of emigration were directly connected with the difficult economic climate of the early 1780s.[124]

Emigration on this unprecedented scale and of this largely unprecedented character was important in itself. No less important was the publicity given to the emigration issue. In its initial phase, this took the form of a propaganda war between mercantilist opponents of emigration and the apostles of America as the land of freedom and opportunity. The basic argument of the former was that a high population (the case of Holland was usually cited)[125] made for economic prosperity. John King, writing in 1783, ascribed the weakened economy of Great Britain as a whole to high levels of emigration, and angrily rebuked those who left the country. He had especially harsh words for America, which he likened to an ungrateful child who, having shaken off all connection with the mother country, "is embowelling the nation of her most useful inhabitants."[126] The opposite view was expounded most effectively by the Frenchman de Crèvecoeur (writing under the pseudonym J. Hector St John) and by Franklin. De Crèvecoeur, whose Letters from an

American farmer were first published in London in 1782 and reprinted
in Belfast in 1783, depicted America in the now-familiar guise of an
"asylum" where all the nations of Europe could mix, live, and work
in peace and religious freedom. The only cautionary note he sounded
was that the Scots, because they "are frugal and laborious," had a
greater chance of being successful in America than the Irish, because the latter "love to drink and quarrel and to take to the gun,"
and because they "labour under a greater degree of ignorance in hus-
bandry than...others."[127] The message from Franklin in his Information to those who would remove to America complemented de Crèvecoeur's: America welcomed the hardworking farmer and the industri-
ous artisan, but not the indolent or the officeseeker.[128] The former colonies enjoyed a generally sympathetic press in Ireland in
early and mid-1783.[129] But as the Irish newspapers strongly opposed emigration, the sympathy did not survive the renewed diaspora.
Thereafter, much more emphasis was given to the attraction of Gene-
vese exiles to Ireland than to extolling the virtues of America;
and the latter were depicted as political liberty rather than economic prosperity. The antiemigration propaganda of the newspapers
was more sorrowful than aggressive in 1783, with frequent lamenta-
tions of the prospect of Ireland becoming "a deserted kingdom" be-
set by the abuse of "rapacious" and "absentee" landlords.[130] It
was firmly insisted, without the least premonition of the demographic catastrophe that was to strike Ireland in the 19th century,
that "the strength and prosperity of a country depends on its population."[131] The generally accepted and oft-recommended cure for
the ill of emigration was the encouragement of employment. To this
end, demands were made for bounties to encourage industry and,
toward the end of 1783, for protecting duties.[132]

The second phase of the propaganda war over emigration followed the Irish Parliament's rejection in late March and early
April 1784 of both protecting duties and (for the second time)
parliamentary reform. In this second phase, the emigration issue
was blurred, in that both the government and "popular" press dis-
approved of it, the latter seeking to maximize its extent and
demonstrate that the exodus was attributable to government policy,
the former seeking to minimize its extent and demonstrate that conditions in America were far worse that those prevailing in Ireland.[133] The government-sponsored Volunteer Evening Post spear-
headed a strong propaganda campaign against emigration by delib-
erately denigrating the independent colonies and by publishing
ostensibly true stories of the fate of Irish emigrants there. Its
favorite theme was that American treatment of arriving Irish emigrants was akin to slavery. From the beginning of May 1784, Irish
indentured servants were described as "white slaves," and soon
terms like "white slave trade," "unfit for market," and "American
slavers" appeared regularly in newspaper columns. Similarly, the
government press made much of the dangerous passage: the odds are
"at least four to one they will have to encounter jail fever, famine

and every other inconvenience which results from close confinement, bad accommodation and unsound provision...."[134] Neither the <u>Volunteer Journal</u> of Dublin nor the <u>Dublin Evening Post</u> (the foremost popular papers of the capital) attempted to refute these allegations, as well they might have done. It was simply not their wish to encourage emigration. They did, however, continue to give fairly detailed accounts of emigrant ships and the number of passengers on board; thus, for example, a note about the departure of a bevy of Dublin silk weavers was accompanied by strong criticism of "their tyrannic masters."[135] This served their purpose by providing tangible evidence of the government's neglect of industry. Only infrequently, when truly angered, did the <u>Volunteer Journal</u> comment on the advantage of settling in "the new world, the land of liberty and brotherly love, where no tyrants vex, no representatives betray the constitution, or invade the rights they are elected to defend."[136]

The collapse of the protectionist agitation and the parliamentary reform movement toward the end of 1784--plus the departure of Mathew Carey, former proprietor of the <u>Volunteer Journal</u>, for an illustrious publishing career in Pennsylvania[137]--brought a slow decline in the virulence of feeling between the Dublin newspapers. But the propaganda against emigration continued unabated, with the difference that it was now voiced to a greater or lesser degree by all papers, Castle and popular, the latter now feeling free to articulate their opposition. This third phase in the publicity given to emigration was thus characterized by near unanimity of sentiment, one striking consequence of which was a decline in the coverage given to passenger vessels leaving the country. Only rarely was the self-censorship broken: for instance, in March 1785 the <u>Dublin Evening Post</u> reported that "multitudes continued to emigrate."[138] Generally, all echoed the scare stories of the <u>Volunteer Evening Post</u>. By December 1784, the reports of the misadventures of Irish emigrants in America had reached a new level of sensationalism: they were hunted "like wild beasts," if they escaped slavery, and were "whipped and branded in a worse manner than the negroes" in captivity. Slavery was the dominant theme of the majority of these articles, while the desire of emigrants to return home made for good copy in long, critical accounts of America's climate, taxes, cost of living, unemployment problem, and so on.[139] Two other motifs were mentioned for the first time in 1785: the "approaching anarchy" in America and what may conveniently be called the Indian factor. Because it was the more colorful, the latter attracted greater attention. Irish emigrants, it was confidently predicted, if they received any land at all, would find themselves "on the borders of the Indian country,...subject to the incursions of those savages, who fire houses, plunder and massacre without distinction of age or sex."[140] It was even asserted by the <u>Volunteer Evening Post</u> in July 1787 that "taxation and tyranny were never felt [in America] till introduced by a Congress."[141]

With the widespread and nearly unanimous publication of such opinions, it is not surprising that by the end of 1785 enthusiasm for emigration had declined greatly from its 1784 level, although it had by no means evaporated, at least in Ulster. Even there, how-ever, and from the unlikely quarter of the radical Presbyterian clergyman Rev. William Bruce, sentiments highly unflattering to the United States were expressed. Writing to a fellow radical in Octo-ber 1784, Bruce commented:

> Redford [a friend recently returned from a visit to the United States] admired nothing in America but Washington. I have lately imbibed very mortifying opinions concerning the charac-ter of the Americans. I would not have believed them whilst they [i.e., the Americans] were in danger. They are rude with-out honesty and dissipated without civilization....The only good thing I ever heard of the Virginians is their Citizen Bill. It confers the rights of citizens on Irishmen after a residence of two years, which puts them on a level with all the nations of the world except the British dominions: Eng-lishmen are not naturalized till after a residence of five years, and a Scotchman must reside thirty years in Virginia to qualify for enjoying the rights of a free citizen.[142]

In view of Bruce's commendation of the Virginia Citizens Bill, it would seem that in his case hostility to emigration was not the motive for hostility to America. With most others, emigration--once a powerful element in the benevolent sympathy felt in Ulster and elsewhere in Ireland for the American colonies during the 1770s--had operated no less powerfully by the mid-1780s to create quite the opposite feeling toward the United States.

On April 19, 1780, in his first declaration of Irish rights, Grattan had described Ireland as "dreading the approach of a general peace, and attributing all she holds dear to the calami-tous condition of the British interest in every quarter of the globe."[143] A year earlier, the pseudonymous pamphleteer Owen Roe O'Nial had warned of the dangers of a union of the Parliaments of Great Britain and Ireland, by which Ireland would "lose our legislative assembly and take the readiest way of destroying the only one [as he erroneously imagined] in the empire."[144] Earlier still, in 1774, Josiah Tucker, dean of Gloucester, "the most astute of conservative English observers of the American crisis," had com-bined these two Irish apprehensions in one remarkable prophecy: "I make not the least doubt but that a separation from the colonies, and also another right measure, viz. a complete union and incor-poration with Ireland, however unpopular either of them may now appear, will both take place within half a century; and perhaps that which happens to be first accomplished will greatly accelerate the accomplishment of the other."[145] Burke, an imperialist with an

Irishman's feeling for the colonial point of view, desired neither consummation, and he had hoped that Ireland could instead contribute to averting "a separation from the colonies." Writing to his principal Irish correspondent, Charles O'Hara, in July 1775, Burke observed: "No bounds ever were set to the parliamentary power over the colonies...; but the reason and nature of things, and the growth of the colonies, ought to have taught parliament to set bounds to the exercise of its own power." In particular, he hoped that Parliament might be taught something by the Irish example--it was, after all, an example, however awkward and unsatisfactory, of the king-in-parliament acting simultaneously as king in a subordinate parliament. In January 1776, after the Irish Parliament had voted 4,000 troops to support the war in America, Burke (obviously writing under the influence of Congress's Address...to the people of Ireland) lamented to the same correspondent that Ireland had betrayed its mediating role:

> Our [the British Parliament's] conduct to America, though wicked and foolish, yet is natural wickedness and folly; yours [the Irish Parliament's] is a species of turpitude not decent to name....You were in the situation in which you might act as the guardian angels of the whole empire, and...[have] appeared in mediatorial character of the utmost dignity and benevolence, and with all certainty at once have secured your own liberties and given peace to our general country.[146]

If Burke was being unrealistic in assigning to Ireland such a positive role (even in the special circumstances of the autumn of 1775), he was right in thinking that Ireland's liberties were bound up with the fortunes and fate of the whole empire. There was such a symmetry in the First British Empire that events in one quarter of the globe could trigger the most unexpected consequences in another. Thus, the financial difficulties of the East India Company gave rise, in 1773, to a revenue measure, which in turn gave rise to the Boston Tea Party, which in turn gave rise to armed conflict with the American colonies and to American independence, which in turn "helped to make India the fulcrum of empire...."[147] Likewise (and more relevant to Ireland), the fact that the Irish establishment bore the cost of what was, in effect, the strategic reserve of the empire, altered the history of both Ireland and America in the decade after the Seven Years' War. On the one hand, the concessions made to Ireland to induce its Parliament to augment that reserve meant that "the imperial problem of the American frontier profoundly influenced the rise of Irish [strictly speaking, Anglo-Irish] nationalism." On the other hand, the earlier failure to extract an augmentation from the Irish Parliament "impaired the ability of the Irish establishment to meet its responsibility as a strategic reserve and led directly to the decision by the crown to create an American establishment...funded...with a series of revenue measures that immediately became 'taxation without representation' in American eyes...."[148] Ireland had suffered much in the past from this symmetry of empire. Indeed, as Professor Harlow has wisely observed, "there was in fact no place in a mercantilist empire for a 'plantation' which, being situated on the doorstep of the parent state, was debarred by climate from producing exotic commodities, and whose natural production overlapped, actually or potentially, with those of Britain."[149] However, the symmetry of empire had redounded, on balance, to Ireland's advantage. Great Britain's war with America caused far less disruption to the Irish economy than used to be imagined and, of course, served as the means of extorting from the mother country major economic and fiscal concessions.[150]

The best security that Ireland would retain all these advantages would have been an adjustment in the constitutional relationship between Great Britain and its American colonies, an adjustment making the relationship more nearly parallel to that between Great Britain and Ireland. A transatlantic parallel for the pre-1782 constitution of Ireland was adumbrated in George Grenville's half-hearted proposal of 1764-65, Lord North's belated proposal of 1775, and Lord Shelburne's chimerical proposal of 1776 that the American colonies should tax themselves for the purposes intended by British parliamentary taxation upon them;[151] a parallel for the Constitution of 1782 was adumbrated in the Carlisle Commission's peace proposals to the colonies in 1778.[152] The failure of the latter was put to good polemical use by opposition pamphleteers and parliamentarians in Ireland, who argued--plausibly, if nearsightedly--that Britain could best convince "the colonists...[of] the sincerity of the ministry in offering them terms" by adopting "a candid and liberal Irish policy"; moreover, Britain ought not to deny to "the loyalty of Ireland" those concessions that had been offered to "the resistance of America."[153] The deeper significance of the failure of the Carlisle peace proposals, however, was that it meant the constitution subsequently extorted by Ireland was unique and had no transatlantic parallel and therefore guarantee. Ironically--in view of his role in the conflict with America--Carlisle's next appointment was as lord lieutenant of Ireland (1780-82). There he presided over the last (and lost) opportunity to give Ireland a constitution that, though unique within the empire, would presumably have followed the treaty prototype of Carlisle's American proposals. To that extent, it would have been more durable than "the most bungling, imperfect business" that in fact ensued in 1782, after Carlisle's recall. Still more ironically, it was Lord Cornwallis, whose surrender at Yorktown in 1781 heralded the recognition of American independence, who was made lord lieutenant of Ireland in 1798, with instructions to carry out the union that was effected in 1800. Thus the symmetry of empire acted through the agency of individuals in a manner reminiscent of Greek tragedy to bring about the fulfillment of Josiah Tucker's prophecy that "a separation from the colonies" would accelerate "a complete union and incorporation with Ireland."

Yet this perspective is distorted. It ignores Ireland's role, for the 18 years that it had one, in the Second British Empire. In this period, Ireland was far from having, as Owen Roe O'Nial imagined, "the only...legislative assembly...in the empire." In 1784—the year not only of the ratification of the Treaty of Paris but also of the establishment of the separate colony of New Brunswick—what remained of British North America could boast three legislative assemblies, those of Nova Scotia (1758), Prince Edward Island (1773), and New Brunswick itself. Bermuda had enjoyed a legislative assembly since 1620; long-established assemblies also existed in the Bahamas, Barbados, the Leeward Islands, and Jamaica, and more recent ones in the Windward Islands were ceded to Britain after the Seven Years' War (most notably, and controversially, in Grenada).[154] Partly because of the loss of the American colonies, and partly because of the new autonomy conferred by the Constitution of 1782, Ireland—still more in the Second British Empire than in the First—was "in theory the most important area of sovereignty... within the British Empire outside of Britain."[155] Indeed, as if in imitation of Ireland, two West Indian colonies, Barbados and Jamaica, both made notable constitutional advances against the mother country in 1782, the latter securing, like Ireland, a modification in the tenure of its judges and "thus making distinct legal history...[with] the first colonial law of its kind ever to win acceptance [from the British Privy Council]."[156] Significantly, when Corsica was somewhat unexpectedly annexed to the British Crown in 1794, it was to the Constitution of 1782 that British ministers and officials hastily looked for the prototype of a British constitution for Corsica.[157]

In imperial theory, "the Irish revolution came to raise a question the American had not, the question of the responsibility of the ministers of the Crown to the legislature. The question could arise in Ireland because Ireland had a Crown in its own right, as America did not, and because Ireland threw off the legislative sovereignty of the British Parliament while retaining its allegiance to the Irish Crown." It also could arise in Ireland, and nowhere else in the First British Empire (or in the Second prior to the Canada Act of 1791), because uniquely in Ireland, before 1782 as after, the Privy or Executive Council was distinct from the legislature and did not double with the legislature's upper house or second chamber.[158] In consequence, the Irish constitution—rather than the new and highly artificial constitutions of Upper and Lower Canada—has been scanned for embryonic traces of responsible government of the 1846 Canadian type. In particular, the Irish type of "responsibility" (meaning a Treasury Board of Irish parliamentarians was accountable to the Irish House of Commons, an arrangement first proposed in the Irish Parliament in 1790 and put into effect in 1793-95) has been scrutinized for hopeful, precocious signs of the Dominion status of the future. Without union in 1800, it has been boldly asserted, "Ireland, not Canada, would have been first in obtaining responsible government," since "for Ireland that would have been the fruitful result of over a hundred years of constitutional activity, a logical and natural development." "The anticolonial, reform objective of the Irish Whigs [of the 1790s] consisted essentially of the attainment of an Irish responsibility evolving into an independent executive." "The Irish had by 1800 a theory of cabinet government far in advance of anything expressed in the British Parliament or by British publicists....It is possible,...perhaps probable, that the idea of 'responsible government' came to the Canadas from Irish sources."[159]

This line of argument, though tempting—particularly to an Irish historian anxious to find a wider, imperial significance in the soon-blighted promise of Grattan's Parliament—is hard to reconcile with the practical realities of Irish politics between 1782 and 1800. The reminder has recently been issued, in another 18th-century context, that "constitutional precedents, far from being the natural expression of principled motivation..., are secreted in the interstices of political practice."[160] For a period in 1792-93, the political situation in Great Britain and Ireland and the tactics of the British government nearly gave rise to a form of Irish responsibility that would have been a constitutional precedent of major imperial import. But by the time Irish responsibility had actually been established in the form of the Treasury Board of 1793-94, the mountain had dwindled to a mouse. Nor is there much sign of "principled motivation" or even of long-term strategy in the Irish Whigs' pursuit of "responsibility." They may well have espoused it in the first instance as a temporary means to other ends, and they certainly subordinated it to their principal end—gaining office in Ireland by changing the British government, a means that was in itself the very negation of "an independent executive." In short, they sought power, with or without "responsibility."[161] In fact, it was in the assemblies of the West Indian colonies, whose "contribution...to the common political experience of the eighteenth century has been too often underrated," that the principle and practice of "responsibility" (in this primarily financial sense) had made the greatest advances. In Jamaica, for example, "the assembly by 1750 had become ...virtually an administrative organ: in all essence it was the Treasury Board of the island...." In the West Indies in general "there was [by 1783] considerable similarity between assembly strivings...and the development of cabinet government in Britain..., [though] the English device ultimately brought all administration and policy within the control of parliament, whereas in the islands the assembly's control was confined to matters directly or indirectly dependent upon finance."[162]

For all the potential of the unique Irish constitutional position, therefore, Ireland made less impact on the Second British Empire than the Second British Empire made on Ireland. The most important point of all is that Ireland, in the minds of British governing circles, belonged in the Second British Empire more literally than it had in the First, simply because the Anglo-Irish elite's threat of separation by force of arms in 1782 had compromised their claim to special, West-British consideration.[163] Rather, their recent record invited comparison with selfish planter-elites in the West Indies, whose ambivalent loyalty during the Revolution was rightly suspected to have derived from their shrewd awareness "of their continuing dependence upon British arms and commerce." Maroon uprisings in Jamaica in the 1730s--and slave revolts in Bermuda in 1761, Monserrat (nearly) in 1768, Grenada and Tobago in 1770, and Jamaica (nearly) in 1775-76--had acted as a brake on planter separatism. That brake had been lacking since the 1690s in Ireland and, with exceptions such as Virginia in 1723, in most of mainland America.[164] Moreover, colonial administration of territories formally ceded in 1763, and bitter military experiences during the Revolution, had brought Britain into fruitful contact with non-Anglo-Saxon races with which it had apparently less in common than it had with the Catholic masses of Ireland. The process of hammering out constitutions for Grenada and Quebec in the second half of the 1760s and the first half of the 1770s had accustomed the British government, acting on the earlier precedent of Nova Scotia, to waiving the Oath of Supremacy and the Declaration against Transubstantiation in order to accommodate both Roman Catholic majorities and those of non-Anglo-Saxon origin. Of major portent for the contest over "Catholic Emancipation" in Ireland in the 1790s was the fact that, in the case of both Grenada and Quebec, the king's Coronation Oath had been raised as an objection to concession, and dismissed. George III did not think the oath applied across the Atlantic, and until 1795, or indeed 1801, it remained to be seen where and to what extent within the British Isles he felt it did apply.[165] During the American Revolution, the loyalty of French Canadian habitants fell far short of expectations, and the cooperation of the Canadian Catholic Church was, and continued to be until about 1800, bought at a price not authorized by the British government. But the myth of French Canadian loyalty lived on, and was given substance by the contrasting conduct of planters of impeccably English stock in the rebellious American colonies and elsewhere.[166] More effective as allies of Britain than the French Canadians, and even more alien to the Anglo-Saxon race and Anglo-Saxon culture, were the Negro slaves of the southern American colonies. Serving in graphically self-explanatory bodies like "the Ethiopian Regiment" and "the Black Pioneers," they "far exceeded the war record of their fellow-Loyalists of a fairer complexion," in addition to considerably disrupting the southern economy by the withdrawal of their labor. Hard military necessity, not ideology or humanitarianism, forged the alliance between the British and the blacks. But the alliance undoubtedly accelerated the British government's ideological and humanitarian commitment to the emancipation of slaves, the more so as its debt to many of the black Loyalists of the American Revolution was paid in the form of transshipment from Nova Scotia to Sierra Leone in 1792.[167] In any case, the one thing "emancipation" in the Irish sense of the 1790s had in common with the West Indian sense of the 1830s was that both could be justified

on the ground of hard military (and financial) necessity. Both
were constructive alternatives to the blood (and treasure) shed as
a result of the monopolizing and/or repressive policies of planter-
elites. This seeming truth must have been reinforced by the coincidence, in 1798, of a Catholic peasant uprising in Ireland and a
slave revolt in Jamaica.[168]

These imperial analogies, of varying degrees of falseness, had
some general bearing on British policy toward Ireland. That policy,
however, was determined by the fact that, geographically and stra-
tegically, if no longer emotionally, Ireland was still West Britain.
It was also still West Britain politically--reforming measures, if
enacted in one part of the British Isles, had implications and
repercussions for the others. One exception was the repeal of the
Sacramental Test in Ireland in 1780, which had no English precedent
and did not create a precedent for England, in spite of similar
measures introduced at Westminster in 1787, 1789, and 1790.[169] Policy toward Catholics stood on a different footing, in large measure
because it had a Continental and diplomatic dimension. In the mid-
and late 1780s, Pitt was (erroneously) convinced that the leaders
of the Irish Catholics were bent on "regaining property and power,"
that their "designs...[were] formulated and supported by foreign
powers," and that the wisest course was "to unite the Protestant
interest against them" by means of a parliamentary reform exclusive
to Protestants. Perhaps his conviction had been assisted by the
sheer convenience of an Irish policy that accorded with his British
policy. Perhaps, too, the Gordon Riots of 1780 had provided a vivid
reminder of the inflammability of anti-Catholic sentiment in England
(no equivalent of the 1778 Catholic Relief Acts had been attempted
for Scotland).[170] From 1788, when the English Catholic Committee
began to press for a further measure of relief in keeping with the
Irish Acts of 1782 ("and even not so extensive..., the Catholic
bishops being there recognized by law"), Pitt and his government
were placed in a difficult position. Disingenuous or not, their
response was to plead that they "did not see any difficulty in
government" going even so far as to restore English Roman Catholic
freeholders to the parliamentary franchise, "but that it was a
great political question with regard to the Irish of that description, who certainly in consequence would demand a removal of the
same obstructive laws."[171] This response was less than prophetic.
It postulated the exact reverse of the legislative position as it
would stand between 1793 and 1829. Nevertheless, it acknowledged
the seesaw relationship between concessions in each kingdom. In
1791, a mild measure of further relief for the English Catholics
(Mitford's Act) was at last passed, and with near unanimity--mainly
because of its timing--"in 1791 the Catholics were the beneficia-
ries of a distrust of the French Revolution which could yet live,
at this stage, with an effort for 'liberal improvement.'"[172] The
measure fell far short of the parliamentary franchise, but by admitting Catholics to practice law and to fill some local offices,
it went far enough to cap the 1782 Irish Acts and so constitute a

precedent for a further Irish measure. The home secretary, W.W. Grenville (formerly chief secretary for Ireland, 1782-83), hastened to assure the lord lieutenant in early March 1791

> that the consideration of what is doing here ought [not] to influence government in Ireland, because I have ever held the whole of that question to be [a] matter of expediency, not of right, except as far as relates to toleration only, strictly so-called. It does not by any means follow that what is right and expedient to be done here would be expedient to be done in Ireland under circumstances so extremely different.[173]

Once more, the sentiment was either disingenuous or remarkably un-prophetic.

What is more significant about it, however, in the context of the present discussion, is that the Home Office then numbered re-sponsibility for the colonies among its functions, and that Gren-ville was the author of the Canada Act and had, just a few days previously, introduced it into the House of Commons. Yet neither at this stage nor later in the year, by which time he had complete-ly changed his mind about the expediency of making concessions to the Irish Catholics, does Grenville seem to have made reference to the precedent of the Canada Act or discussed Catholic relief, ex-cept in the European context of the British Isles and the French Revolution. It was actually not Grenville but his successor as home secretary, Henry Dundas, who tolled the bell for the Anglo-Irish elite by describing them (in December 1791) as only "one description of Irishmen," whose contest with another for "monopoly or pre-eminence" was far from being a vital interest for Great Britain. Nevertheless, the sentiment was Grenvillian, in that it had a little earlier been expressed more trenchantly in a letter to Grenville from his brother, the first Marquess of Buckingham (who, as Lord Temple, had also been his principal in the Irish administration, 1782-83). Buckingham's frame of reference, too, was European, although it also possessed an unusual Irish dimension: during a second term as lord lieutenant, 1787-90, he had conceived a hatred for many of the Anglo-Irish magnates that literally drove him to a nervous breakdown. In addition, he had the unusual bias, or perhaps insight, that derived from being married to an Irish Catholic. However much these considerations may have influenced him, his ostensible and statesmanlike concern was that of Grenville, Dundas, and, presumably, Pitt: to prevent the political alliance between Catholics and Protestant Dissenters in Ireland that the formation of the Society of United Irishmen in November seemed to foreshadow.

> It is no longer a question in Ireland whether you will give the Catholics the English benefits, for it is not possible to refuse that extension....If the great object of their wishes leads (as it does) to the privilege of voting at county elec-tions, I profess I see no ground of policy on which you can

refuse it, as the refusal will certainly interest them to support any struggle for any new system by which they can hope to gain it. And the groundwork of your proceedings is the conviction that, from the change in their political tenets, they are entitled to an interest in their government, and that their opinions will assist you in your hopes of maintaining the Irish legislature against the new-projected republic or French mode of government.[174]

This policy was, for a variety of reasons, not pursued. Instead, Catholic relief was administered in two, hesitant, ungracious doses —"the English benefits" (broadly speaking) in 1792, and the county franchise, the right to bear arms, and eligibility for various civil and military offices (short of the highest, including seats in Parliament) in 1793.

This absence of any specific imperial derivation for the policy of breaking open the near-monopoly of the Anglo-Irish elite is a warning against seeking to define too precisely Ireland's place in the Second British Empire. It is impossible that the mainly traumatic imperial experience from 1763 did not alter attitudes to Ireland. Yet, in the wake of a major imperial development such as the Canada Act, and over a short time sequence such as March-December 1791, that alteration proves incapable of precise documentation. Part of the problem may be that imperial developments affected Ireland, not directly but via Great Britain. In the present instance, for example, the concession of representative institutions to recently hostile French Canadians made indefensible the continued refusal of far slighter concessions to long-loyal and thoroughly English Roman Catholics. And this in turn made the refusal of concessions to less deserving but politically much more important Irish Catholics almost as hard to defend. Moreover, imperial developments affected Ireland through the thought processes of British ministers, in whom the very fact of having embarked on a policy of constructive concession for Canada may have induced a certain habit of mind. This seems, at any rate, to have been the case with Grenville. In formulating his Canadian proposals in 1789, he had stressed the need to "make...concessions at a time when they may be received as [a] matter of favour...rather than to wait till they shall be extorted from us by...necessity." In October 1791 he expressed the fear that the Irish administration would give way "too late" on the Catholic question, "without either having the credit of liberality or deriving the benefit of attaching to English government that body which composes the effective mass of the people of Ireland." And, true to form, he set his face in October 1792 against the concessions subsequently made in the Catholic Relief Act of 1793, on the ground that the conduct, partly of the Irish administration and Parliament but mainly of the Catholics themselves, had been such that the time for "voluntary and gratuitous" concession was past.[175] Even without an explicit statement of affinity, it is obvious that the same optimistic spirit—that Roman Catholics were subject to their own aris-

tocratic leadership, favorable to monarchy, and susceptible, therefore, to subtle anglicization and even anglicanization--animated
both the Canada and the Irish Catholic Relief Acts. British ministerial misunderstanding of the tenurial system in French Canada invested the French Canadian "seigneurs" with a leadership they had
never really possessed, and British ministerial unmindfulness of
the effects of the Penal Laws invested the surviving Catholic aristocracy and gentry of Ireland with a leadership they had exercised
in the late 1770s but were unable to sustain in the early 1790s.
(In November 1791, even before the "split" that led to a temporary
secession from the Catholic Committee by the aristocratic party,
the lord lieutenant waspishly described Lord Fingall as one "who
had considerable influence in the Catholic body when aristocracy
was part of the creed.")[176] In both instances, the policy had some
of the futility of Napoleon's call to the boyars as he approached
Moscow.

It was in the implementation rather than the inspiration that
policy toward Canada and Ireland differed. It was a crucial part
of the provisions of the Canada Act that French Canadian Catholics
should be elected to the Assembly of Lower Canada and eligible for
appointment to the Legislative Council (or upper house) and the
Executive Council. This provision had been based in part on very
recent experience in Grenada, where the frustration of the British
government's efforts to have some token spokesmen of the French
majority in Grenada elected to its assembly and appointed to its
council had led to the departure of the French planter community.[177]
The Irish Catholic Relief Act, by contrast, allowed Catholics to
be electors, but not to be elected, and did not allow the surviving
Catholic aristocracy to take their seats in the House of Lords or
make Catholics eligible for the Irish Privy Council. In this respect, the only possible bearing the Canada Act had on the measure
was in strengthening the case for following, in Ireland as in Canada, the time-honored English 40-shilling freehold qualification for
the county franchise, despite very strong, locally based Irish ar-
guments to the contrary. Imperial precedent allowed some diversity
in qualifications for the franchise, but the recentness of the Canada Act probably made it impossible to take advantage of this, even
if the British government had been so disposed.[178] But there is
little sign that they were, and none that they ever contemplated
admitting Catholics to seats as well as votes in 1793. This failure, in the traditional and still-fashionable Leckian view,[179] deprived the Catholic 40-shilling-freehold peasantry of the natural
leadership of the Catholic aristocracy and gentry, and thus ran
counter to the optimistic, aristocratic spirit that animated the
Canada Act. One possible explanation for the contrast is that the
presence of Catholic peers and MPs in the Irish Parliament would
have complicated the negotiation of any subsequent union between
the Parliaments of Ireland and Great Britain. The idea of a union
had been the British government's initial response to the first
symptoms of Anglo-Irish separatism in 1779-80. It bobbed to the
surface again on various occasions during the 1780s and 1790s. And

it was fairly consistently in view after 1793.[180] This adds a further complication to any assessment of the place in the Second British Empire of a country Great Britain had to treat both as an undependable dependency and a potential component.

When first sounded by the British government in October 1798 about his attitude to a union, John Foster, a forthright defender of the Anglo-Irish Ascendancy, stated insuperable objections (which he was to maintain to the end) and then went on to attack the policy of the lord lieutenant, Lord Cornwallis, in relation to the reconstruction of the country after the '98 Rebellion.

> The rebels being dispersed, it should have been the object of those in power to have endeavoured to induce them to return to their allegiance and become peaceful subjects again, and so far as pardon could attain this, it was attempted. But what was the pardoned man to do?...My wish was instantly to have had great works begun, such as navigation of the Barrow, new roads through the mountains, draining of bogs, etc., at the public expense...: in short, to have every channel opened for giving full employment to every man who would work; and I did presume that after the misery they had experienced, they would have thus become interested against new tumults, and learn to respect the government that not only pardoned, but gave them easy means of subsistence, not as beggars, but by honest industry. Instead of this, a commission was appointed to enquire into the losses of the loyalists, and only to enquire, grounded on the model of your measure for the American loyalists, without adverting to the want of the similarity in the two cases. There, you had only one object--the American loyalist--for you had lost the country. Here, we had other objects: to restore the country from the ravages of the rebellion, and to reclaim the rebels, as well as to compensate the loyalists.[181]

This use of the term "loyalist," which was officially enshrined in the name of the commission, seems to have been unique (outside North America) to Ireland. Earlier in the 1790s in Great Britain, a "loyalist association movement" had flourished, but this appears to be a historian's term, and not to have found its way into the titles of any of the associations.[182] In Ireland it was widely used, not so much by Foster (who preferred "loyal men"), but by other Anglo-Irish magnates and their political followers, and by humbler loyalists as well. The term invites comparison with surviving British North America, where the British authorities had settled refugee Loyalists and placed them in some of the principal colonial offices, but where the broad, mainly federal, political thinking of these Loyalists was consistently ignored. In a way, this was strikingly like Ireland in the 1790s, where the British government had need of the ability, experience, and assistance of leading members of the Anglo-Irish elite like Foster, but no use for their broader concepts of an Ascendancy and of the Protestant Constitution in Church and State. It may perhaps be more than a verbal coincidence that Ireland had a "Castle," and Lower Canada was to develop a "Chateau," clique, both composed of loyalists in some sense of the word.[183] When to compensation for losses in the '98 Rebellion was added compensation for boroughs and offices abolished by the Act of Union in 1800, it began to look as if the Irish loyalists were being compensated into otium cum dignitate and that the country, though not lost, was as good as lost to them. This effect was delayed, in part because George III resolutely maintained that his Coronation Oath precluded him from sanctioning the admission of Catholics to seats in Parliament, and because the pauper county electorate unleashed by the Relief Act of 1793 continued to return sprigs of the Anglo-Irish elite to the United Parliament at Westminster until the mid-1820s and beyond. The delay has obscured the loyalist parallel and, more generally, the remoter effects of the Treaty of Paris on Ireland.

NOTES

1. Quoted in V.T. Harlow, The Founding of the Second British Empire, 1763-1793, 2 vols. (London, 1952 and 1964), 1: 267.

2. Quoted in C.C. O'Brien, "Edmund Burke and the American Revolution," in O.D. Edwards and G. Shepperson, eds., Scotland, Europe and the American Revolution (Edinburgh, 1976), pp. 115-16.

3. J. Cannon, The Fox-North Coalition: Crisis of the Constitution, 1782-4 (Cambridge, England, 1969), pp. 12-13; Harlow, Second British Empire, 1: 545-46.

4. O.D. Edwards, "The American Image of Ireland: A Study of Its Early Phases," in Perspectives in American History (Cambridge, Mass., 1970), 4: 219-20.

5. J.G. Simms, Colonial Nationalism, 1698-1776: Molyneux's the Case of Ireland...Stated (Cork, 1976), p. 63.

6. Simms, William Molyneux of Dublin, 1656-1698, edited by P.H. Kelly (Dublin, 1982), pp. 73-90, 110; Edwards, "American Image of Ireland," pp. 204, 215-18, 220.

7. M. Flaherty, "The Case for Ireland: Readings in English, American and Irish Political Thought in the 18th Century" (Yale University dissertation prospectus, August 1982, kindly made available to me in typescript by Mr. Flaherty), p. 26.

114

8. Edwards, "American Image of Ireland," pp. 229-31. See also Edwards, "Ireland and the American Revolution," in Scotland, Europe and the American Revolution, p. 125, and "The Impact of the American Revolution on Ireland," in The Impact of the American Revolution Abroad (Washington, D.C., 1976), pp. 128, 151.

9. Edwards, "American Image of Ireland," pp. 234-35.

10. D.N. Doyle, Ireland, Irishmen and Revolutionary America, 1760-1820 (Dublin, 1981), p. 1.

11. Edwards, "American Image of Ireland," pp. 205-6; G.R. Preedy, The Life of Rear-Admiral John Paul Jones..., 1747-1792 (London, 1940), pp. 85-88.

12. Quoted in M.R. O'Connell, Irish Politics and Social Conflict in the Age of the American Revolution (Philadelphia, 1965), p. 27.

13. Ibid., p. 210; Simms, Colonial Nationalism, pp. 34, 55-56; Flaherty, "Case for Ireland," p. 26.

14. Edwards, "American Image of Ireland," pp. 213-14, 224-28.

15. Flaherty, "Case for Ireland," pp. 26, 35-36; J.P. Reid, In a Defiant Stance: The Conditions of Law in Massachusetts Bay, the Irish Comparison and the Coming of the American Revolution (Pennyslvania State University Press, 1977), p. 12.

16. Simms, Colonial Nationalism, p. 35. (See also n. 31.)

17. William Pulteney (MP for Shrewsbury and brother-in-law of Governor Johnstone, a member of the contemporary Carlisle Commission), Thoughts on the present state of affairs with America and the means of conciliation, 4th ed. (Dublin, 1778), pp. 45-46.

18. Birr Castle, Co. Offaly, Rosse Papers, F/21: draft by Flood for a speech on the address [October 1765?]. The speech is remarkable in that Flood tries, in the same passage, to make the American comparison as well as assert the antiquity of the Irish Parliament: "The worm will turn when it is trod upon, and why should not the parliament of Ireland? If there be a deposit more sacred than any other, it is that which is lodged in the representatives of the people alone to tax the country which has sent them to parliament. Yet, even this right has been denied you by Ministers....But it has not been attempted in act? There is no man so mad as to attempt to rob a nation of its freedom till he see whether they are likely to bear it or not. It has been thrown out to sound [us]. The same doctrine was thrown out with respect to the American colonies before it was enacted. But shall any Minister consider this country in that light? This country which

stands with Magna Charta in her hand for near 600 years, with the
laws of England and the parliamentary constitution adopted at the
instance of the Irish, as the record of Henry II expresses it, and
by the fairest, the fullest, most ancient and best attested national
compact which any nation has to boast as the ground of its constitution? Shall this nation be enslaved by the dictum of a First Lord
of the Treasury?"

19. Quoted in O'Brien, "Burke and the American Revolution,"
p. 115.

20. Quoted in R.B. McDowell, Irish Public Opinion, 1750-1800
(London, 1944), p. 48.

21. Flaherty, "Case for Ireland," p. 37.

22. R.J. Barrett, "A Comparative Study of Imperial Constitutional Theory in the Age of the American Revolution" (Ph.D. thesis,
Dublin University, 1958), quoted in O'Connell, Irish Politics and
Social Conflict, pp. 30-31. See also Reid, In a Defiant Stance,
p. 11, and Doyle, Ireland, Irishmen and Revolutionary America,
p. 251.

23. O'Connell, Irish Politics and Social Conflict, pp. 30-31.

24. T.M. O'Connor, "The More Immediate Effects of the American
Revolution on Ireland, 1775-1785" (M.A. thesis, Queen's University of
Belfast, 1938), pp. 65-68; Doyle, Ireland, Irishmen and Revolutionary
America, pp. 51-74.

25. McDowell, Irish Public Opinion, p. 48.

26. O'Connell, Irish Politics and Social Conflict, p. 31.

27. Edwards, "Impact of the American Revolution on Ireland,"
p. 144. See also M. Elliott, Partners in Revolution: The United
Irishmen and France (Yale University Press, 1982), p. 11. For a
different view, Doyle, Ireland, Irishmen and Revolutionary America,
pp. xviii, 153-79.

28. Edwards, "Ireland and the American Revolution," p. 122;
R.R. Palmer, "The Impact of the American Revolution Abroad," in the
volume of the same name, p. 6.

29. Edwards, "Ireland and the American Revolution," p. 122;
T.W. Moody, "The Irish Parliament under Elizabeth and James I: A
General Survey," in Proceedings of the Royal Irish Academy, vol. 14,
sec. C, no. 6 (December 1939), passim; A.P.W. Malcomson, "The Foster
Family and the Parliamentary Borough of Dunleer, 1683-1899," in Co.
Louth Archaeological and Historical Journal 17 (1971): 157; R.D.
Simmons, The American Colonies from Settlement to Independence
(London, 1976), pp. 20-74, 192-94.

30. J.C. Beckett and A.G. Donaldson, "The Irish Parliament in the 18th Century," in Proceedings of the Belfast Natural History and Philosophical Society, 2d ser. 4 (1951): 30, and C.B. Fergusson, "The Colonial Policy of the 1st Earl of Liverpool as President of the Committee for Trade, 1786-1804" (D.Phil. thesis, Oxford University, 1952), p. 13. Both are quoted in M.G. O'Brien, "The Exercise of Legislative Power in Ireland, 1782-1800" (Ph.D. thesis, Cambridge University, 1983), pp. 6-7, 95.

31. L.W. Labaree, ed., Royal Instructions to British Colonial Governors, 1670-1776, 2 vols. (reprint ed., New York, 1967), 1: 125; E.M. Johnston, Great Britain and Ireland, 1760-1800: A Study in Political Administration (reprint ed., Westport, Conn., 1978), pp. 99-103; J.L. McCracken, The Irish Parliament in the 18th Century (Dundalk, 1971), p. 14; B. Bailyn, The Origins of American Politics (New York, 1968), p. 67; A.G. Olson, "Parliament, Empire, and Parliamentary Law, 1776," in J.G.A. Pocock, ed., Three British Revolutions: 1641, 1688, 1776 (Princeton, 1980), pp. 291-93, 302; J. Blow Williams, British Commercial Policy and Trade Expansion, 1750-1850 (Oxford, 1972), p. 17.

32. Reid, In a Defiant Stance, pp. 8-16, 18-19, 87, 113, 137. However, the effect in practice of the "seemingly potent" Whiteboy Act was minimal; see J.S. Donnelly, "Irish Agrarian Rebellion: The Whiteboys of 1769-76," in Proceedings of the Royal Irish Academy 83, sec. C, no. 12 (1983): 317-31.

33. Ibid., pp. 118, 190-91; Simmons, American Colonies, pp. 144-49, 245-67; Bailyn, Origins of American Politics, p. 106. For another slant see Olson, Anglo-American Politics, 1660-1775: The Relationship between Parties in England and Colonial America (Oxford, 1973), pp. 161-72.

34. Olson, "Parliament, Empire, and Parliamentary Law," p. 294; R. Middlekauff, The Glorious Cause: The American Revolution, 1763-1789 (Oxford, 1982), p. 26 and, more generally, pp. 23-28, 38-42; W.L. Morton, "The Local Executive in the British Empire, 1763-1828," in English Historical Review 308 (July 1963): 438-39; Bailyn, The Ordeal of Thomas Hutchinson: Loyalism and the Destruction of the First British Empire (reprint ed., London, 1975), pp. 176-84.

35. Malcomson, "Absenteeism in 18th-Century Ireland," in Irish Economic and Social History Journal, vol. 1 (1974), passim; F.G. James, "The Irish Lobby in the Early 18th Century," in English Historical Review, vol. 81 (1966), passim; Olson, "Parliament, Empire, and Parliamentary Law," p. 314; J.E. Ross, ed., Radical Adventurer: The Diaries of Robert Morris, 1772-1774 (Bath, 1971), pp. 3-6, 23; Lady Llanover, ed., The Autobiography and Correspondence of Mary Granville, Mrs Delany, 1st ser., 3 vols. (London, 1861), 1: 359-60; D. Burnett, Longleat: The Story of an English Country House (London, 1978), pp. 117-18.

36. Doyle, Ireland, Irishmen and Revolutionary America, pp. 25, 31-32, 34; Bailyn, Origins of American Politics, pp. 74, 88-91; P. Haffenden, "Colonial Appointments and Patronage under the Duke of Newcastle, 1724-1739," in English Historical Review 308 (July 1963): 422-24, 428-29, 431-35; D. O'Donovan, "The Money Bill Dispute of 1753," in T. Bartlett and D.W. Hayton, eds., Penal Era and Golden Age: Essays in Irish History, 1690-1800 (Belfast, 1979), pp. 86-87; J.L. Collins, Jr., "Irish Participation at Yorktown," in Irish Sword 15, no. 58 (Summer 1982): 3; Malcomson, John Foster: The Politics of the Anglo-Irish Ascendancy (Oxford, 1978), pp. 239-45; Reid, In a Defiant Stance, p. 19; Simmons, American Colonies, pp. 242-44; D.M. Clark, The Rise of the British Treasury: Colonial Administration in the 18th Century (Newton Abbot, 1960), pp. 42-43, 114, 125-27, 131-33, 137-38, 168, 182-85, 188-90.

37. Edwards, "American Image of Ireland," pp. 212-13; Bailyn, Thomas Hutchinson, pp. 330-31, 392; Bailyn, Origins of American Politics, pp. 77-79.

38. Olson, Anglo-American Politics, pp. 75-105, 113-18, 148-53. The best, though voluminous, authority for Devonshire's lord lieutenancy is the Public Record Office of Northern Ireland's calendar of his viceregal papers, ref. T.3158/630-1484. See also O'Donovan, "Money Bill Dispute," passim, and J.C.D. Clark, "Whig Tactics and Parliamentary Precedent: The English Management of Irish Politics, 1754-1756," in Historical Journal, vol. 21 (1978), passim.

39. D.M. Clark, British Treasury, pp. 109, 125-30, 195-96, 199-202; T. Bartlett, "The Augmentation of the Army in Ireland, 1767-1769," in English Historical Review, vol. 380 (July 1981), passim; Collins, Irish Participation at Yorktown, pp. 3-4; Harlow, Second British Empire, 1: 511-13.

40. Bartlett, "The Townshend Viceroyalty, 1767-72," in Penal Era and Golden Age, pp. 110-11; Olson, "Parliament, Empire, and Parliamentary Law," pp. 301-11; Olson, Anglo-American Politics, pp. 137-141.

41. James, "The Irish Lobby," pp. 555-57; McDowell, Ireland in the Age of Imperialism and Revolution, 1760-1801 (Oxford, 1979), pp. 309-39; Bailyn, Origins of American Politics, pp. 92-95; Olson, Anglo-American Politics, pp. 136-38, 177-79; Olson, "Parliament, Empire, and Parliamentary Law," pp. 313-16.

42. J.E. Tyler, ed., "A Letter from the Marquess of Rockingham to Sir William Mayne on the Proposed Absentee Tax of 1773," in Irish Historical Studies, vol. 8 (1952-53), passim; T.W. Copeland et al., Correspondence of Edmund Burke, 9 vols. (Chicago/Cambridge, 1958-70), 2: 464-96. One principal difference between the two agitations was that Lord Shelburne "very creditably" (in view of his huge Irish possessions) supported the absentee tax, but of course joined forces

with the Rockinghams in opposition to the American war. See P. Brown, The Chathamites: A Study in the Relationship between Personalities and Ideas in the Second Half of the 18th Century (London, 1967), p. 82. See also Anon., A Letter to a Member of Parliament on a Tax upon Absentees (Dublin, 1783), pp. 15-16.

43. For Franklin's penetrating and entertaining accounts of his interviews with the slower-witted Hillsborough, see C. van Doren, Benjamin Franklin (New York, 1938), pp. 383-90. For Hillsborough as an advocate of union, and more generally, see Malcomson, "The Gentle Leviathan: Arthur Hill, 2nd Marquess of Downshire, 1753-1801," in P. Roebuck, ed., Plantation to Partition: Essays in Ulster History in Honour of J.L. McCracken (Belfast, 1981), p. 103.

44. J.T. Main, The Social Structure of Revolutionary America (Princeton, 1965), pp. 270, 286-87; Simmons, American Colonies, p. 320; J.M. Murrin, "The Great Inversion, or Court versus Country: A Comparison of the Revolution Settlements in England (1688-1721) and America (1776-1816)," in Three British Revolutions, p. 412.

45. Van Doren, Franklin, pp. 392-93; Doyle, Ireland, Irishmen and Revolutionary America, pp. 15-18.

46. See, for example, W.H. Crawford and B. Trainor, eds., Aspects of Irish Social History, 1750-1800 (Belfast, 1969), p. 34; D. Dickson, C. O'Grada, and S. Daultrey, "Hearth Tax, Household Size and Irish Population Change, 1672-1821," in Proceedings of the Irish Royal Academy, vol. 82, sec. C, no. 6 (1982), passim, but especially p. 169.

47. O'Connell, Irish Politics and Social Conflict, pp. 266-81; D. Dickson, "Middlemen," in Penal Era and Golden Age, pp. 162-85.

48. Malcomson, John Foster, "The Gentle Leviathan," and The Pursuit of the Heiress: Aristocratic Marriage in Ireland, 1750-1820 (Belfast, 1982), passim; P. Roebuck, "Landlord Indebtedness in Ulster in the 17th and 18th Centuries," in J.M. Goldstrom and L.A. Clarkson, eds., Irish Population, Economy and Society: Essays in Honour of the Late K.H. Connell (Oxford, 1981), passim; W.A. Maguire, "Lord Donegall and the Hearts of Steel," in I.H.S., vol. 31, no. 84 (September 1981), passim; E. Hewitt, ed., Lord Shannon's Letters to His Son: A Calendar of the Letters Written by the 2nd Earl of Shannon to His Son, Viscount Boyle, 1790-1802 (Belfast, 1982), passim. The "claret to a chamber pot" epigram is quoted in Reid, In a Defiant Stance, p. 13. For William Hare and Henry Bruen, see: Public Record Office of Northern Ireland, Belfast, Farrer Papers, D.585/7, 8, 16, rental and partial survey of Hare's Ennismore estate, Co. Kerry, 1777-79, and purchase calculations concerning [the rest of?] the Kerry estate acquired from Lord Kerry, May 20, 1779; and Historical Manuscripts Commission Report on the Dropmore Papers (London, 1892 and 1894), 1: 359, and 2: 14, Marquess of

Buckingham to W.W. Grenville, October 18, 1788, and Earl of Westmorland to Lord Grenville, January 12, 1791.

49. Quoted in L. Gottschalk, Lafayette and the Close of the
American Revolution (Chicago, 1942), p. 53.

50. For the Volunteers, in their home-guard and political
roles, respectively, see P. Smith, "'Our Cloud-Cap't Grenadiers':
The Volunteers as a Military Force," in The Volunteers of 1778:
Commemorative Issue of The Irish Sword 13, no. 52 (1978 and Summer
1979): 185-207, and "The Volunteers and Parliament, 1779-84,"
in Penal Era and Golden Age, pp. 113-36. The Volunteers of
Ireland also includes: K.P. Ferguson, "The Volunteer Movement and
the Government, 1778-1793," pp. 208-16, and P.O. Snoddy, "Some
Police and Military Aspects of the Irish Volunteers," pp. 217-19.
The latter contains (p. 219) a striking instance of a Volunteer
corps intervening to prevent a gaol-rescue of men convicted and
sentenced to death for acts of violence connected with the enforcement of an American-style nonimportation agreement in Dublin.

51. For two case histories, the Skeffington family of Antrim
and the second earl of Clanbrassill, see Malcomson, "Election
Politics in the Borough of Antrim, 1750-1800," in I.H.S. 17, no. 65
(March 1970): 35-38, 46-47, and "The Struggle for Control of Dundalk
Borough, 1782-92," in C.L.A.J. 17, no. 1 (1969): 23-31.

52. J.J. Kelly, "The Irish Parliamentary Reform Movement:
The Administration and Popular Politics, 1783-5" (M.A. thesis,
University College, Dublin, 1981), p. 84, passim.

53. Doyle, Ireland, Irishmen and Revolutionary America, p. 158.

54. Edwards, "Impact of the American Revolution on Ireland,"
p. 128 and, more generally, p. 128-37. For an entertaining (yet
significant) example of Episcopalian hatred of Presbyterians (or,
as the pamphleteer calls them, "Ultonian sectaries," "a faction whose
principle of political existence is opposition, reasonable or unrea-
sonable"), see Anon., Fragment of a letter to a friend relative to
the repeal of the [Sacramental] Test (Dublin, 1780), passim.

55. McDowell, Irish Public Opinion, p. 40.

56. Edwards, "American Image of Ireland," p. 208; Bailyn,
Thomas Hutchinson, p. 346; E.S. Morgan, The Birth of the Republic,
1763-89, rev. ed. (Chicago, 1977), p. 6. In a sense, however,
Catholicism ceased to be a wholly external threat when the British
government, by the Quebec Act of 1774, extended the boundaries of
Quebec province to the Ohio and the Mississippi rivers. As Andrew
Kippis, D.D., a defender of the Treaty of Paris, declared in his
Considerations on the provisional treaty with America and the pre-

liminary articles of peace with France and Spain (London, 1783), p. 36: "That was an act which was calculated for tyrannical purposes and which was particularly hostile to the North Americans...."

57. E. O'Flaherty, "The Catholic Question in Irish Politics, 1774-1795" (M.A. thesis, University College, Dublin, 1981), pp. ii-iii, 7-14.

58. Doyle, Ireland, Irishmen and the American Revolution, pp. 69-74, 168-75.

59. Ibid., pp. 127-31.

60. O'Connell, Irish Politics and Social Conflict, pp. 34-35.

61. This, and the subsequent comment in this paragraph on the Catholic Relief Bill, is taken from: O'Connell, Irish Politics and Social Conflict, pp. 103-25; O'Connor, "More Immediate Effects of the American Revolution on Ireland," pp. 108, 133-148; R.E. Burns, "The Catholic Relief Act in Ireland, 1778," in Church History (June 1963), pp. 181-205; and O'Flaherty, "Catholic Question," pp. 14-37. For the extraordinary case of James Willson, see J.S. Reid, History of the Presbyterian Church in Ireland..., new ed. in 3 vols. (Belfast, 1867), 3: 341, 343.

62. O'Flaherty, "Catholic Question," pp. 40-45, 73-74, 112; Edwards, "Impact of the American Revolution on Ireland," pp. 128-29; C. Royster, A Revolutionary People at War: The Continental Army and the American Character, 1775-1783 (Chapel Hill, 1979), p. 124.

63. The substance of the speech delivered by Henry Beaufoy Esq. in the [British] House of Commons upon the 28th of March 1787 on his motion for the repeal of the Test and Corporation Acts (London, 1787), p. 33, passim. See also n. 54.

64. Cannon, Fox-North Coalition, pp. 90-91; Kelly, "Irish Parliamentary Reform Movement," pp. 330-31.

65. Edwards, "American Image of Ireland," p. 232.

66. Malcomson, John Foster, p. 415 and, more generally, pp. 350-432; M. Wall, "The United Irish Movement," in Historical Studies, vol. 5, Papers Read before the 6th Conference of Irish Historians (London, 1965), pp. 122-40; Kelly, "The English Government and Ireland after Legislative Independence" (typescript of a hitherto unpublished paper read in November 1982 at the Irish Historical Society's symposium on Grattan's Parliament); Harlow, Second British Empire, 1: 631-35; J. Ehrman, The Younger Pitt: The Years of Acclaim (London, 1969), pp. 363-70.

67. Ehrman, The British Government and Commercial Negotiations with Europe, 1783-1793 (Cambridge University Press, 1962), p. 4.

68. Brown, The Chathamites, p. 441.

69. See n. 95 and, for other examples of nerviness explicitly deriving from the American experience, see duke of Rutland, ed., Correspondence between the Rt. Hon. William Pitt and Charles, Duke of Rutland,...1781-1787 (London, 1890), p. 26, Rutland to Pitt, July 24, 1784, and H.M.C. Rutland Papers (London, 1894), 3: 147, Rutland to Pitt, November 14, 1784.

70. Thomas Day, Reflections upon the present state of England and the independence of America, 4th ed. (London, 1783), pp. 77-78.

71. Edwards, "American Image of Ireland," pp. 201-2.

72. Ibid., p. 209.

73. Harlow, Second British Empire, 1: 496-501; R.B. Morris, The Peacemakers: The Great Powers and American Independence (New York, 1965), pp. 148-49. The anonymous, and surely eccentric, author of A plan of reconciliation with America..., humbly inscribed to the King (London, 1782), pp. 20-25, 29, took the view that the Constitution of 1782 might bring the Americans to follow the Irish example! In his view, the failure of the negotiations of 1778 was the fault of the Carlisle Commission: "The object of the commission was an indignity to the legislature, and the Commissioners were an insult to the Americans..., and the Governor [Johnstone, one of the Commissioners] absolutely a burlesque upon the commission." The king should not offer the Americans "a government of their own and a legislature upon the principles of the Irish nation.... North America will be a separate nation, but not an independent one, as it will be legislatively dependent on Great Britain, as Ireland is." Further inducements to the Americans would be the sending of a viceroy and "the creation of peers from the leading men of Congress and the army." This pamphlet must surely represent the most extreme development of the analogy between Ireland and America.

74. Edwards, "American Image of Ireland, p. 209, and "Impact of the American Revolution on Ireland," p. 129; Doyle, Ireland, Irishmen and Revolutionary America, p. 181.

75. Doyle, Ireland, Irishmen and Revolutionary America, pp. 52, 109-12, 137, 142-44. For a refutation of the notion "that poverty and revolutionary ideals were mutually exclusive," see Royster, Revolutionary People at War, pp. 373-78.

76. P.O. Snoddy, "The Battle of Camden, 1780," in The Volunteers of 1778: Commemorative Issue of The Irish Sword, p. 269; McDowell, Ireland,...1760-1810, pp. 239-40.

77. Edwards, "American Image of Ireland," pp. 231, 240.

78. Quoted in C.R. Ritcheson, Aftermath of Revolution: British Policy Toward the United States, 1783-1795 (Dallas, 1969), p. 33. For the contrast between this and American expectations, see Hutson (this volume), pp. 6-9.

79. Harlow, Second British Empire, 1: 238-311; G. Stourzh, Benjamin Franklin and American Foreign Policy (Chicago, 1954), pp. 96-104, 147-213, 238-59, especially p. 255; van Doren, Franklin, pp. 289-93; Edwards, "American Image of Ireland," pp. 233-40; Cannon, Fox-North Coalition, p. 15. See also Hutson (this volume), pp. 10-12.

80. J.C. Rainbolt, "Americans' Initial View of Their Revolution's Significance for Other Peoples, 1776-1788," in Historian 19, no. 3 (1973): 418-33, especially pp. 427, 429, 432. See also Hutson (this volume), pp. 12-13.

81. See n. 128.

82. P.J. Jupp, "Earl Temple's Viceroyalty and the Renunciation Question, 1782-3," in I.H.S. 17, no. 68 (September 1971): 499-520, especially pp. 507-8, 511, 515-18; Public Record Office, London, H.O. 100/8, ff. 10-11, Temple to T. Townshend, January 4, 1783.

83. Dublin Evening Post, January 28 and 30, 1783. I am indebted to Mr. J.J. Kelly for these references.

84. R.D.C. Black, ed., A Catalogue of Pamphlets on Economic Subjects, 1750-1900, in Irish Libraries (Belfast, 1969), p. 74, no. 1277. I am grateful to Dr. M.G. O'Brien for drawing my attention to this point.

85. The parliamentary register, or history of the proceedings and debates of the House of Commons of Ireland, 1781-97, 17 vols. (Dublin, 1782-1801), 2: 1-9.

86. Malcomson, "Speaker Pery and the Pery Papers," in North Munster Antiquarian Journal 16 (1973-74): 46, 58 (n. 72); O'Connor, "More Immediate Effects of the American Revolution on Ireland," pp. 58-65; McDowell, Irish Public Opinion, pp. 78-80; McDowell, Ireland..., 1760-1801, pp. 291-92.

87. Irish Parliamentary Register, 2: 27-28; Ritcheson, Aftermath of Revolution, pp. 4-11.

88. Ehrman, Commercial Negotiations with Europe, p. 4.

89. Kelly, "Irish Parliamentary Reform Movement," pp. 221-22.

90. W.A. Miles, A political mirror for the year 1780, with notes explanatory and historical..., inscribed to Sir Edward Newenham, Knt, representative and trustee in parliament for the electors of the county of Dublin, 3d ed. (Dublin, 1780), p. 38.

91. Ehrman, Commercial Negotiations with Europe, pp. 5-16, 148-50, 173-76; Irish Parliamentary Register, 1: 211-32.

92. P.R.O., H.O. 100/8, f. 3, Temple to Townshend, December 30, 1782. I am indebted to Dr. M.G. O'Brien for this reference and point.

93. Ritcheson, Aftermath of Revolution, p. 17.

94. H.M.C. Dropmore Papers, 1: 190, Temple to W.W. Grenville, February 9, 1783.

95. Harlow, Second British Empire, 1: 545.

96. Jupp, "Renunciation Question," pp. 515-20.

97. J.H. Plumb, "The Impact of the American Revolution on Great Britain," in The Impact of the American Revolution Abroad, pp. 70-71.

98. Kelly, "Irish Parliamentary Reform Movement," passim, especially pp. 32-42. For the preliminary stirrings of the Irish movement, see O'Connell, Irish Politics and Social Conflict, p. 283.

99. O'Connor, "More Immediate Effects of the American Revolution on Ireland," pp. 84-85, especially p. 83.

100. Kelly, "Irish Parliamentary Reform Movement," p. 141.

101. H.M.C. Dropmore Papers, 1: 189, Temple to Grenville, February 9, 1783; H.O. 100/8, ff. 3-4, 140-42, Temple to Townshend, December 30, 1782 and February 2, 1783.

102. H.O. 100/9, ff. 149-54, opinion of the law officers, May 29, 1783.

103. P.R.O.N.I. Foster/Massereene Papers, D.562/8431, John Foster to Lord Northington (Temple's successor as lord lieutenant), August 28, 1783.

104. Ibid.

105. D.562/8446, Foster to Waddell Cunningham, October 23, 1784; Irish Parliamentary Register, 2: 269, 272. (I am indebted to Mr. D. Lammey and Mr. J.J. Kelly, respectively, for these references.) For examples of the Irish legislation, see 23 and 24 Geo. III, caps. 6 and 9, and 26 Geo. III, caps. 6 and 16.

106. Malcomson, John Foster, pp. 49-58.

107. National Library of Ireland, Dublin: Bolton Papers, MS. 16351/35, D. Daly to E. Cooke, June 14, 1785. I am indebted to Mr. J.J. Kelly for this reference.

124

108. Malcomson, John Foster, pp. 58-60, 367-69; Ehrman, Commercial Negotiations with Europe, pp. 1-4.

109. C. Gill, The Rise of the Irish Linen Industry (Oxford, 1965), p. 180.

110. See n. 102; Harlow, Second British Empire, 1: 448-92; Blow Williams, British Commercial Policy, pp. 217-28; Ritcheson, Aftermath of Revolution, pp. 1-17; Ehrman, Pitt: The Years of Acclaim, pp. 332-39.

111. R. Refaussé, "The Economic Crisis in Ireland in the Early 1780s" (abstract of a Ph.D. thesis, University of Dublin, 1982), in Irish Economic and Social History 9 (1982): 76-77. See also L.I. Cochran, "Scottish-Irish Trade in the 18th Century," in T.M. Devine and D. Dickson, eds., Ireland and Scotland, 1600-1850: Parallels and Contrasts in Economic and Social Development (Edinburgh, 1983), pp. 152-53, 158.

112. Blow Williams, British Commercial Policy, p. 223; Ritcheson, Aftermath of Revolution, pp. 19-20, 188-89.

113. Ritcheson, Aftermath of Revolution, pp. 189-203; Malcomson, ed., An Anglo-Irish Dialogue: A Calendar of the Correspondence between John Foster and Lord Sheffield, 1774-1821 (Belfast, 1975), pp. 8-11, 75-80.

114. This and the succeeding five paragraphs are derived, almost verbatim, from J.J. Kelly, "The Resumption of Emigration after the American War of Independence, 1783-86" (unpublished typescript, forthcoming in article form). I am most grateful to Mr. Kelly for the liberal use of his paper he has permitted me. As it is not yet accessible to a wider audience, I have repeated his citation of authorities.

115. W.H. Crawford, ed., Letters from an Ulster Land Agent, 1774-85 (Belfast, 1976), pp. 39, 41-42.

116. Dublin Evening Post, February-May 1783, especially February 18 and 20 and April 22.

117. Irish Parliamentary Register, 3: 198-99; Faulkner's Dublin Journal, May 8, 1784; Volunteer Journal (Dublin), May 21 and 24 and June 2, 1784; M.A. Jones, "Ulster Emigration, 1783-1815," in E.R.R. Green, ed., Essays in Scotch-Irish History (London, 1969), p. 51.

118. V.J. (Dublin), March 26, 1784; V.E.P., April 29, 1784.

119. D.E.P., March 18 and May 4 and 11, 1784; V.J. (Dublin), April 23 and May 5, 1784; V.E.P., March 2, 1784.

120. D.E.P., April 22, June 3, and July 3, 1783; R.J. Dickson, Ulster Emigration to Colonial America, 1718-75 (London, 1966), pp. 86-87; Jones, "Ulster Emigration," p. 52; V.J. (Dublin), June 28 and July 28, 1784.

121. N.L.I. Bolton Papers, MS. 15827/3, Stephenson to T. Orde, June 7, 1784; P.R.O.N.I. Abercorn Papers, T.2541/IA1/14/25, James Hamilton to Lord Abercorn, May 16, 1784.

122. V.J. (Dublin), September 15 and November 20, 1784.

123. Dickson, Ulster Emigration, p. 64; V.J. (Dublin), May 5, 7, and 28, June 7 and 28, and July 28, 1784; D.E.P., June 3 and 12, 1784.

124. Jones, "Ulster Emigration," pp. 52-53.

125. [J. Knox], A view of the British Empire, more especially Scotland... (London, 1784), p. 32.

126. J. King, Thoughts on the difficulties and distresses in which the peace of 1783 has involved the people of England..., 5th ed. (London, 1783), passim.

127. [M.G. de Crèvecoeur], Letters from an American farmer..., reprint ed. (Belfast, 1783), pp. 37, 46-47, 51.

128. B. Franklin, Information... (London, 1784), as excerpted in V.J. (Dublin), November 10, 1784.

129. See, for example, D.E.P., June 5, 1783.

130. D.E.P., February 18 and 20 and June 3, 1783.

131. D.E.P., August 9, 1783; Kelly, "Irish Parliamentary Reform Movement," pp. 133-79.

132. D.E.P., June 12, July 15, and December 13, 1783.

133. Whether due to policy or absent-mindedness, the government proceeded against emigration by propaganda rather than by statute. The Irish Act of 25 Geo. III, cap. 17, against "seducing artificers and manufacturers" or their tools to foreign countries, did not apply to the United States until the following year (1786), and in any case excluded many crucial sorts of "artificers" (for example, linen weavers).

134. V.E.P., May 1, June 5, 6, and 31, August 10, and November 2 and 22, 1784.

135. D.E.P., July 29, 1784; V.J. (Dublin), June 7, 1784.

126

136. <u>V.J.</u> (Dublin), June 2, September 15, and October 20, 1784.

137. <u>V.J.</u> (Dublin), November 10, 1784.

138. <u>D.E.P.</u>, March 12, 1785.

139. <u>V.E.P.</u>, December 7, 1784, May 4 and September 13, 1785; <u>D.E.P.</u>, December 23, 1784 and February 10, 1785.

140. <u>V.E.P.</u>, August 30, September 13, November 24 and 26, and December 24, 1785.

141. <u>V.E.P.</u>, July 3, 1787.

142. Linenhall Library, Belfast: Joy Papers, MS. 14/19, Bruce to [Henry Joy], October 7, 1784.

143. <u>The speeches of the Rt Hon. Henry Grattan in the Irish and in the Imperial Parliament, edited by his son</u>, 4 vols. (London, 1822), 1: 40.

144. Quoted in O'Connor, "More Immediate Effects of the American Revolution on Ireland," p. 179.

145. Quoted in Harlow, <u>Second British Empire</u>, 1: 207; J.G.A. Pocock, "1776: The Revolution Against Parliament," in <u>Three British Revolutions</u>, p. 282.

146. Quoted in R.J.S. Hoffman, <u>Edmund Burke, New York Agent, with His Letters to the New York Assembly and Intimate Correspondence with Charles O'Hara, 1761-1776</u> (Philadelphia, 1956), pp. 589, 612-13.

147. Morgan, <u>Birth of the Republic</u>, pp. 57-59; Plumb, "Impact of the American Revolution on Great Britain," p. 73.

148. See n. 39.

149. Harlow, <u>Second British Empire</u>, 1: 505.

150. O'Connor, "More Immediate Effects of the American Revolution on Ireland," pp. 95-103, 118-23, 169.

151. Middlekauf, <u>The Glorious Cause</u>, pp. 70-74; Morgan, <u>Birth of the Republic</u>, pp. 19, 67; Harlow, <u>Second British Empire</u>, 1: 214.

152. Harlow, <u>Second British Empire</u>, 1: 496-501. But cf. n. 73.

153. Quoted in McDowell, <u>Irish Public Opinion</u>, p. 60, and O'Connor, "More Immediate Effects of the American Revolution on Ireland," p. 188.

154. Morton, "Local Executive in the British Empire," pp. 445–49; Harlow, Second British Empire, 2: 670-675, 774, 789-91; H.C. Wilkinson, Bermuda in the Old Empire: A History of the Island..., 1684-1784 (Oxford, 1950), passim; F.G. Spurdle, Early West Indian Government, Showing the Progress of Government in Barbados, Jamaica and the Leeward Islands, 1660-1783 (Palmerston North, N.Z., [c. 1950]), passim; E.M. Johnston, "Grenada, 1775-79," in P. Roebuck, ed., Macartney of Lisanoure, 1737-1806: Essays in Biography (Belfast, 1983), pp. 99-106.

155. Edwards, "Ireland and the American Revolution," p. 122.

156. Spurdle, Early West Indian Government, pp. 56-57, 92-93; Harlow, Second British Empire, 2: 790.

157. Ehrman, The Younger Pitt: The Reluctant Transition (London, 1983), p. 346.

158. Morton, "Local Executive in the British Empire," pp. 441, 446-47; Harlow, Second British Empire, 2: 758.

159. T.J. Kiernan, History of the Financial Administration of Ireland to 1817 (London, 1930), p. 336; D. Kennedy, "The Irish Whigs, Administrative Reform and Responsible Government, 1782-1800," in Eire-Ireland: A Journal of Irish Studies 8, no. 4 (1973): 66; Morton, "Local Executive in the British Empire," pp. 444-45.

160. J.C.D. Clark, The Dynamics of Change: The Crisis of the 1750s and English Party Systems (Cambridge, England, 1982), p. 456. The same point is made, less pithily but with immediate relevance to the present discussion, in Malcomson, John Foster, pp. 376-77.

161. Ibid., pp. 378-81; Hewitt, ed., Lord Shannon's Letters to His Son, pp. 77-79; O'Brien, "Exercise of Legislative Power in Ireland," pp. 163-71.

162. Spurdle, Early West Indian Government, pp. 122, 215.

163. For some discussion of the post-1783 British government's attitude to the Anglo-Irish ruling class, see Malcomson, John Foster, pp. 381-84, 394-95.

164. Harlow, Second British Empire, 2: 789; Wilkinson, Bermuda, p. 252.

165. Johnston, "Grenada, 1775-79," p. 101; Harlow, Second British Empire, 2: 701; Morton, "Local Executive in the British Empire," p. 447; H. Neatby, Quebec: The Revolutionary Age, 1760-1791 (Oxford, 1966), pp. 108-18, 123-33, 136-41; Malcomson, John Foster, pp. 424-27.

128

166. Neatby, Quebec, pp. 142-58; Harlow, Second British Empire, 2: 707-9, 714-15, 721; H.T. Manning, The Revolt of French Canada, 1800-1835: A Chapter in the History of the British Commonwealth (London, 1962), pp. 35-38.

167. R.W. Winks, The Blacks in Canada: A History (Yale University Press, 1971), pp. 24-61, 96-113; J.W. St. G. Walker, The Black Loyalists: The Search for a Promised Land in Nova Scotia and Sierra Leone, 1783-1870 (Dalhousie University Press, 1976), pp. 1-12, 32, 57, 86-87, 135-38, 388-89, 392, 395.

168. Malcomson, ed., Catholic Emancipation, 1793-1829: P.R.O.N.I. Education Facsimiles, nos. 241-60 (Belfast, 1976), p. 7; F. Cundall, ed., Lady Nugent's Journal: Jamaica 130 Years Ago... (London, 1934), pp. 39-41.

169. Ehrman, Pitt: The Reluctant Transition, pp. 57-73.

170. O'Flaherty, "Catholic Question," pp. 89, 99; Ehrman, Pitt: The Reluctant Transition, pp. 82-84.

171. O'Brien, "Exercise of Legislative Power in Ireland," pp. 235-37.

172. Ehrman, Pitt: The Reluctant Transition, p. 83.

173. State Paper Office of Ireland, Westmorland Correspondence, Letterbook 1, p. 13, Grenville to earl of Westmorland, March 24, 1791.

174. See n. 66; H.M.C. Dropmore Papers, 2: 237, Buckingham to Grenville, December 11, 1791; ibid., pp. 212-15, 221-22; Pembroke College Library, Cambridge, Chatham Papers, Pitt to Lord Auckland, December 14, 1791.

175. Neatby, Quebec, pp. 157-58; H.M.C. Dropmore Papers, 2: 215, Grenville to Dundas, October 24, 1791; Duke of Buckingham, ed., Memoirs of the Courts and Cabinets of George III from Original Family Documents, 4 vols. (London, 1853 and 1855), 2: 220, Grenville to Buckingham, October 11, 1792. I am indebted to Dr. P.J. Jupp for this last reference.

176. See n. 166; O'Flaherty, "Catholic Question," pp. ii-iii, 12, 123-26; H.M.C. Dropmore Papers, 2: 235, Westmorland to Grenville, November 21, 1791.

177. Harlow, Second British Empire, 2: 754-74; Neatby, Quebec, pp. 257-63.

178. Harlow, Second British Empire, 2: 770; O'Flaherty, "Catholic Question," pp. 128, 163-64; Malcomson, John Foster, pp. 297-304, 411-12; Wilkinson, Bermuda, pp. 172-73.

179. W.E.H. Lecky, History of Ireland in the Eighteenth Century, cabinet ed. in 5 vols. (London, 1903), 3: 348-68.

180. G.C. Bolton, The Passing of the Irish Act of Union (Oxford, 1966), pp. 6-7, 20. The question of the 1779-80 proposals is fully explored in D. Lammey, "A Study of Anglo-Irish Relations between 1772 and 1782, with Particular Reference to the 'Free Trade' Movement" (Queens University of Belfast thesis nearing completion), chap. 7.

181. P.R.O.N.I. (originals in Keele University Library) Sneyd Papers, T.3229/2/36, Foster to Lord Auckland, October 21, 1798.

182. D.E. Ginter, "The Loyalist Association Movement of 1792-93 and British Public Opinion," in Historical Journal 9, no. 2 (1966): 179-90; Malcomson, John Foster, p. 351; Malcomson, "The Gentle Leviathan," p. 118 (referring to the second marquess of Downshire, who may have been particularly prone to use the term because his father, as Lord Hillsborough, had been secretary of state for the colonies, and one of his followers in the Irish House of Commons, Colonel Robert Ross, had fought in the American War); G. Taylor, An history of the rebellion in the county of Wexford in ...1798, to which is annexed the author's account of his captivity and merciful deliverance, 2d ed. (Dublin, 1800), p. 185.

183. See Condon (this volume), pp. 189-94; Malcomson, John Foster, pp. 412-15.

THE PEACE OF 1783: A FRENCH VIEW

Claude B. Fohlen

After seven years of war, peace was at last restored in 1783 with the so-called Treaties of Paris and Versailles. Americans usually refer to the first, while the French mention the second. One might think that the French do not want to be reminded of the Treaty of Paris of 1763. That is true, but there were actually two separate treaties completed on the same day in 1783: the Treaty of Paris, signed by the Americans and the British, and the Treaty of Versailles, signed by France and her allies on one part, by the British on the other.[1] This is not the only instance in which a coalition ended with more than one treaty. The Treaties of both Utrecht and Rastadt ended the War of the Succession of Spain in 1713 and 1714; the second Treaty of Versailles and the Treaty of Neuilly, Saint-Germain, Trianon, or Sèvres in 1919 and 1920 marked the end of the First World War. These treaties of 1713-14 and 1919-20 were preceded by a general conference at which the former belligerents (excluding the Germans in 1918) drafted the final act.

Such was not the case in 1782-83. There were not only two separate treaties, but also two separate negotiations. The Americans conducted their own negotiations with the British in Paris during the last months of 1782, while the French simultaneously negotiated with the British in London. Neither effort was officially recognized by the other, despite the Franco-American alliance. Why was this so? Why did the Americans distrust the French when peace was at hand, yet rely on them during the war and continue to rely on them when in need of money? This last question derives from the irony that Benjamin Franklin, on the very day he met with Vergennes to inform him about the preliminaries of peace just signed with the British, reminded the French minister for external affairs that the United States needed further subsidies. Franklin pleaded his somewhat embarrassing case with customary skill and thoroughness: "The whole structure (of the nation) will collapse immediately if, for that reason, you refuse to give us additional assistance." Vergennes acquiesced, of course, and immediately granted him Ł600,000 out of a fund of Ł6 million set aside for the young republic.

In the treaty of alliance signed between France and the United States in 1778, Article VIII stated: "Neither of the two parties

132

shall conclude either truce or peace with Great Britain without the
formal consent of the other first obtained; and they mutually engage
not to lay down their arms until the independence of the United
States shall have been formally or tacitly assured by the treaty or
treaties that shall terminate the war." Thus, it seems clear that
the countries agreed not to sign a separate peace or even conclude
a truce without the consent of the other. This pledge was further
cemented by the Congress, which appointed commissioners to France
and instructed them to keep the French informed of any progress in
the negotiations. Did the American commissioners break their country's pledge? Did they betray the French?

Such questions have been discussed at great length by American
historians--much less so by the French--who argue that there was no
breach of faith, even less a betrayal. These historians contend
that the commissioners had good reason to disregard their instructions from Congress, which were in line with Article VIII of the
treaty of 1778. The commissioners suspected that the French were
conducting secret negotiations in London. They had learned about
the September 7, 1782 departure for London of Rayneval, the deputy
minister for foreign affairs and confidant of Vergennes, and were
much alarmed that he would neglect their true interests. They
were even more alarmed three days later when they received a copy
of a letter written to Vergennes by Barbé-Marbois, French consul
in Philadelphia, cautioning him against giving the Americans a
share in the fisheries on the coast of Newfoundland and the Gulf of
Saint Lawrence. The Americans--particularly residents of Massachusetts, including the highly vocal Samuel Adams--had argued that,
having shared the fisheries when they were a colony, they were
therefore entitled to the same rights once liberated from the
British. In this they were in conflict with the French, who sought
to regain title to the fisheries, which they had lost in the Treaty
of Paris of 1763.[3]

The Americans also thought they could obtain a better territorial deal if they negotiated directly with the British. They
may have been right. The French were quick to accommodate Spanish
designs on Florida and wanted to avoid a conflict with the British
over the border between Canada and the United States. According to
La Luzerne, the Americans ended up rejoicing that their neighbors
to the south were the Spaniards instead of the British.[4] As for
the border with Canada, the Americans got an excellent deal, which
was surprising because it had been an idée fixe of Vergennes not
to intervene in Canada, even at the price of cheating the Americans,
as he made clear in a dispatch to La Luzerne:

You know our plan with regard to Canada: it is unalterable;
thus, everything which prevents the conquest of this country
is crucial for us; but you are aware that this line of thought
must be entirely hidden from the Americans. It would be a
crime for which they would never pardon us; it is better to
leave them with their illusions....[5]

La Luzerne's response shows he knew how generous the British would be about their territory in the north:

> The plenipotentiaries, in pushing the territorial line to include the Lake of the Woods, create for their posterity in the distant future an opening to the Pacific Ocean....This line gives the Americans a vast commerce with the natives and puts in their hands the forts of Oswego, Niagara, Detroit, and Michillimakinac, four strongholds that they never took during the course of this war....[6]

It is doubtful the French would have supported the Americans in getting these four important military and commercial positions.

While the American commissioners had obvious reason to skirt their French allies in starting their own negotiations with the British, French diplomats had been suspicious of the Americans long before they began these separate discussions. In the spring of 1782, Barbé-Marbois told Vergennes of the threat of a separate agreement:

> It is a critical matter for us that the United States persists steadfastly with those principles that they have followed up to now, that is to say that their alliance with the King remains solid, and that they follow the example His Majesty has given them of refusing to make a separate agreement with the Court in London.[7]

He suggested his minister remind the Americans of numerous French "sacrifices" for the American cause, but to no avail.

The British government sought also to divide the allies of France. While the British knew that disassociating Spain from France would be difficult because the two had common interests, they realized this would be an easier game to play with the Americans. The Americans shared their culture, and the British knew that many Americans feared an alliance with two papist kingdoms that had absolute monarchies. The American struggle was a struggle for liberty, and the two countries on which America relied were hardly sanctuaries for that. Franklin and Jefferson were great admirers of France, but John Adams and John Jay were not. The alliance between France and the United States was based more on self-interest than on sentiment, and the British knew this and took advantage of it, so that it was easy for them to persuade the Americans to negotiate separately. Vergennes and La Luzerne understood this as early as the summer of 1782. Vergennes, in a dispatch alluding to the change of ministry in England, reaffirmed the solidarity of France and Spain while denouncing maneuvers with the Americans:

> It is presumed that the [British] minister continues to hold the illusion of their perseverance, and that he will not cease attempts to mislead the Congress or the American people until peace is actually signed.[8]

Referring to proposals by Carleton to General Washington, La Luzerne, about the same time, expressed his anxiety about the future:

> The following phrases in Mr. Guy Carleton's letter: "Mr.
> Grenville will first propose the independence of the thirteen
> colonies rather than making it a condition of a general treaty"
> are suspect and equivocal....Their purpose is also to divide
> France and the United States and to set each of them up for a
> quick attempt to deprive either of its ally....[9]

Even if it came as no surprise to the French, Vergennes resented
American softness in the face of British pressure, as he made clear
in a letter to Franklin, after he had been told about what the
Americans had done:

> You have fixed the preliminary articles without informing us,
> even though the instructions of Congress proscribe your doing
> anything without the King's participation. You will produce
> a sure gleam of hope for peace in America without knowing the
> state of our negotiation.[10]

Did the American commissioners fall into a trap set by the
British? French diplomats thought so. But it was actually John Jay
who started the negotiations, not the British. Jay seized the initiative with John Adams not yet back from Holland, and, he believed,
with Franklin too ill to act, and with the fourth commissioner, Henry
Laurens, incapacitated by the death of his son, who had been killed
in an obscure action in South Carolina almost a year after Yorktown.
Jay had been humiliated in Madrid and had little sympathy for France.
He was resentful of Vergennes for using power politics to support
the American cause. "Vergennes," wrote Richard Morris, "seemed to
make it painfully evident that he was more interested in trimming
the British Empire down to size than in establishing a new nation
along new principles and with durable prospects." Jay, for his
part, took "a strong stand against [those] instructions of Congress
[that subordinated] the peace commissioners to the King of France,"
according to Morris.[11] "If the instructions conflict with America's
honor and dignity," Jay is said to have told Franklin, "I would break
them like this," and with that he hurled his clay pipe into the fire.

Jay was the first to get the British to formally recognize the
former colonies as an independent state. Though Franklin tended to
minimize this move, Jay felt the glory was his for having won independence from the British. Notwithstanding disagreements over further particulars, Jay's fellow commissioners could not but follow
Jay's lead and agree to sign the separate peace, which Franklin
announced to Vergennes on November 29, 1782: "I have the honour,"
Franklin wrote, "to acquaint your Excellency that the Commissioners
of the United States have agreed with M. Oswald on the Preliminary
Articles of the Peace between those States and Great-Britain. To-
morrow I hope we shall be able to communicate to your Excellency a
Copy of them...."[12]

Did the commissioners violate their instructions? The best answer is Edward Corwin's:

> Technically, of course, the violation by the commissioners of their instructions was a matter exclusively between them and the Congress....[But] the action of the commissioners [did not] technically violate the pledge given in the Treaty of Alliance, that the United States would conclude neither truce nor peace with Great-Britain without first obtaining the formal consent of France. The Provisional Articles were not a separate peace nor did they "hold out a certain hope of peace." It may be admitted, however, that they were intended to convey a warning that the United States reserved the right to make a separate peace, if a final peace should be obstructed by France for reasons not covered by the Treaty of Alliance.[13]

Vergennes was furious, of course, and Franklin did his best to appease him. "We have committed a breach of courtesy in not consulting you before signature," he wrote a few days later, "but it is not out of lack of respect for the King, whom we all affectionately honor, and we hope that we will be pardoned."[14] Vergennes had some reason to rejoice, however. His American allies had gotten an excellent deal, more than "I could have thought possible," he said. He sought a general peace, and signing the preliminaries --whether or not the French had been excluded--appeared to hasten that conclusion. French finances had been in very bad shape for years, and Vergennes had long had to overcome opposition to expenditures in America. While the king supported him, he knew opposition to his policy was sufficiently strong that he could not ignore the calls for peace much longer.

Further, it was consistent with French policy to reach a compromise with the British and to avoid a peace founded on military strength. With the independence of the United States in hand, there was no reason to prolong the conflict.[16] The British had recognized the new nation, and the French had gotten their revenge for the humiliation of 1763.

More important still, Vergennes knew he could use the preliminaries as a lever against the Spaniards and the Dutch, who, disappointed by the turn of events, wanted to prolong the war. "It still remains to reconcile Spain's interests and those of the Dutch," wrote Vergennes. "I have reason to hope that we'll soon reach agreement among ourselves as to the first....As for the Dutch, I fear that their business will cause us delay and embarrassment." Up to that point, Spain had been uncompromising, claiming, among other acquisitions, Minorca, Gibraltar, and Florida. But the subsequent failure of the Franco-Spanish forces to recapture Gibraltar was a major blow to their ambitions and put pressure on Floridablanca to enter negotiations with the British. That left the Dutch isolated in the coalition, unable to satisfy their territorial desires. Thus, for Vergennes, the signing of the preliminaries gave added reason for persuading his allies to shorten the war.

Vergennes's most persuasive argument for bringing hostilities to a close and accepting the challenge of the Americans, however, was the mounting tension in Eastern Europe. In November 1782, with the consent and cooperation of Joseph II of Austria--who had designs on the Balkans--Catherine II of Russia sent Turkey an ultimatum calling on the Turks to relinquish Crimea.[17] A former ambassador to the Porte, Vergennes knew of the Ottoman Empire's weakness and of the dangers of partition. A Russo-Austrian alliance could threaten the European balance of power, weaken France's position in the Mediterranean, and even provoke a general European conflict.

This interpretation--that the French had plenty of reason to favor a quick end to hostilities with the British--has recently been challenged by the Duc de Castries in one of the rare books in French devoted to the American Revolution.[18] Castries is very critical of the American negotiators, especially Jay, whom he compares to Benedict Arnold and accuses of having betrayed the allied cause with a "double jeu américain." Castries argues that better terms of peace could have been obtained later on, because the French were victorious on the coasts of India.

While this may be true, the position of the French in the West Indies had worsened after the defeat of the French Navy at the Saintes (April 1782) and the capture of de Grasse, Yorktown's real winner. Victory in India could not compensate for this misfortune. It came too late, in any case; the preliminaries had already been agreed upon.

Castries's view fails to take into account the rising storm in Eastern Europe and the desire on the part of Vergennes and the king not to abort the peace process already under way. Nothing could change Vergennes's determination to erase the memories of 1763 and avoid any further conflict with the British. France had already renounced interest in Canada, in the West Indies, and in the Indian Ocean. Vergennes, looking far ahead, sought final reconciliation of the two long-time enemies, not better terms on which to continue the struggle.

The Treaty of Versailles affected mainly France's relations with the United States and Great Britain, but this is difficult to assess because only six years elapsed between the signing of the treaty and the outbreak of the French Revolution. Therefore, it seems reasonable to investigate the intentions of the French government, rather than the treaty's accomplishments.

Despite the misunderstandings of 1782 between the American commissioners and Vergennes, the Franco-American alliance of 1778 remained in effect until 1800, when the convention signed by the French and the Americans formally cancelled all former engagements. But the alliance was much loosened and weakened as early as 1783, because the French had supported American independence only to avenge the humiliation of 1763.

There was no genuine interest among the French in the American cause as such, except among a minority of liberals, especially within the aristocracy, and some philosophers and writers, all considered dangerous to the monarchy. What Vergennes had in mind was preserving the balance of power in Europe and the colonial world, not supporting any moral or ideological cause. He made this obvious in his famous Mémoire of March 29, 1784, as did Rayneval as early as 1781.[19]

In renouncing its intent to reconquer Canada and to claim Louisiana (ceded to Spain in 1763)--and in agreeing to cede Florida to Spain--France was without interests on the American continent. It retained St. Domingue and some smaller islands, however, and received Tobago. It hoped to develop trade between the United States and the French West Indies, a goal supported by American merchants who had called on ports there during the war. But the French refused to break with the colonial practice of restricting trade with its colonies to the mother country, and no French West Indies port was subsequently opened to American ships, a gesture the Americans resented.

The Franco-American treaty of commerce was still valid, but it had little effect for either side once the war was over. For almost two centuries, Americans had relied on the British market, and they were accustomed to goods manufactured and provided by the English. The French proved unable to unseat them as British goods inundated the American market, to the great satisfaction of the American consumer. The French had built their commerce on war supplies and, for several reasons, were unable to retool in time. First, the British had accumulated goods in their ports and were ready for the first opportunity to ship them to the United States. Second, the French were unequipped to manufacture the hardware and fabrics Americans wanted. Third, long-established commercial ties between English firms and their American clientele were difficult to break, especially when these firms gave credit to their patrons, something the French could never do. Fourth, Americans, as they had during the war, found French goods second-rate. Finally, the new republic had accumulated a large debt as a consequence of its many French loans. To pay the interest on these loans, it would have been necessary for the United States to develop substantial trade with France, but this was difficult, given the dominance of the Anglo-American commercial relationship and the fact that Americans sold only staples, including tobacco, tar, furs, and other raw materials. While the Americans actually exported more to France than they imported, the resulting trade surplus was never large enough to cover their debts.

Several of the French firms engaged in the U.S. trade went bankrupt, and on both sides of the Atlantic eagerness to develop trade quickly declined—great expectations at the end of the war to the contrary—even before the French Revolution began.[20]

The French, especially Vergennes, had higher hopes for improved commercial relations with Great Britain. In his recent book, Orville Murphy showed us a new side to the French diplomat, a desire to develop French commerce. Vergennes has always been seen as the classic diplomat, adept at political maneuvers, but Murphy found him more farsighted than is usually assumed. Great Britain may have wanted to forget the Seventy-Eighth Article of the Treaty of Versailles, which provided that "France and England name commissioners ...to negotiate new commercial arrangements" by 1786, but Vergennes did not. He was adamant on this point, for he could not foresee any improvement in relations with the British except in the commercial sphere. This was clearly indicated in a note dated 1783 and possibly written by Rayneval:

> The moment of peace must be seized to establish between the two nations all possible lines of friendship, commerce, and good behavior. This [argument] has certainly not escaped Count Vergennes, since he appears to be occupied already in carefully giving English manufactured goods advantages in the French market on condition that England returns the favor in the wine trade with France, and this is of critical importance.

The author went on to suggest that one way of diminishing tensions between the two countries was to establish "in their American colonies a reciprocal freedom of trade among the French, the English, and the Americans of the United States."[21]

Vergennes was especially keen on signing a treaty of commerce with the British. He knew they were not ready to accept defeat and were in fact already preparing for the next round. In his Mémoire of March 29, 1784 he advised the king:

> England is not losing sight of the need to rebuild its navy, and she applies to the task abundant funds, and the work of her shipyards and arsenals. She pursues these with an energy that differs little from war, and soon, thanks to the new construction she has begun in all her yards, her fleet will be more numerous and stronger than it was at the moment of peace.[22]

But there was little enthusiasm for such a treaty on either side. The British still adhered to the provisions of the Treaty of Utrecht and saw no serious reason to change them; the French were afraid of English imports, which had become fashionable among its upper classes. Vergennes applied pressure on the British to approve a treaty by closing French markets to certain British manufactured goods, including carriages, hardware, woolens, cottons, and hosiery. He wanted to make it clear that all commercial relations would have to be reciprocal, and that, if the English government refused, the French could retaliate. Vergennes's tenacity paid off, and the treaty was at last signed on September 26, 1786, almost three years after the pledge at Versailles and one year after the deadline. While the treaty did give France "most-favored-nation" status, withheld by the English because they had signed the Methuen Treaty with Portugal, it was, as Murphy pointed out, "unusual in its attempt to further an Anglo-French rapprochement by establishing rules and principles to govern the relations between the two states, as well as among the subjects of both sovereigns."[23]

Vergennes thus succeeded in getting a treaty with liberal provisions, one that would improve future relations between the two countries. For the French, this was the greatest achievement to be drawn from the Treaty of Versailles, and no minor accomplishment for Vergennes.

According to Jonathan Dull, "French participation [in the American Revolution] was a mistake for France, a failure of tragic dimensions. Its benefits to France were illusory, its victories hollow, its accomplishments pointless."[24] Dull's view could only come from knowing that the generation that experienced the treaties of Paris and Versailles of 1783 also witnessed the French Revolution. In the short run, these treaties were revenge for the humiliation of 1763. They confirmed the return of France to the international scene as a major broker in the balance of power. They marked the beginning of a new era when friendship between nations would be based not only on military or political considerations, but on the fruits of liberalized trade relations. Nobody could have predicted that a revolution would destroy the treaties' profits. Nobody has been able, so far, to forecast a revolution; those who have, have always been wrong. Hazard belongs to history.

NOTES

AMAE: Archives du Ministère des Affaires Etrangères, Paris.

CP: Correspondance politique

1. The signing of the Treaty of Paris is marked by a plaque at 56 rue Jacob in Paris. It reads:

140

En ce batiment jadis hotel d'York le 3 septembre 1783 David
Hartley, au nom du roi d'angleterre, Benjamin Franklin, John
Jay, John Adams au nom des Etats-Unis d'Amerique ont signe
le traite definitif de paix reconnaissant l'indépendance des
Etats-Unis.

2. AMAE, CP, E.U., 22, Franklin to Vergennes, Passy, December
17, 1782; Vergennes to La Luzerne, Versailles, December 21, 1782.

3. Ibid., Vergennes to La Luzerne, Versailles, August 12, 1782.
In this dispatch to La Luzerne, the French minister in Philadelphia,
Vergennes explained that the French government had been informed of
agitation in New England over the fisheries, but that it did not
intend to prolong the war to satisfy the Americans.

4. Ibid., 23, La Luzerne to Vergennes, Philadelphia, March 26,
1783.

5. Ibid., 22, Vergennes to La Luzerne, Versailles, October 14,
1782.

6. Ibid., 23, La Luzerne to Vergennes, Philadelphia, March 19,
1782.

7. Ibid., 20, Vergennes to La Luzerne, Philadelphia, March 23,
1782.

8. Ibid., 22, Vergennes to La Luzerne, Versailles, August 12,
1782.

9. Ibid., 22, La Luzerne to Vergennes, Philadelphia, August 15,
1782.

10. Ibid., 22, Vergennes to Franklin, Versailles, December 15,
1782.

11. On the role of Jay, Richard B. Morris, The Peacemakers (New
York, 1965), especially chap. 13, "The long clay pipe of Mr. Jay."
For a different view of Jay, see Orville T. Murphy, Charles Gravier,
Comte de Vergennes (Albany, 1982), pp. 328-29, 391-93. Also,
William C. Stinchcombe, The American Revolution and the French
Alliance (Syracuse, 1969), chap. 13, "From Yorktown to Peace." For
a historiographical background of American diplomacy during the War
of Independence, see Alexander Deconde, "Historians, the War of
American Independence, and the Persistence of the Exceptionalist
Ideal," International History Review 3 (August 1983): 399-430. The
most recent discussion on the role of Benjamin Franklin in the
negotiations is found in Jonathan R. Dull, "Franklin the Diplomat:
The French Missions," Transactions of the American Philosophical
Society 72, pt. 1 (1982): 53-64.

12. AMAE, CP, E.U., 22, Franklin to Vergennes, Passy, November 29, 1782.

13. Edward S. Corwin, French Policy and the American Alliance of 1778 (Princeton, 1916), pp. 341-42.

14. Ibid., 22, Franklin to Vergennes, Passy, December 17, 1782.

15. Ibid., 22, Vergennes to La Luzerne, Versailles, December 19, 1782.

16. AMAE, Memoires et Documents, France, no. 587, Vergennes to the king, March 29, 1784:

L'indépendance de l'Amérique assurée, la guerre devenait sans objet pour la France comme pour l'Angleterre et l'on aurait pu vouloir la prolonger de notre part sans demasquer un système d'ambition bien opposé à l'esprit de modération de Votre Majesté.

17. For a general view of this conflict, refer to Orville Murphy, op. cit., chap. 27, "The crisis of 1783."

18. Duc de Castries, La France et l'Indépendance américaine, Librairie academique Perrin (Paris, 1975), chap. 12, "Le traite de Versailles."

19. AMAE, Mémoires et Documents, France, no. 587, Rayneval to Louis XVI, 1781.

20. Claude Fohlen, "The Commercial Failure of France in America," Two Hundred Years of Franco-American Relations (Newport, R.I., September 1978), pp. 93-120.

21. AMAE, Memoires de Documents, France, no. 587, 1783.

22. Ibid., Vergennes to the king, March 29, 1784.

23. Orville T. Murphy, op. cit., p. 443.

24. Jonathan R. Dull, "France and the American Revolution Seen as a Tragedy," in Two Hundred Years, p. 6.

III

Reverberations in the Americas: Does the Revolution Continue?

THE IMPACT OF THE TREATY OF PARIS
ON SPANISH AMERICA

Peggy K. Liss

I begin in an unlikely locale--that now fashionable intellectual watering hole, 18th-century Scotland--with a member of what
John Pocock has called "the Scottish school of sociological historians."[1] He is William Robertson, whose History of America,
published in 1777, deals almost exclusively with Spanish America.

Pocock has described the great achievement of these Scots--the
best known being Adam Smith--as "the recognition that a commercial
organization of society had rendered obsolete much that had been
believed about society before that."[2] Not surprisingly, Robertson
and Smith, whose Wealth of Nations preceded Robertson's History by
a year, assumed that applied principles of political economy were
central to all human activity and that economic growth was a prefer-
able starting point for achieving the well-being of a society.
Both men invested material existence with great moral worth. What
may be surprising is that similar assumptions were at work in the
changing Spanish imperial system Robertson portrayed.

Spain's America policies began to be systematically overhauled
in the 1760s under the enlightened despot Charles III. A comprehensive reform program was drawn up, based on Nuevo sistema de gobier-
no económico para la América (A New System for the Economic Government of America), a plan put forth in 1743 by José Campillo y Cosío,
a former minister of the treasury. Campillo outlined "a system
equally political and economic," one meant to benefit everyone by
increasing royal authority, augmenting the treasury, and promoting
public well-being in Spain and its America. At the system's heart
was commerce, "the fundamental principle of all the other interests
of the monarchy, for it is the invigorator of agriculture, the arts,
and trade, and of manufactures and industry." Spain, Campillo wrote,
must first rid American government of traditional abuses, then take
steps to do two things--regain control of imperial trade, and build
up its America, still officially known as the Indies, as a source
of raw materials and a market for imports. Here lay the route to
prosperity and power.[3]

Charles III and the ministers who implemented his proposals
wed faith in material progress to an avowed enlightened way of looking at the world that included an enthusiasm for reform sponsored
by the state, a commitment to intellectual and moral progress, and
a reliance on reason. They shared the enlightened belief that

studying useful knowledge would uncover universal laws, and that applying such knowledge could harness nature and enable a more just and reasonable social existence. They were fervent and future oriented, and they sent like-minded officials to America. The Spanish program for reform was in accord with Robertson's principles: "The nation," he wrote approvingly, "has adopted more liberal ideas." But "the commercial regulations of Spain with respect to her colonies are too rigid and systematical to be carried into complete execution." Noting the flow of contraband, Robertson wrote further: "A spirit of corruption has infected all the colonies of Spain in America."[4]

Robertson's history, though neglected today, is an excellent and judicious contemporary account, as far as it goes. He came to realize that Spaniards were not sufficiently zealous in removing trade restrictions and monopolies in American commerce and that they relied too much on mining projects. (He cited Smith as an authority on these issues, repeating Smith's general theories on national wealth.)[5] Yet at bottom, he blamed the lack of greater success in reform within America on the persistence of the past. We shall see that he overlooked some other stumbling blocks.

He got first-hand information from within the Spanish Empire, acknowledging the help of such well-placed Spaniards as the Conde de Campomanes, an architect of the reform program, and Dionisio Alcedo y Herrera, a high official in South America. Robertson also relied on Creoles for information, but in his history said almost nothing about them. Creoles come across only as passive actors, and there Robertson went wrong, for Spanish Americans, including his Creole informants, were integral to the story he wanted to tell.

The Creoles whom we associate with Robertson--José Antonio Rojas of Chile, the Quito-born Antonio de Alcedo, and Francisco Javier Clavijero of Mexico--are now least remembered for their contacts with him. Rather, they are recalled as early spokesmen for a new variety of creolism, or Spanish American self-awareness. This criollismo would come to characterize the sentiments of the leaders of the movements for Spanish American independence.

In the 1760s, Rojas, Alcedo, and Clavijero were young, educated, and talented, imbued with enlightened self-interest. They aspired to prominence. Rojas and Clavijero addressed themselves to bettering society, Alcedo to its defense (he joined the Imperial Army). The Bourbon reforms of the period promised both: economic expansion for their communities and greater opportunities to forward their careers in either the royal bureaucracy or the military. Throughout the empire, education--not to mention the general atmosphere--was becoming more secular. The state discarded the old imperial ideology, including the notion that all change was insidious, and began instead to endorse reform in the name of progress.

The three Creoles were enchanted and intoxicated by the new spirit, both critical and positive, that enveloped the new policies. Clavijero, a Jesuit, carried the banner for regional economic development and educational reform. Rojas worked under the new reforming viceroy in Peru, Manuel de Amat, then traveled to Spain, and finally returned home to Santiago, where he became a force for Creole rights on the cabildo ("town council"). Alcedo, the son of Dionisio Alcedo, attended a Spanish military academy and studied medicine before joining the Spanish Army and rising through its ranks.[6]

In America over the next 20 years, Rojas and other Creoles grew increasingly critical of the imperial regime. The new reforming rhetoric itself encouraged criticism, to a point, and Creoles soon saw that the new program meant for tighter political and fiscal control, greater numbers of Spaniards in American government, and increased levies for America. They saw, too, that in the course of implementing new policies, officials pushed especially hard (and often harshly) for those measures designed to benefit the metropolis; as for those measures designed to aid America, the state could never quite afford them.[7]

Clavijero fell victim to another reform: Charles III's assertion of state authority over the clergy. The Mexican was deported from his homeland in 1767 when the Jesuits were expelled from the empire. In exile in Italy, he published History of Mexico (1780-81), which reinforced what has been called "the classical antiquity of the Mexican creoles," that is, a pride in the pre-Hispanic, indigenous high civilizations. Also, he took Robertson to task for giving insufficient credit to the achievements of America's great cultures, and he noted that Robertson's myopia owed a good deal to the philosophes Buffon and DePauw. He could have added that it extended to Robertson's view of Creoles.

It was probably because Robertson focused on the Spanish imperial system that he wrote little about the inhabitants of Spain's America, except for the Indians (and that, as Clavijero complained, he got wrong, so it is probably just as well). Yet in saying nothing else, he left the long-standing impression that Spanish America was a dismal swamp, mired in apathy. Taken up by subsequent generations of historians, this erroneous verdict by default remained the standard view, and it hampered efforts to make sense of Spain's empire in the late colonial period and beyond.

A generation later, another European savant, Alexander von Humboldt, filled in some gaps left by Robertson, but because Humboldt was seen as an authority on his own period, his comments on the preceding decades were given little heed. Humboldt traveled widely in America and had read Clavijero and Robertson. He not only got information from Creoles but singled out the scientific activities of a number of them as evidence of American intellectual vitality, warning Spain that American complaints and aspirations

were valid and potentially explosive. Most important for our purposes, Humboldt pinpointed the moment when "creoles [began] to
say 'I am not a Spaniard; I am an American.'"[9] That moment came
with the signing of the Treaty of Versailles, which, together with
the Treaty of Paris, signified the success of the American Revolution.

Thus, as Robertson was writing on the eve of 1776, only a small
group of forward-looking young Creole intellectuals had taken up
las luces and precepts of political economy and begun to call for
reform. By Humboldt's time, the first decade of the 19th century,
the winds of change had enveloped not only intellectuals throughout
Spanish America but a new breed of Creole entrepreneurs, and they
had fanned a newly assertive Creole patriotism, still hyphenated,
but with a greater emphasis on America. In all this the onset and
the successful conclusion of the American Revolution played an important part.

Immediately, between 1776 and 1783, two things happened: Creolism became more narrowly associated with Americanism, and inter-
American contacts, especially commercial ones, multiplied. Spain's
entry into the war in 1779 and the resulting British blockade stimulated both internal production in Spanish America and the U.S.
carrying trade. Anglo-American ships sped down to Patagonia. (They
would soon round Cape Horn, sail up to the Pacific Northwest, and
venture to China.) What happened in Spanish America was varied and
complex.

Propertied Cubans prospered. Havana was the main base of Spanish and French naval operations, and after 1776, as Franklin Knight
has pointed out, the United States became Cuba's largest trading
partner; the years between 1779 and 1783 marked the true initial
impulse of Cuban economic expansion.[10] Cubans became, and remained,
economically oriented toward the United States.

Spanish American productivity during the war years was generally up. The numbers of Creole merchants rose rapidly, and together
with planters and ranchers they thirsted for less restricted trade
--although planters and ranchers wanted it restricted to noncompeti-
tive imports. The call for free trade, comercio libre, was a key-
note of the new creolism, and it was heard, for instance, when Creole merchants realized that Anglo-American flour undersold Mexican
flour in Havana because Spanish restrictions hampered effective competition. At the same time, Creoles admired the prosperity and the
economic sagacity of the people they called bostoneses, and they
wanted to beat them at their own game. Some reforming Spanish ad-
ministrators in America felt the same way, and encouraged more open
commerce in order to export surplus, expedite supply, and discourage
smuggling--especially in Havana and in the marginal areas beginning
to come into their own, including Buenos Aires, New Orleans, and

Caracas. Thus, Caracas's Spanish governor, Francisco de Saavedra, wrote to Jose de Gálvez, the minister of the Indies, that trade with foreigners was necessary and would be lucrative. It would enable Venezuelans to export fruits of the land and cows and mules, he said, for, after all, "what can we do with over 10,000 mules?"[11] In short, by 1776, Spain's America program had abetted American economic expansion and disseminated knowledge of the principles and goals of reform. Then, during the American Revolution, Spain's international policies created conflict among its priorities in Spanish America. One result was a mule crisis for Venezuela; others were more ominous.

Spain's entry into war in 1779 placed an additional, resented burden on its American dependencies. Recruitment was stepped up; military pay and privileges were thus made more uncertain. These steps, combined with the abrasive measures with which reform was instituted, led in 1780-81 to revolution, contemporary with the Anglo-American, but unsuccessful. In the Andes and in northern South America, thousands of people--Creoles, mestizos, and Indians --rebelled (ultimately to be pacified by government promises, largely unkept, and, in some areas, by white fears of race war). These rebels knew of the other American revolution. From New Granada (now Colombia) in 1781, the viceroy reported that "news of the independence of the English colonies of the north goes from mouth to mouth among everyone in the uprising."[12] And from Caracas, José de Abalos, its intendant, warned Gálvez that South American rebellion was connected to "the sad and lamentable rising in the United States of North America," and he predicted catastrophe if Spanish Americans were not both better treated and more closely tied to the metropolis.[13]

Saavedra, in Mexico in 1781 as Gálvez's envoy, found broader influences. He noted that Creoles there had become enlightened in a very short time and that "the zeal for religion which was the most powerful brake to contain them weakens by the moment."[14] French books abounded, he reported, and were "making a species of revolution in their mode of thinking." Among the inflammatory French authors Saavedra listed: Voltaire, Rousseau, Raynal, and Robertson. (Raynal had much to say about Britain's American colonies and the causes of 1776; Robertson probably had been translated into French.) Saavedra's error corroborates what we have surmised--a conjuncture of the French and Scottish enlightenments in the perception of inhabitants of the Spanish Empire. He also provides evidence to a more general trend, that shortly after 1776 "revolution" became lodged in the vocabulary of Spanish reformers, and often its use was in reference to America.

The Conde de Aranda, for example, who was Spain's minister in Paris during the peace negotiations, expressed apprehension about "the menace of the revolutionary spirit represented by the United States." He went on to predict that the new nation would become a giant threatening Spain in America. Though Aranda's authorship has been questioned, his remarks echoed reports from Saavedra, Abalos, and other Spanish officials in the Indies.[15]

Humboldt thought that one reason Creoles began in 1783 to make an issue of being American was that they got the impression that Aranda and other Spanish ministers treated the victorious Americans with new respect. Also, Humboldt's writings corroborate the evidence that U.S. material well-being nurtured among Creoles a growing sense of optimism about America's natural wealth, about its being the land of the future. America increasingly became the symbol of infinite possibility. The Revolution of 1776 changed relations among all Americans and much within the Americas. In Spanish America, a species of revolution affected Creole hearts, minds, and pocketbooks, and was for some a step toward political independence; both economic and political alternatives finally seemed to be at hand. For most, it was a step at least toward greater regional autonomy.

While Robertson's American-born correspondent, Antonio Alcedo, distinguished himself at the siege of Gibraltar, another Spanish officer of less acceptable lineage in imperial society (his father was a Canary Islander) and of more restless and flamboyant disposition deserted his post in Havana to flee first to the United States and then to Europe. He was Francisco de Miranda, now known as the Precursor of American Independence. In a diary he kept in 1783-84 while traveling in the fledgling United States, Miranda admired its great statesmen, its prosperity (particularly its thriving commerce and agriculture), and the industriousness of its people, though he thought them too egalitarian; he did not enjoy finding his servant at table with him at a Connecticut inn. These travels, he said later, persuaded him to work toward independence for Spanish America, and to model that effort on the United States (in which, as had Adam Smith, he discerned the perseverance of the British constitution). "Good God!" Miranda wrote of America in his diary. "What a contrast to the Spanish system!"[16] Miranda went on to become the architect of a revolutionary Creole network in Europe and America. Just a decade earlier, Robertson had seen the potential for progress in Spain's America. His Spanish and Creole informants, too, had been guardedly optimistic. Yet with the end of the Revolution of 1776, many people had come to see Spanish rule as an impediment to America and Americans.

Yet war had left Spain with less power and more problems; with peace, Creoles again found themselves flatteringly courted, as royal ministers made American defense and development their pressing concern. Aranda and the Conde de Floridablanca, chief royal minister, worried that the rambunctious inhabitants of the United States would swarm down the Mississippi River and gain access to the Gulf of Mexico and even Mexico itself. Because a rocketing Spanish debt necessitated the quick extraction of as much specie as possible from its colonies—and required that America pay for its own maintenance, defense, and development—Spain, as Gálvez explained to Saavedra, must make Americans feel they "have influence in their own happiness."[17] It thus switched to a policy of reform after the signing of the Treaty of Paris, proposing to Creoles a kind of alliance for progress.

Accordingly, a much broader spectrum of Creoles was invited, during the 1780s and 1790s, to cooperate actively with authorities in developing the economies of their own regions of the empire, and many did so for the next 20 years. They responded eagerly, forming or bolstering several sorts of approved regional associations dedicated to self-help. In collaboration with officials, they instituted more consulados ("merchant guilds") and new economic or patriotic societies (these designations were significantly interchangeable). Cabildos became more active. Gazettes proliferated. Creole self-awareness, self-reliance, self-esteem, and public spirit were championed. That new American nation, the United States, was a developmental inspiration. Patriotism was terribly fashionable, and was most frequently couched in language associated with the Enlightenment and with political economy. And while still hyphenated, it was centered on America—its growth, even its perfectibility.

Alcedo, then a colonel, was permitted to publish in Madrid a multivolumed Diccionario geográphico-histórico de las Indias, o América. This encyclopedia of hemispheric information extolled the breadth and variety of his native America. It provided facts about the United States and focused on events leading to its having "separated from the dominion of the court of England after a bloody war."[18] The encyclopedia became very popular in Spanish America, as did Clavijero's Mexican history and other literary mirrors of the new creolism.

We have known for some time that the Enlightenment penetrated Spanish America, that it brought faith in progress and a vision of a rosy future that would be achieved through the application of useful knowledge. It is less well known that everywhere the major emphasis of the Enlightenment, beginning in the 1760s, was increasingly on the primacy of an economic upswing; that within Spanish America there was indeed concern with philosophical, literary, and theological themes, but there prevailed—in theory and as a guide to action—an intermeshing of those themes with political initiative and economic goals. What are now understood as enlightened notions were wed to tenets of political economy, to what Robertson called "liberal ideas," which were most often associated, particularly from the 1780s on, with Creoles who knew of Adam Smith and understood how things worked in the United States. Thus, in the Gazeta de Literature he edited in Mexico City, Antonio Alzate, a Creole Humboldt admired, praised the inventiveness of the Anglo-Americans as he wrote about the ways applying useful knowledge could improve Mexican agriculture, ranching, mining, and industry, and about the need for freer commerce. Thus, too, Jacobo de Villaurrutia, who founded the Guatemalan economic society and also its gazette (which he used to win support for freer commerce, including trade with the United States), addressed fellow members as "illustrious patriots." He told them they must promote material progress, widen the internal market, and perform "a sacred role"--that of embracing all useful knowledge and working for the good of mankind and the glory of Guatemala, which would bring about "a happy revolution."[20] Villaurrutia, like other reform-minded officials and concerned Creoles, echoed Adam Smith and Robertson's censure of monopolies and their support for fewer restrictions on commerce.

Consciously or not, Villaurrutia's term "happy revolution" paraphrased Adam Smith's "revolution of greatest importance to the public happiness," by which Smith meant a turn of events that would bring about the commercial organization of society. "Happy revolution" had entered the language of reform by 1789, when Floridablanca insisted that through wise policy "a happy revolution" had been achieved in Spain's regaining its trade with America.[21] Small matter that Spain's first minister paid no attention to contrary reports; the wish-embodying phrase stuck. It signified that Spain's proposed alternative to the American and French revolutions was a peaceful commercial and economic turnabout, and it was taken up in America. To America, Creoles applied the view of Campillo, Robertson, and Smith--that economic and commercial advances were prerequisites to widespread well-being. Happy revolution became a Creole gospel, eliding into holy revolution. Spanish American circumstances and the old Hispanic tendency to interlace sacred and profane gave a very different flavor to the Scottish concoction.

While the clergy had once counseled concern only for the next world--and patience in this one--some of them were now to be found in the forefront of American reform, espousing an 18th-century forerunner of liberation theology--or at least preaching change in accord with the latest social ideals. Alzate, for example, the editor of the Mexican gazette, was a priest. Regalist, reforming bishops sent to America in the 1760s had influenced many provinces, buttressing other reforming authorities through the new emphases they brought to their old function as mediators between the people and the civil government. Thus, we also have the priest José Antonio Pérez Calama, who had come to Mexico in the 1760s in the entourage of the reforming bishop of Puebla. In 1784, Pérez Calama presented the young seminarian Miguel Hidalgo with a gold medal for his paper on reforming scholastic theology. The next year he helped the Mexican bishops apply Alzate's precepts of political economy, in order to offset the widespread ravages of famine and plague. They in turn collaborated closely with the popular young viceroy Bernardo de Gálvez (who was viewed as a war hero for his victories against the British at Mobile and Pensacola, in cooperation with the Anglo-Americans).

In 1789, Pérez Calama became the bishop of Quito, where he founded and directed the economic society. In his address inaugurating that society, Pérez Calama urged quiteños to build regional wealth through commerce by exchanging their grains and wool for cash. He assured them that "the grand art of making money" was the spirit and political soul of cultured peoples.[22] The Lima patriotic society's Mercurio Peruano printed his speech, commenting that it represented "a happy revolution of ideas!"[23]

Clearly, Bourbon recourses provided emerging Creole leaders with experience in adapting the hortatory language of the period to their American situations. Equally important, Creoles got a taste of self-reliance, of regional responsibility, and of economic planning. But complications set in after 1789, particularly with the radical phase of the French Revolution, the execution of Louis XVI, and the black and mulatto rebellion on St. Domingue. The French and Haitian revolutions heated up American criticism of imperial arrangements, and the tendency to assert Americanism, according to Humboldt, intensified. These uprisings also brought strict state repression of all dissent, and Spain's war with France in 1793 made Francophiles traitors and gave even greater immediacy to extracting funds. At its outset, the French Revolution was seen by young Creoles in public life as a reinforcement of the principles of the revolt of 1776. Thus Manuel Belgrano of Buenos Aires recalled that while studying in Spain from 1789 to 1793 the rage for political economy and the "ideas of the French Revolution" (which he saw as liberty, equality, security, and property) had been major influences on him. He was taken, he added, by the theories of Campillo, Campomanes, Smith, and the French physiocrat Quesnay, and he returned home "infatuated by the brilliant prospects for America."[24] Later, as secretary of the consulado, Belgrano saw himself as being in glorious partnership with the government, avidly compiling reports on the province as a basis for development—just such a mission, he explained, "was the intention of an enlightened minister like Diego Gardoqui, who had lived in the United States."[25] But Belgrano soon became disillusioned, complaining of progress being thwarted by entrenched wholesalers "who knew only to buy at four and sell at eight." He did, however, get newer, more enterprising merchants to cooperate with wheat farmers and ranchers in petitioning the Crown for more open trade and for tax advantages. Moreover, new elements within the consulado and new segments in society came to the fore in the 1790s in Buenos Aires and elsewhere. In 1808, they would seize political power.

Antonio Nariño, a young Creole well placed in the Bogotá bureaucracy, was probably sincere in saying, during his trial in 1794 for publishing a Spanish edition of the French Declaration of the Rights of Man of 1789, that he believed its immediate antecedent to be the American Bill of Rights. He was also accused of plotting to put into effect there "the Constitution of Philadelphia."[26] Nariño and other Creoles culled notions of popular sovereignty from the

French and American revolutions to strengthen their argument that
their tie to Spain's monarchy was a defined, constitutional one,
permitting them great latitude in American self-government.

As the 1790s progressed, even disenchanted Creoles tended to
disavow the more radical phase of the French Revolution. Francisco
de Miranda, in a letter to a confederate in Trinidad, summed up a
widely held Creole outlook of the later 1790s when he wrote: "Two
great examples lie before our eyes: the American and the French
revolutions. Let us discreetly imitate the first; let us carefully
avoid the disastrous effect of the second." Many adopted a political stance some reform-minded Spaniards had taken up during the
American Revolution: attempting to replace the absolutism of what
we now call enlightened despotism by insisting a constitution governed their society's relations with the monarchy. Indeed, reports
of the causes and course of the Revolution of 1776 had helped to
spread throughout the Spanish Empire North American and British concepts of political economy and of natural, constitutional rights.
The rising young royal minister Melchor Jovellanos called the British the best economists in the world. In 1781, he spoke to the
Royal Academy of History about the existence of a working though
unwritten constitution whose origins lay in medieval institutions
and the workings of the <u>cortes</u> (the Spanish "parliament"). Campomanes and the Conde de Cabarrús, a leading economic advisor to
Charles III and a great fan of the American patriots, took much
the same tack: during the American Revolution, both expressed belief
in the interlocking nature of economic and political life and saw
their proper organization as governed by an unwritten but functioning constitution. Campomanes not only wanted a general overhaul
of society and the imperial system, but also to incorporate America
into a single Spanish national body.[27] The early constitutional
phase of the French Revolution later gave corroboration, a Catholic
context, a more congenial spirit, and a closer analogy to the idea
of constitutional monarchy in Spain. Reacting to much the same
stimuli, Creoles instead fell back upon an American constitution
linking them only to the Spanish monarchy, not the Spanish nation.

Creoles invited to aid in developing and defending their regions became increasingly eager to wield at least regional political
authority as well. Those who did talked more and more of an existing, American constitution, combining beliefs embedded in traditional criollismo with some more recent interpretations of popular
sovereignty. From the 16th century on, Creoles had claimed repeat-
edly that they were the legitimate lords of the land and its peoples, for, they said, the king had made a pact to that effect with
their Spanish progenitors who had conquered America--and, some tra-
ditionalists added, civilized it. Their tie to Spain was to the
monarchy only.

The new creolism that was visible by the 1760s, while more ac-
tivist, intellectual, and entrepreneurial, intersected with this

more conservative, older variety of creolism in emphasizing the primacy of American tradition; in Mexico, it took an admiring view of the old indigenous civilization, a view probably owing much to the mestizo origins of many of its proponents. The belief in an American constitution was thus a meeting ground for proponents of both the entrenched creolism--chiefly owners of mines and large estates, and privileged merchants whose privileges were often the target of Bourbon reforms--and the new creolism, which growth and Spain's emphasis on reform had, if somewhat inadvertently, helped to shape. Thus old oligarchs and newer merchants, bureaucrats, and people in the professions agreed on Creole home rule, leaving unsettled the question of who would rule at home. This question would be addressed later in each regional-center-become-republic, along with deciding what form and content the American constitutions should take.

When England blocked Spanish trade with America in 1797, Creoles received a double dose of U.S. influence. Inter-American contact through commercial exchange surged, driving home the reality of a shared Americanness distinct from Europe, as well as the efficacy of what they thought the United States stood for. The United States, said one admiring South American, is "a nation which by simple and just means and by cultivation and trade has rapidly achieved power and greatness, public felicity and a spread of wealth."[28] Spain opened its ports to neutrals in 1797; by 1800, the bulk of U.S. trade was with Latin America. There were massive shipments of flour, legal and otherwise, to Havana and elsewhere. North American ships carried cargoes between Latin American ports and brought in reexports, including the products of England's industrial revolution.

From then on, Spain's direct contact with its colonies virtually ended. The rhetoric of reform, unity, and equality grew stale. Spanish schemes for tapping colonial wealth became ever more urgent and byzantine. In 1805, Rojas's brother-in-law, Manuel de Salas, a prominent civic leader in Chile, demonstrated Creole awareness of this state of affairs: "The hope of reform having disappeared," he wrote to Belgrano (with care to avoid subject and object), "there has come to substitute for it the execution of a fiscal project."[29] And from Mexico the bishop-elect of Michoacán, Manuel Abad y Queipo, warned of unrest and concluded that "nothing increases discontent so much as the demand for money."

Some Creoles had gotten the bit between their teeth and now wanted the reins as well. In Buenos Aires new entrepreneurs owned ships and meat-salting plants. Hide exports were up. Support for new enterprise was voiced, for instance, in Semanario de agricultura, industria, y comercio (The Weekly of Agriculture, Industry, and Commerce). Its editor, Juan Hipólito Vieytes, often cited Campillo and Jovellanos and, in a long exposition on Adam Smith's ideas, argued that American capital should be invested in America;

economic freedom, he said, was a step toward greater political liberty.[30]

In the early 1800s, Alexander von Humboldt arrived in America to find networks of Creoles with a developed sense of self-interest stemming from their awareness of world events and of America's actual and potential role in them. One such Creole was José Ignacio Pombo, with whom Humboldt stayed in New Granada. Pombo was at once an entrepreneur, an intellectual, and a patriot. He came of a distinguished provincial family, had studied philosophy and law at a Bogotá academy, and, with peace in 1784, had started what became a highly successful import-export firm in Cartagena. He underwrote scientific research into developing the natural wealth of the viceroyalty. He also founded Cartagena's economic society and wrote reports on economic, fiscal, and scientific matters to its consulado and the government; Jovellanos, Campomanes, Edmund Burke, Adam Smith, and Thomas Jefferson were all cited in support of his views. It is likely that Pombo did business with North Americans in competition with the merchants of British Jamaica and Trinidad. The English, he said, were pirates; commercial alliances with the United States, on the other hand, were desirable.

While Pombo worked within the imperial framework as long as possible, his nephew, Miguel de Pombo, became a leading junta member and an advocate of independence; he published a book in Bogotá in 1811 containing economic data from the United States and a Spanish translation of its Constitution. The younger Pombo referred to "our brothers of the North" and invoked a spirit of broad, hemispheric patriotism.[31] This sort of generational transition--from espousing reform for economic development to embracing revolution for political independence--was not necessarily the rule in Spanish America, but it certainly was not the exception.

Still, the outstanding exception was Cuba. Ignacio Pombo pointed to the spectacular growth of Cuba's sugar industry as proof of what happened when a region was freed of monopolies and could trade with the United States. Cubans, through a combination of special concessions and business acumen (demonstrated, for example, in smuggling), managed to maintain formal loyalty to Spain and a free-wheeling relationship with the United States. Of all the Creoles, propertied Cubans had the greatest power and standing in public affairs. A case in point is Francisco de Arango y Parreño, a spokesman for sugar planters and a founder of Havana's consulado, its economic society, and its gazette. He was also a correspondent of the American Philosophical Society of Philadelphia and a follower of Adam Smith. Because state policies of the period linked freer trade and lower taxes in Cuba to higher royal income, Arango, in a speech on commercial agriculture, informed his compatriots of ways those policies could be used to advance their own interests as well. To this end, he traveled in Europe, finding a better strain of sugar cane he later introduced in Cuba, as well as steam engines for the sugar mills there.

Joined by his Cuban sponsors and his confidant the Spanish governor, Arango sought with a good deal of success to establish regular trade with the United States, exchanging sugar for flour, and, with labor scarce and sugar mills thriving, to have more Africans brought in as slaves. One Cuban historian has estimated that some 93,000 blacks arrived in Cuba between 1790 and 1805.

Eighteenth-century Creole revolutionaries embraced only relative equality: Miranda, you will remember, was troubled by his servant's dining with him at a Connecticut inn. Many Cubans, like Arango, saw slavery as an economic necessity; for others, fears of a race war (à la St. Domingue) dampened their enthusiasm for rousing the populace. The sheer numbers of blacks and Indians presented revolutionary whites and white-leaning mestizos with a rather different situation from their Anglo-American counterparts. If nothing else, it meant that no Creole would ever disguise himself as an Indian and throw bales of tea into Veracruz Harbor. Creole self-assertion had to take other tacks.

Elsewhere, frustrations mounted. When France invaded Spain in 1808, some old Creole critics turned revolutionary, while the old revolutionaries reminded their fellow Spanish Americans of the happy outcome of revolt in Anglo-America. In the forefront of the juntas, which Creoles formed in the name of their regional communities to fight first against the French ruling Spain and later for independence, were men shaped by the era of Bourbon reform and buoyed by U.S. successes. They proposed an American solution. Yet we can see that it owed much to a confluence of ideas and ideals flowing from France, Britain (and especially Scotland), and Spain itself, and that this European notion strongly affected the kind of American precepts the juntistas recognized. These precepts came from the dynamic interplay of acceptance and rejection, of Creole aspirations and Spanish American perceptions of Western political and economic theory.

From 1808 to 1810, two themes predominated in the language and goals of the largely propertied, urban, "prudent" men who took control of their regions: constitutionalism (spoken of as self-government within a constitutional monarchy), and more advantageous commercial exchange. The first Spanish American declaration of independence was issued July 5, 1811 by the Caracas junta, formed by members of the consulado and the patriotic society. Simón Bolívar belonged to the first, Miranda to the second. In Buenos Aires, the Spanish Creole officer José de San Martín emerged as war leader, his career reflecting the legacies of reform and exigency, as well as an emphasis on defense combined with both Creole self-awareness and the more recent imperative of Creole self-reliance. In Mexico, the call to revolution came from Miguel Hidalgo, the gold medalist of 1784 who had become a village priest and a radical social visionary.

Hidalgo's injunctions to the clergy for reform translated into work-shops for his villagers, and he interpreted the invasion of Spain by the ungodly French as a call to rid Mexico of their Spanish co-horts there. Hidalgo, who had probably seen a Spanish version of the U.S. Constitution, called for a congress to rule the nation and hoisted the banner of the Virgen de Guadalupe. He was hailed in the insurgent press as "el nuevo Washington."[33]

Surely Robertson would not have savored Spanish America's blend of the liberal ideas he admired. Thomas Jefferson and John Adams did throw up their hands. Small wonder that their compatriots have often failed in trying to sort out the strands of the Spanish American past, for in disentangling them, that past is lost. It is the bundle they form that is history.

Questions about the ongoing impact in independent Spanish America of the triumph of an American revolution--which is what the Treaties of Versailles and Paris ultimately signified to Spanish Americans--are best left for another day. It is clear, however, that by 1784 Spanish Americans had perceived correctly, if through a filter of intermeshed Western concepts, that the first American nation was an important republic and that it stood for enlightened self-interest, a better, freer life for its citizens, and untram-meled economic advance. They also had begun to see the United States as a colossus, an economic competitor and even a threat, and they reacted with admiration and envy, with fear and with hope.

NOTES

1. J.G.A. Pocock, "Machiavelli, Harrington, and English Po-litical Ideologies in the Eighteenth Century," William and Mary Quarterly 22 (1965): 582.

2. Ibid.

3. Campillo, Nuevo Sistema, first published in Madrid, 1789, pp. 11, 64, 156. And see my Atlantic Empires: The Network of Trade and Revolution, 1713-1826 (Baltimore: Johns Hopkins University Press, 1983), chaps. 3, 4, 6-8 for the history of 18th-century reforms within the Spanish Empire.

4. Robertson, 10th ed. (London, 1803), 4: 4, 114-16.

5. Ibid., 4: 66-67, 80, 84; cites "Smith's Inquiry," 2: 155, 171.

6. Ibid., 4: 90, 92, 359; and see Charles Ronan, "Antonio de Alcedo: His Collaborators and His Letters to William Robertson,"

The Americas 34 (1978): 490-510; Ciriaco Pérez-Bustamante, estudio preliminar to Antonio de Alcedo's Diccionario geográfico-histórico de las Indias, o América (Madrid, 1967); Francisco Javier Clavijero, S.J., "Frutos en que comercia o puede comerciar la Nueva España," and "Proyectos utiles para adelantar el comercio de la Nueva España," in Mariano Cuevas, S.J., ed., Tesoros documentales de México: siglo XVIII (Mexico, 1944), pp. 363-98; Charles Ronan, Francisco Javier Claviiero, (1731-1787) (Chicago: Loyola University Press, 1977); Miguel Luis Amunátegui, La crónica de 1810 (Santiago, 1876), 2: 21-97; Diego Barras Arana, Historia General de Chíle, 16 vols. (Santiago, 1884-1902), 7: 513-16, 546-49; and Roland D. Hussey, "Manuscript Hispanic Americana in the Harvard College Library," Hispanic American Historical Review 17 (1937): 274.

7. Gaspar Melchor de Jovellanos, for example, the young royal minister whose writings in the 1770s reflected the high tide in Spain of enlightened optimism and liberal faith in social progress through material advance, was comfortable with presuppositions of the Enlightenment, political economy, and nascent liberalism. But he most often cited them as general rules to which the problems of his day must for the moment be excepted.

8. Clavijero, Sioria Antica del Messico, 4 vols. (Cesena, 1780-81); Ronan, Claviiero, pp. 288-89, 292-96; Antonello Gerbi, The Dispute of the New World (Pittsburgh: University of Pittsburgh Press, 1973), pp. 158-59, 166-68. Robertson responded to Clavijero in his 1788 edition, admitting some errors of fact. This rejoinder appears in vol. 4, pp. 343-49, of the 1803 ed. Wrote Clavijero: "I protest...to all of Europe that the spiritual and mental qualities of the Americans are in no way inferior to those of Europeans"; if present-day Greeks did not show signs of their ancient glory, why judge outstanding Indians of the past by Indians of today? (Ronan, Claviiero, p. 292).

9. Alexander von Humboldt, Political Essay on the Kingdom of New Spain, trans. John Black (London, 1811), 1: 205; Gerbi, p. 158.

10. Franklin W. Knight, "Origins of Wealth and Sugar Revolution in Cuba, 1750-1850," Hispanic American Historical Review 57 (1977): 231-53.

11. Mercedes M. Alvárez F., Comercio y comerciantes y sus provecciones en la independencia venezolana (Caracas: Vargas, 1963), p. 139.

12. Francisco Posada, El movimiento revolucionario de los comuneros neogranadinos en el siglo XVIII, 2d ed. (Mexico: Siglo XXI, 1975), p. 24.

13. Carlos E. Muñoz Oraá, "Pronóstico de la independencia de América y un proyecto de monarquia en 1781," Revista de Historia de America 50 (1960): 439-73.

14. Francisco Morales Padrón, "México y la independencia de hispano-américa en 1781 segun un comisionario regio: Francisco de Saavedra," in Homenaje a D Ciriaco Pérez-Bustamante (Madrid: Instituto Gonzalo Fernández de Oviedo, CSIC, 1969), pp. 335-58.

15. Aranda, "Dictamen reservado que el conde de Aranda dió al Rey sobre la independencia de los colonias inglesas, después de haber firmado el tratado de paz ajustado en Paris en el año de 1783." A copy is in the Yale University library.

16. Francisco de Miranda, The New Democracy in America: Travels of Francisco de Miranda in the United States, 1783-84, trans. Judson P. Wood, ed. John S. Ezell (Norman: University of Oklahoma Press, 1963), pp. xx, 5, 19, 30-32, 46, 81, 147, 156.

17. Eduardo Arcila Farías, El Real Consulado de Caracas (Caracas: Instituto de Estudios Hispanoamericanos, Facultad de Humanidades y Educación, Universidad Central de Venezuela, 1957), p. 34.

18. Alcedo (Madrid, 1967), 2: 57-59.

19. José Antonio Alzate y Ramírez, Gacetas de Literatura de Mexico, 4 vols. (Puebla, 1831); and see my "Revolutionary Language and the Breakup of Empire," in the feschtschrift for Charles Gibson, Bibliotheca Americana (forthcoming).

20. Robert J. Shafer, The Economic Societies in the Spanish World (1763-1821) (Syracuse: Syracuse University Press, 1958), pp. 353-54.

21. Conde de Floridablanca, "Memoria presentado al Rey Carlos III y repetido al Rey Carlos IV...renunciado al ministerio," in Biblioteca de Autores Españoles (Madrid, 1952), 59: 336.

22. Germán Cardozo Galué, Michoacán en el siglo de las luces (Mexico: El Colégio de México, 1973), pp. 49, 91-92.

23. Ibid.

24. Belgrano, Estudios Económicos (Buenos Aires, 1954), pp. 13-47.

25. Ibid., p. 49. From 1790 to 1794, Gardoqui was a director of the Finance Ministry bureau dealing with the treasuries and trade of the Indies. He had been a merchant during the American Revolution and later Spanish envoy to the United States.

26. Servando Teresa de Meir, Memorias, 2 vols. (Mexico: Porrua, 1946), 1: 26.

27. Richard Konetske, "La condición legal de los criollos y las causas de la independencia," Estudio Americanos 2 (1950): 45; John H.R. Polt, "Jovellanos and his English Sources," Transactions of the American Philosophical Society 54 (1964): 5-74; Conde de Cabarrús, "Discurso sobre la libertad de comercio concedida por S.M. a la America meridional" (read on February 28, 1778), in Memorias de la Sociedad Económica (Madrid, 1787), 3: 282-94; and José Antonio Maravall, "Las tendencias de reforma política en el siglo XVIII," Revista de Occidente, 2d ser. 5 (1967): 53-82.

28. José Ignacio Pombo, in Rafael Goméz Hoyos, La revolución granadina, ideario de una generación y una época, 2 vols. (Bogotá: Temis, 1962), 2: 267-68.

29. Miguel Luis Amunátegui, Los precursores de la independencia de Chile, 3 vols. (Santiago: Imprenta Barcelona, 1909-10), 3: 49. Salas was a great admirer of Benjamin Franklin.

30. Ibid., 3: 445-49; Semanario, fasc. (Buenos Aires, 1928, 1937), passim.

31. Javier Ocampo, El proceso ideológico de la emancipación; Las ideas de génesis, independencia, futuro e integración en los orígenes de Colombia (Tunja: Universidad Pedagógica y Tecnológica de Colombia, 1974); Gómez Hoyos, 2: 267-97.

32. Francisco de Arango y Parreño, De la factoria a la colonia (1808) (Havana: Talleres de Cultural, 1936).

33. El Despertador Americano, fasc. (Mexico, 1964), passim. Its full name was El Despertador Americano, Correo Político Económico de Guadalajara.

COMMENTARY

Franklin W. Knight

Peggy Liss puts the Treaty of Paris—as well as preceding events—into a context in which they become, at the same time, symptom, symbol, and catalyst for change. The Treaty of Paris was neither the alpha nor omega of American nationalism in the hemispheric sense. It was the most radical expression of political engineering in an increasingly secular age.

There are two things Liss's paper does. First, it traces the intellectual ferment and interconnections of what she has elaborated on in Atlantic Empires. Ideas about man, nature, social order, and political systems were undergoing broad-based review from a number of people in a number of places.

Adam Smith and William Robertson were not prophets. They were merely unusual, sensitive observers of a rapidly changing milieu. And they were not alone. The climactic changes imposed by the commercial revolution and changing characteristics of technology, especially naval technology, affected not only their native Scotland, but a vast number of port cities in every country that had been integrated in the South Atlantic System, what Fernand Braudel would call "the Atlantic economy world."

Second, the paper traces, examines, and explains the changing nature of the Spanish state system toward the end of the 18th century. This is of critical importance, for in Spain as in Spanish America, the 18th century was a watershed.

The essence of Spanish enlightened reformism, especially during the age of Charles III, was certainly to effect the type of commercial and administrative revolution about which so much has been written.

"Spain," says Liss, paraphrasing Campillo, "must first rid American government of traditional abuses, then take steps to do two things—regain control of imperial trade, and build up its America, still officially known as the Indies, as a source of raw materials and a market for imports. Here lay the route to prosperity and power." If I part company with her at this point, it is merely a question of degree, of emphasis.

I would go further. I would describe the Atlantic ferment—not only among European metropolitan reformers but also among the creolized upper sector of their American empires--as the inevitable consequence of imperialism and colonialism. That is how Adam Smith, the Abbé Raynal, and Edward Long saw it in the 1770s. The empires were maturing.

If I am correct, there is not much difference between the sentiments felt and expressed in 1776 by English colonial North Americans and Spanish American Creoles. Why the Spanish Americans were not ready for war is another matter.

The precursors of the literary and economic societies of the 1780s and 1790s in the Spanish world--José Antonio Rojas, Antonio de Alcedo, and Francisco Javier Clavijero--were men whose intellectual foundations were established in the 1760s, at the same time the revolutionaries at Philadelphia were beginning to question the nature and convenience of English imperialism. It is perhaps worth pointing out that Alcedo's extraordinary Diccionario, though initially published in 1887, was begun in 1867. I am not saying that events between 1776 and 1783 did not have a tremendous impact on Spanish America. That is accepted. But why such an impact?

Here one has to return to the reality of the Spanish American Empire during the later 18th century. One aspect of Spanish reformism that has not been explored as fully as the others is the concept of political sovereignty. Unlike the English and French American empires, the Spanish American Empire was a patrimonial empire. The vast Indies were, to a certain extent, the personal domain of the monarchs of Castille.

If the claims had not worn thin by 1776, certainly the statutory legitimacy was inconvenient. Therefore, when the enlightened Spanish reformers approached this subject, they sought to make, for the time, a radical--if not revolutionary--transformation. The reorganization of political power in Spain and the Indies had, as its master design, the conversion of the patrimonial monarchy into a national monarchy; but the implications were certainly greater, for the Spanish nation states of the Americas would become almost coequal to those of Spanish Iberia. It was not to be a true confederation.

According to Liss, this represented "a kind of alliance for progress." But that was a peninsular view. Spanish American Creoles, especially after their experiences in Spain and during the wars of the 1760s and 1770s, preferred an "Operation Bootstrap," but not under Spanish metropolitan auspices. The political metropolis, after all, need not coincide with the economic metropolis.

Such political changes facilitating the expansion of commerce and further stimulating local economies were welcome. But only unrestricted free trade could be entirely satisfactory--and that bore some economic perils for Spain.

The political tragedy of late 18th-century Spanish America is that the reforms failed to create a Spanish commonwealth, the only system that could restrain the centrifugal forces of late 18th-century imperialism and provide an adequate compromise for the nature of sovereignty.

This, then, is where the Treaty of Paris made a difference. In legitimizing a new form of sovereignty in the Americas, it made a crucial difference for Spanish American political thought, and thus brings Liss's discussion full circle.

The patriotism of the English North Americans survived seven years of war. It brought measurable economic benefits both to the ex-colonies and the ex-metropolis. It was therefore justified on economic grounds. But above all, it legitimized the artificial creation of political authority. Yet we must bear in mind that this realization, occurring when it did, was qualified by the confusing reality of the French Revolution and even more qualified by the frightful reality of the Haitian Revolution. Nevertheless, the Treaty of Paris of September 3, 1783 symbolized and legalized state formation in Latin America. The new Constitution of the United States resonated throughout the hemisphere until another Treaty of Paris—that of December 10, 1898—eclipsed Spanish political influence. In this sense the Treaty of Paris of 1783 ushered in a new age.

THE CULTURAL PATRIMONY
OF THE NEW UNITED STATES

Marcus Cunliffe

By the 18th century, treaties were usually couched in two or
more languages, those of the principal parties. This is true, for
example, of the 1778 treaty of alliance between France and the United States. The manuscript copy, preserved in the National Archives,
has two parallel columns, with the French version in one column and
the English text in the other. The Anglo-French, Anglo-Spanish, and
Anglo-Dutch peace treaties of 1783 also have dual texts in this fashion. Not so the Anglo-American Treaty of Paris, which was composed in a single language, English.

If pressed to comment on the significance of the single text,
many people, I suspect, would respond in one of two standard ways--
the Hands-across-the-Sea response and the American-Patriot or Star-
Spangled-Banner response. A Hands-across-the-Sea reaction to the
linguistic form of the Treaty of Paris might be: "How nice." In
this amiable interpretation, the American Revolution tends to be
regarded as a puzzling, regrettable, but fortunately temporary dis-
agreement. Yes, there was a quarrel, but merely a family quarrel:
behold, we are still of the same family, big and happy, and able to
make exchanges within essentially the same discourse. You import
Masterpiece Theatre, a British person might remark, we buy Dallas;
we get T.S. Eliot, you can have Aldous Huxley, Christopher Isher-
wood, and a longish run of W.H. Auden.

The American-Patriot reaction is to dramatize the history of
the widening gap between English English and American English. The
process supposedly leads to the emergence of an American language
sharply differentiated from the old mother tongue in vocabulary,
pronunciation, mood, and even syntax. The distance between the two
forms of English, according to some scholars, was already quite
marked before the Revolution. The lexicographer Noah Webster is
often credited with doing much, in the early years of the Republic,
to codify, legitimize, and propagate the youthful American language.
Mark Twain deserves even greater credit. He perfected so distinctive an American style, informal and supple as a buckskin hunting
shirt, that he could declare 100 years ago: "There is no such thing
as the Queen's English. It is a joint-stock company, and we hold
the bulk of the shares." Who has not heard anecdotes about how, for
instance, joint planning in World War II was threatened with chaos
when the British who spoke of "tabling" a document meant that it
was to be discussed, while their American colleagues meant that it
should be deferred or shelved--the opposite definition?

The Hands-across-the-Sea notion is of a cultural heritage, exemplified by language, that could be comfortably shared. Patrimony, the term used in my title, signifies, according to the OED, "property, or an estate, inherited from one's father or ancestors; heritage, inheritance." Webster's first dictionary (1806) defines patrimony in the same way. The American cultural patrimony handed down from Great Britain might thus (leaving aside inheritance from other countries) include Shakespeare, the King James Bible, and the works of Bunyan, Milton, and Alexander Pope. These could all, in a sense, be regarded as "American" through ancestral conveyance.

On the other hand, the American-Patriot interpretation stresses the theme of rejection or repudiation rather than continuity and assimilation. It is the theme not of patrimony but almost patricide. Thus, an essay by Winthrop Jordan on the symbolic behavior of 1776 is called "Familial Politics: Thomas Paine and the Killing of the King." The suggestion is that Paine's pamphlet Common Sense demythologized monarchy with such savage skill that it amounted to a rhetorical slaying of the sovereign, George III, in the name of a universal or popular sovereignty. Jordan describes various ceremonies of 1776 in which coffins or effigies represented the British king (Paine's "royal brute"). These objects were held up to ridicule, and burned or smashed. A royal statue was toppled in Manhattan, and its metal melted down for bullets. Paintings or sculptures of royal crests were torn down; so were inn signs relating to the monarchy: Fragments of the broken material were sometimes distributed among the crowd, as if to symbolize the transfer of prerogative, from one person to the whole population.[1]

The rejection of monarchy in favor of republicanism likewise signified a repudiation of a traditional form of government. So did the prohibition of titles of rank, and the various moves within the former colonies to separate church and state. In a good deal of rhetoric there was an emphasis on pristine novelty: the New World turning its back upon the Old. What becomes of the idea of patrimony in such an atmosphere?

As far as language was concerned, Americans of the Revolutionary era were fertile in jokes and suggestions--the latter of which were, it must be said, mostly farfetched. Perhaps understandably, their French allies showed particular interest in schemes to abandon the English tongue. Chastellux claimed that there was in the 1780s a serious American proposal to substitute Hebrew for English:

> The proposal was, that it should be taught in the schools, and made use of in all public acts. We may imagine that this project went no farther, but we may conclude from the mere suggestion, that the Americans could not express in a more energetic manner, their aversion for the English.[2]

Chastellux's fellow countryman, Brissot de Warville, pondered the matter in 1788, during a voyage across the Atlantic. The Americans, he decided, must necessarily "detest the English," and try to "erase every trace" of the British connection. They must accordingly "introduce innovations into their language as they have in their constitution." And they must make this new language as universal as possible. Why not, Brissot speculated, encourage Americans to use _French_ words and idioms? Through this _franglais_, or _framéri-cain_, the new nation would escape the linguistic patrimony: "they will create a language of their own; there will exist an American language."[3] According to a later, perhaps apocryphal story, a member of the wartime Continental Congress "proposed that the young republic should complete its independence by adopting a different language from that of the mother-country, 'the Greek for instance'" --to which Roger Sherman of Connecticut is said to have retorted that "It would be more convenient for us to keep the language as it was, and make the English speak Greek." Some echo of the debate, in fact, persisted into the 20th century. In 1923, Washington Jay McCormick, a Republican representative from Montana, laid before Congress a bill to establish "American" as the official language of the United States: "I would," declared Representative McCormick, "supplement the political emancipation of '76 by the mental emancipation of '23." He urged America to think its own thoughts "in a language unadorned with gold braid. It was only when Cooper, Irving, Mark Twain, Whitman, and O. Henry dropped the Order of the Garter and began to write American that their wings of immortality sprouted." McCormick's bill died in committee. But State Senator Frank Ryan persuaded the Illinois legislature to pass a similar bill in the same year (1923), which enacted that the "official language of the State of Illinois shall be known hereafter as the 'American' language, and not as the 'English' language." So far as I know it is still on the statute book of President Reagan's home state.[4]

Americans after the Revolution sought to express their national separateness in other ways--for instance, by devising a national flag and national anthems. There was, too, a sort of quest for a symbolic figure, conspicuously, self-evidently, and solely of the American continent. The foremost candidate was the native American or American Indian. When the young Pennsylvania artist Benjamin West went to Italy in 1760, he was shown the celebrated statue of the Apollo Belvedere. Acting out his proto-American role, West exclaimed of the figure: "How like a Mohawk Indian!"[5] The Indian had already acquired other symbolic identities. There was, for example, Tammany or Tamenund, a 17th-century Delaware chief who had been a trusted ally of William Penn. Chief Tammany, it has been said, was adopted as a kind of patron saint--Saint Tammany, indeed--by Pennsylvanians in the 1770s, a contrasting figure to the Saint George, Saint Andrew, or Saint David of various Philadelphia fraternal orders. A 1776 stage comedy, "The Fall of British Tyranny; or, American Liberty Triumphant," included a song about Saint Tammany:

170

> Of St. George, or St. Bute, let the poet Laureat sing,
> Of Pharaoh or Pluto of Old.
> While he rhimes forth their praise, in false, flattering lays,
> I'll sing of St. Tamm'ny the bold, my brave boys....

The Massachusetts men who staged the Boston Tea Party in 1773 disguised themselves as "Mohawks," in quasi-Indian garb and painted faces. The style was imitated by other groups of American protesters, such as the Whiskey Rebels of western Pennsylvania (1794), and--decades afterward--by the Anti-Renters of New York State.[6]

Yet the element of prank or burlesque in such instances may conceal some unprecedented and quite painful difficulties. The United States was the first society in modern history to achieve political independence in an upsurge of revolutionary nationalism. It shared with other societies of the 18th and 19th centuries a characteristic blend of radical and traditional sentiments. These included the attribution of tyrannical and alien qualities to the enemy nation or nations opposed to claims for autonomy. They also included an emphasis on the new nation's identifying heritage--heroic ancestors, folkloric traditions, and the like.

Cultural nationalism burgeoned throughout the Western world in the second half of the 18th century. The nation was portrayed as an immemorial bond, of the kind expressed in the German word Volk, reemerging in latter-day conceptions of the "race," the patri, the People, and, of course, the Fatherland (or Motherland) and the Muttersprache ("mother tongue"). Early in the 19th century, Friedrich Schlegel insisted: "There is nothing so necessary to the...whole intellectual existence of a nation, as the possession of a plentiful store of those national recollections and associations, which are lost in a great measure during the dark ages of infant society, but which it forms the great object of the poetical art to perpetuate and adorn."

That process was well under way in the British Isles. Thomas Percy's Reliques of Ancient English Poetry (1765) appeared in the same decade as James Macpherson's supposed translations from the Gaelic of the Scottish 3rd-century bard Ossian, the son of Fingal. In the next generation Walter Scott, and such figures as James Hogg, the "Ettrick Shepherd," helped to create an international vogue for Scottish balladry and minstrelsy.

Similar processes were at work elsewhere. Thomas Comerford's History of Ireland (1751) tried to link Gaelic culture to that of ancient Greece. Charles Vallancey's Essay on the Antiquity of the Irish Language (1772) sought to trace Gaelic back to Punic or Carthaginian roots. "It was from this time," according to R.F. Foster, "that the currency of thought, running on antiquarian and historiographical lines, familiarised the Irish mind with shamrocks, wolf hounds, round towers, the cult of Brian Boru, and the image of an ecumenical St. Patrick." In Wales a comparable upsurge led to the revival of the moribund annual national Eisteddfod ("bardic assembly") in 1822. The Swiss linked the exploits of William Tell with the newer patriotic deeds of Andreas Hofer. The Germans rediscovered Hermann, or Arminius, the ancient warrior who had defied the Roman legions; and, via the Brothers Grimm, they explored the great treasure of German folk tales. Hans Christian Andersen was soon to perform the same office for Denmark. A history of Italian literature by Tiraboschi, published in 1781, asserted that the national literary pedigree began with the pre-Roman Etruscan people. Russians took pride in the medieval lay of Prince Igor.[7]

The American Revolution was in some degree a stimulus for these manifestations of national sentiment. Yet its own cultural patrimony was, by comparison, sparse and ambiguous. Most of the heritage, to repeat, was overwhelmingly British (like the tune of "God Save the King," borrowed for the American anthem "My Country, 'Tis of Thee"). The "native" patrimony referred mainly to the American aborigines. But the symbolic utility of "Indians" or "redskins," for the United States, was limited and equivocal. For after all, this was a settler revolution, not a native uprising, and on balance, the colonists were less disposed than the Westminster government to respect the rights of native Americans. In popular demonstrations, it is true, a "redskin" disguise tended to indicate protest. After the Revolution, however, protests such as the Anti-Rent War were in their nature simply domestic disputes, not displays of anglophobic patriotism. Much of the Indian iconography of 19th-century America was to be merely picturesque, or commercial (as with the cigar-store Indian), or political-convivial (as with New York's Tammany Hall). In statuary and pictorial art the Indian was invariably depicted as a loser to the white man.

There is a revealing exception to this statement. The pilleus (Phrygian bonnet or "liberty cap") emblem of emancipation from slavery, sometimes shown atop a liberty pole, lingered on for several decades after the American Revolution. But it came to seem either meaningless, or else un-Americanly "French" and radical—and possibly embarrassing too for a nation that still retained chattel slavery. At any rate, in 1859 the U.S. Mint, in what has been described as "a feat of unsurpassed iconographic hypocrisy," ceased to display a bonneted classical female on the coinage, substituting instead an Indian maiden with feathered headdress inscribed "Liberty." In the same decade Thomas Crawford's bronze statue "Armed Liberty," designed for the dome of the Capitol in Washington, D.C., was likewise modified: the Liberty bonnet metamorphosed into a curious feathered concoction. Secretary of War Jefferson Davis had objected to the liberty cap as "inappropriate to a people who were born free and would not be enslaved." The art historian Oliver Larkin complained that the resulting hybrid looked like "a pregnant squaw."[8]

Indigenous cultural references were thus not easy to fasten
upon, in the early years of independence. The British or Anglo-
American patrimony was even more perplexing, because it appeared to
contradict any emphatic assertion of American independence. Tom
Paine's Common Sense denied that Britain was the parent of the
American colonies; if there were a lineage, it was, he said, a
genealogy from the whole of Europe. Or (another of Paine's meta-
phorical expedients), the American boy had become a man. Being
mature, he must in the nature of things leave the old home and set
up for himself. Moreover, the relationship was no longer familial,
because the wicked parent had forfeited any claim to affection,
let alone obedience.[9]

But Paine was himself English. He did not arrive in the United
States until he was 37, with a letter of introduction from Benjamin
Franklin, who by 1775 had himself spent some 20 years as a Londoner.
The Boston artist John Singleton Copley had Loyalist family connections, quit the colonies for England on the eve of the Revolution,
and, during the next 40 years, never returned to North America.
Copley's contemporary, Benjamin West, was only 22 when he left for
Europe, where he passed the remaining 60 years of his life, becoming
historical painter to King George III and eventually president of
the Royal Academy. West's American pupil in London, Gilbert Stuart,
lived in high style in London and Dublin through the War of Independence and only returned to the United States in 1792 or 1793--
hoping, it appears, to pay off his English and Irish creditors by
mass-producing portraits of George Washington.[10]

In all the arts, then, and in every aspect of culture, it could
be felt that there was as yet (as some people expressed the problem)
no "American character." Instead there were assertions of difference from Europe; of types of moral superiority over Europe (sometimes called "republican," and by degrees "democratic"); of destined
future greatness (the "rising glory" theme, as this has been termed;
and of the exceptional physical features of Americanness, notably
the figurative and literal abundance of elbowroom in a vast, unen-
cumbered landscape.[11]

The patrimonial aspects, if easier to define, were--for reasons
already outlined--harder to admit. Thus, there was for the Revolutionary era, and in particular for someone like Thomas Jefferson, a
fondness for Anglo-Saxon England--perceived by Americans in the Whig
image of a paradise of freeholders, not yet subjugated under the
"Norman yoke" of 1066. The first ship commissioned by the Continental Congress in 1775 was named the Alfred, after King Alfred. Jefferson thought the study of Anglo-Saxon was desirable within the
curriculum of his projected University of Virginia.[12]

But Anglo-Saxondom was not a very plausible piece of patrimony,
even as a linguistic notion. Let us reconsider, rather, the idea
of an American or Anglo-American language; for here was both the

greatest cultural impediment to a fresh start for America and the most ambitious effort to realize something that might be both an inheritance <u>and</u> a fresh, genuinely American testament. The principal advocate <u>of</u> such an achievement during the Revolutionary era was, as noted, Noah Webster. Webster, a New England scholar and tireless promoter of his own publications, wrote an essay (<u>Dissertation on the English Language</u>, 1789) arguing that there <u>was</u> not only a need for but a real possibility of achieving "a <u>national language</u>, as well as a national government." In the year of the Treaty of Paris, blowing his own trumpet along with that of the young nation, he had prophesied for it "a greatness and lustre, before which the glory of ancient Greece and Rome shall dwindle... and the splendor of modern Europe shall fade into obscurity."

For Webster and some of his fellows, moreover, the greatness and luster were just around the corner. Their speedy attainment would be much aided, Webster said, by means of a nationwide adoption of his own systems of spelling, pronunciation, and grammar, and his own accredited vocabulary of Americanness. The Websterian dream was to create a canon that was simultaneously ancient and modern--in a word, rational. He would include words that had become respectably established in American usage. So when someone criticized him (1816) for sanctioning <u>locate</u> as a verb and <u>location</u> as a noun, although they were not <u>in the</u> English dictionaries, Webster answered: "no Sir, and this was one reason why I compiled mine. How can the English <u>locate</u> lands, when they have no lands to locate!" Similar defenses were made of new Americanisms such as <u>presidential</u> and <u>congressional</u>, also not to be found (or located) in Samuel Johnson's lexicography, though all of these are in the 1806 <u>Webster</u>.

That was the modern side of Webster's prospectus. The ancient feature was that he envisaged Americans as speaking and writing a purer English than that of the old country. In English 18th-century usage, for example, a superfluous final <u>k</u>, which Noah Webster wanted to remove, had been added to <u>musick</u>, <u>Gothick</u>, and other <u>-ic</u> endings. There was no sanction, he decided, for the English <u>u</u> in <u>color</u>, <u>honor</u>, and such words; the <u>-re</u> ending in <u>centre</u> should be reversed to <u>-er</u>. And in the interests of rational pronunciation <u>plough</u> would be better (though not much better?) as <u>plow</u>.[13]

The Websterian aim, then, was in large part to clean up the ancestral language--to purge it of corruption and make Americans the arbiters, a sort of nationwide Académie, of linguistic correctness. "The English language," said the Reverend Ezra Stiles, president of Yale, in a 1783 address, "will grow up with the present American population into great purity and elegance." Indeed all the arts would respond to transplantation, as Stiles claimed had happened following the conquests of Alexander the Great. Under Alexander, Stiles maintained, culture had "immediately flourished in greater perfection" than in the defeated domains. Similarly,

the arts now to be transplanted from Europe and Asia would "flourish
in America with an augmented lustre." (Lustre to be spelt -re, not
-er.)[14]

Webster and like-minded people believed that the salvation of
the language was possible because Americans on average already
spoke and wrote a better English than that of the old country. They
convinced themselves that this improvement would continue, and the
American advantage would thus increase steadily and rapidly. In
Wealth of Nations (1776), Adam Smith had been ready to contemplate
a future transfer of the seat of government from the metropolis to
the increasingly populous and affluent colonies: the periphery could
become the core. This actually took place in 1807-08, when the Portuguese court and royal family, under British protection, moved
across the Atlantic: Rio replaced Lisbon as the capital of the Portuguese Empire. In the sphere of language, Webster's generation
conjured up an analogous inversion: westward the course of English
would make its way.

In later life, Webster, always in some ways a respecter of tradition (like, say, a restorer of old-master paintings) got more and
more conservative. He was forced to realize that his scheme had
never made complete sense. For one thing, it assumed that Great
Britain was set irreversibly on a downward path. But as the years
passed, Britain's power and cultural vitality refused to go into
decline. Again, the reality of a unified, Continental, standard
grammatical English became more and more difficult to believe in.
As an old man, Webster argued with habitual vehemence that American English and English English were virtually identical: "Our
language is the English." Allowing for a "few peculiarities" in
each branch, Webster came to say it was "desirable that the
language of the United States and Great Britain should be the
same."[15]

Webster was perhaps recognizing the inevitable. The old notion
of a completely different American language had showed itself to be
chimerical. This central patrimony was a gift impossible to refuse.
Webster was not the only American to cherish illusions as to the
actual and future state of the national language. James Fenimore
Cooper was a stout defender of his country during his long absence
in Europe. He, too, thought the general standard of English usage
was highest in the United States. From Paris, he set down his opinion that the finest--most refinedly melodious--English speakers of
all were American women of the Middle West. Returning to the United
States in the early 1830s, Cooper changed his mind on that and on
other points of language. His revised view (The American Democrat,
1838) was that there was a great deal of bad and inconsistent usage
in the United States. Among "provincialisms" that Cooper singled
out as "exceedingly vicious" was the pronunciation of new as noo
(Noo York), which (he complained) rendered "the language mean and
vulgar." By the same token, clerk should be pronounced clark, this
being "more in conformity with polite usage." And Cooper, irritated

by what was termed *framéricain*, claimed that the Anglicized French word *lieutenant* should be pronounced *levtenant*, not *lootenant*: for, he noted, "they who affect to say *lootenant* do not say "*lootenant-co-lo-nel*,' but '*lootenant-kurnel*.'"[16]

There is an element of crustiness and social snobbery in such dicta. Yet the English are hardly in a position to fault other people for inconsistencies of usage. Indeed, people of other nations showed themselves credulous and chauvinistic in the Revolutionary era with respect to their various heritages, taking on trust the historical authenticity of Ossians, Igors, and Hermanns who (like William Tell) may never have existed at all. The American equivalent was at least a real figure, George Washington, a sort of instant ancestor: a native-born leader who never left the American hemisphere and who, according to popular folklore, was held in special awe by the American Indians. Himself childless, he was dubbed *Pater Patriae*, the father of his country, and given a quasi-classical pedigree by being linked with the semilegendary Roman soldier-farmer Cincinnatus. In like manner the political leadership of the colonies—in fact, it has been pointed out, a group of remarkably young men—became known as the Founding Fathers. Within a few years of the ratification of the 1787 Constitution, the Founding Fathers were being referred to as venerable sages and their document as time hallowed.[17]

So, what of the patrimonial theme? We have seen that as the first new nation, being also a settler nation, the young United States did not have an easy task in expressing its cultural identity. Political independence, said the poet Philip Freneau, was the work of a few years; cultural independence could take centuries. I have suggested that Webster and his contemporaries seemed to have to abandon the vision of a separate American language, or at least to defer its realization for many years to come. We have also seen that the founding Americans, Washington above all, were even during their lifetimes apotheosized into ancestral monumentality. PATRIMONIES PROVIDED! NO WAITING!

Two other associated points are worth making by way of conclusion. Both have to do with replicatory cultural processes involving the two nations. First, on the matter of language, I believe that neither the Hands-across-the-Sea nor the Star-Spangled-Banner people have quite brought the issue into focus. It is obvious that American English and English English differ from one another, as do other respective cultural aspects. But "differ" is an imprecise word. It can cover small or large divergencies, polite disagreements or bitter quarreling. In important ways, Webster and his associates were, I think, not relinquishing an early patriotic hope when they conceded that Great Britain and the United States essentially shared a common language. It was and is essentially one language. By the

176

1880s Mark Twain was entitled to claim that the Americans held the bulk of the shares. That is even more true of the 1980s (including the spread across this nation and across the Atlantic of "federal prose," or "bureaucratese," the language of Foggy Bottom). The two versions of English have changed, but in so doing have closely influenced one another.

This is obvious enough. Less obvious, perhaps, is that from Noah Webster onward some Americans continued stubbornly to believe that their brand of English was better than the British one. Their patriotic endeavor was _not_ really to evolve a separate language, though they retained the right to indulge in what Jefferson approvingly called "neology." Their principal purpose was, as in Webster's day, to keep good English alive, not out of subservient anglophobia but in some proud and rivalrous way because they _did_ feel the language was their patrimony.

Edgar Allan Poe became known as the "tomahawk man" for his critical reviews of other writers. He did not, however, wield the tomahawk as a native American weapon, in aid of a national vernacular. On the contrary, his concern was to uphold the proper international standards of usage. Often he rebuked Americans for their lapses. His sharpest criticism, though, was directed against English authors. Poe, for instance, condemned the style of a novel by Edward Bulwer-Lytton as "grossly defective--turgid, involved, and ungrammatical." "Mr. Bulwer," said Poe, "cannot express a dozen consecutive sentences in an honest and manly manner. He is king-coxcomb of figures of speech." He has a "mania of metaphor" and an absurd addiction to "little French sentences." (_C'est juste_, etc.) Poe, in short, perceived himself with the utmost earnestness as committed to a sacred duty, a duty to the American Republic as well as to the republic of letters. In a famous obituary tribute, Mallarmé saluted Poe's endeavor: _donner un sens plus pur aux mots de la tribu_, imparting a purer sense (purity again!) to the words of the (Anglo-American) tribe.[18]

Mark Twain was certainly a master of American forms of dialect, and took pride in his keen ear for ordinary speech. I suspect that he took even greater pride, though, in his ability to compose clean, lively, noncoxcombical English prose. He regarded his book on Joan of Arc, written in a careful medley of "historical" and "modern" English, as a masterwork. Twain was correspondingly savage with bad writing. Like Poe, he was savage in the name of civilization--and doubly righteous when the bad style came from an English author, such as Matthew Arnold, whom he assailed without mercy for every sort of error of ignorance and carelessness. It was the lounging slanginess that Twain deplored in Arnold, not any tendency to write in a too high-toned, Order-of-the-Garter manner.[19]

In other words, Americans with a feeling for language accepted from the outset that the language of Shakespeare and Milton was a major, perhaps _the_ major, element in their patrimony from Britain, the maintenance of which would require ceaseless vigilance, sometimes against their own people, sometimes against language-neglect and language-abuse at the hands of the British.

A second concluding suggestion involves another kind of condominium, in which the Americans unconsciously or half-consciously replicated British cultural imagery. A well-known example occurs in Washington Irving's story of Rip Van Winkle. This was borrowed by Irving from an old European tale, though his version eventually eclipsed the original and became an item in _American_ folklore. In Irving's story, Rip, a Catskill villager, falls asleep for 20 years --snoozing, as it happens, right through the American Revolution. When he at last reawakens and stumbles back to his village, many changes have taken place. In the old days, for example, the tavern sign was a crude painting of George III. The uniform has been changed, the name transmogrified--from King George into George Washington.

Here, as it were, is patrimony as palimpsest: the new overlays the old, retaining its basic shape but with altered significance. Another, more conjectural case relates to the Battle of Cowpens, fought between Cornwallis and Daniel Morgan in January 1781. The Americans are more enthusiastic about the encounter than the British, since Morgan defeated Cornwallis. It is also gratifying to Americans because Cornwallis was a professional soldier and an aristocrat, in command of predominantly regular units, while Morgan was an amateur of humble origins, with a scratch force including a high proportion of militiamen. The intriguing detail for our purposes is that, in the darkness before the battle, Daniel Morgan went among his troops, man-to-man, to raise their spirits and convince them they were more than a match for the seemingly stronger, more glamorous enemy. Sure enough, they won.

No doubt most nations have comparable stories of outnumbered yet dauntless heroes who snatch victory out of the jaws of defeat, or if they are beaten will nevertheless fight to the last man. But it is very much within a _British_ patriotic context, of plain folks' gallantry in the face of seemingly impossible odds. In classic Shakespearian form, it is the victory of Agincourt in which, as at Crécy and Poitiers, in British patriotic lore, the longbow in the hands of simple yeomen beats the mounted chivalry of France. Daniel Morgan walks among the campfires in the dark; so, we all know, did Henry V at Agincourt. Figuratively, the American commander's message to his troops was "Cry God for Morgan, America, and George (Washington)!" Had Morgan ever read _Henry V_? We cannot be sure. He did, once, disclaiming education, say he had not had the chance to study "Voltaire and Shakespeare"--an odd pairing. There is a fair chance that given his patrimony, Morgan had at least heard of Shakespeare's version of the battle, and perhaps unwittingly reenacted the scene. Whatever the historical evidence, in a semiotic sense we have a replication of a kind of confrontation deeply satisfactory to the British nation.[20] An American interpretation of the nation's patriotic evolution sits upon a previous English evocation of <u>that</u> nation's record. The early part of the saga is American as <u>well</u> as British. With the Revolution, the American version begins to rely on a similar drama of <u>versuses</u>. John Paul Jones, victorious over seemingly superior forces, is an American reenactment of Francis Drake routing the Spanish Armada in the same coastal waters. But the British are now the villains in the American story. Andrew Jackson, as Henry V, at New Orleans triumphs over a seemingly far superior army led by the duke of Wellington's brother-in-law.

The patrimony has thus been maintained, in a sense, yet reversed in favor of the Americans, though with an extraordinary tangle during the first decades of American independence. Militarily, Wellington and his dogged volunteers defeat Napoleon's imperial conscripts; Nelson, the relatively self-made sailor, vanquishes the proud navies of the Continent. In literature, Americans tend to proclaim the virtues of simple, everyday circumstances over the sophistications of high society. Ralph Waldo Emerson, in his <u>American Scholar</u> address (1837), says: "We have listened too long to the courtly muses of Europe." The new era is concerned with "the literature of the poor, the feelings of the child, the philosophy of the street, the meaning of household life." But he is not able to name a single American who has written thus. His examples—Burns, Wordsworth, Goethe, etc.—are all European, most of them English or Scottish.

A final word about language. Ordinary Americans not professionally concerned with the world of letters were in all probability not much bothered over who held title to what. In the North American context, for most people, "English" was "American." A couple of anecdotes may make this clear. In 1799 a Quaker missionary among the Seneca Indians was asked by them, with some hostility, whether in his religion Indians and whites went to the same place when they died. He answered that there were "but two places, a place for the Good and a place for the Bad, of all Nations of People," and when asked "whether all would be of one Language, when there," he answered, "yes." Heaven and Hell apparently speak the same language; and—not to the surprise of the Indians, we may guess—it turns out to be English, or rather, American.[21]

The other true story is of Carl Schurz, an able and eventually prominent German liberal who emigrated to the United States in 1852. A couple of years later Schurz visited Chicago. He had a dream there of a confrontation with the city's rats. They surrounded him and accused him of trespassing. The rats did not speak German. So he had to answer their charge in broken English. In the dream, despite grammatical errors, he managed to be eloquent, and "so roused their sympathy that they made the lonely foreigner their honored guest." Thus "the Americanization of Carl Schurz" is accomplished when he is able to speak English adequately. But what he speaks to the rats and himself is, in effect, American.[22]

NOTES

1. Winthrop D. Jordan, "Familial Politics: Thomas Paine and the Killing of the King," Journal of American History 60 (September 1973): 294-308.

2. From Travels in North America (1787), cited in Dennis E. Baron, Grammar and Good Taste: Reforming the American Language (New Haven: Yale University Press, 1982), pp. 11-12. See also the opening chapters of H.L. Mencken, The American Language: An Inquiry into the Development of English in the United States (New York: Knopf, 1919, and in several subsequent editions).

3. J.P. Brissot de Warville, New Travels in the United States of America, 1788, ed. Durand Echeverria (Cambridge, Mass.: John Harvard Library, 1964), p. 78.

4. The Greek anecdote was related by Charles Astor Bristed, an American residing in England, in Cambridge Essays, 1855 (1856); see Baron, pp. 12-13. On McCormick, see Baron, pp. 39-40--a borrowing from Mencken, American Language, 4th ed. (1936), pp. 80-84, which supplies other amusing details.

5. Quoted in Van Wyck Brooks, The Dream of Arcadia: American Writers and Artists in Italy, 1760-1915 (New York: Dutton, 1958), p. 2.

6. Alan Leander MacGregor, "Tammany: The Indian as Rhetorical Surrogate," American Quarterly 35 (Fall 1983): 391-407.

7. Marcus Cunliffe, The Age of Expansionism, 1848-1917, History of the Western World ser. (London: Weidenfeld & Nicolson, 1974), pp. 80-84. On Ireland, see R.F. Foster, "History and the Irish Question," Transactions of the Royal Historical Society, 5th ser. 33 (1983): 169-192.

8. The gulf between native and settler Americans is indicated in Brissot (Travels, p. 415). At a Fourth of July ceremony in 1788 in Lexington, Ky., Brissot noted the following toast: "May the Indians, enemies of America, be chastised by the force of arms!" On the U.S. Mint, see Marvin Trachtenberg, The Statue of Liberty (London: Allen Lane, 1976), p. 82. Crawford's commission is discussed in Lillian B. Miller's excellent monograph, Patrons and

Patriotism: The Encouragement of the Fine Arts in the United States, 1790-1860 (Chicago: University of Chicago Press, 1966), pp. 75-76. Jefferson Davis, later to be president of the Confederacy, was involved because commissions came under the aegis of Captain Montgomery Meigs of the Corps of Engineers, who in turn had to report to the War Department.

9. For example: "Britain is the parent country, say some....; but it happens not to be true, or only partly so, and the phrase parent or mother country hath been jesuitically adopted by the king and his parasites, with a low papistical design of gaining an unfair bias on the credulous weakness of our minds. Europe, and not England, is the parent country of America....But, admitting that we were all of English descent, what does it amount to? Nothing. Britain, being now an open enemy, extinguishes every other name and title...." Paine, Common Sense, pt. 3.

10. James T. Flexner is the author of several works on the early evolution of American art, including biographies of Copley and Stuart. Among more broadly interpretive analyses are J. Meredith Neil, Toward a National Taste: America's Quest for Aesthetic Independence (Honolulu: University Press of Hawaii, 1975), and Kenneth Silverman, A Cultural History of the American Revolution: Painting, Music, Literature, and the Theatre,...1763-1789 (New York: Crowell, 1976).

11. On "rising glory," see Silverman, pp. 228-35. Discussions of possible American greatness are to be found also in Michael Kraus, The Atlantic Civilization: Eighteenth-Century Origins (Ithaca: Cornell University Press, 1949), pp. 216-307, and in Joseph J. Ellis, After the Revolution: Profiles of Early American Culture (New York: Norton, 1979), pp. 3-21.

12. Trevor Colbourn, "Thomas Jefferson's Use of the Past," William and Mary Quarterly, 3d ser. 15 (1958): 56-70; Colbourn, The Lamp of Experience: Whig History and the Intellectual Origins of the American Revolution (Chapel Hill: University of North Carolina Press, 1965); Marcus Cunliffe, "The Earth Belongs to the Living: Thomas Jefferson and the Limits of Inheritance," in Winfried Fluck et al., eds., Forms and Functions of History in American Literature: Essays in Honor of Ursula Brumm (Berlin: Erich Schmidt Verlag, 1981), pp. 56-70.

13. Webster's opinions, and those of Stiles and others, are usefully anthologized in Robert E. Spiller, ed., The American Literary Revolution, 1787-1837 (New York: Anchor Books, 1967), and Russel B. Nye & N.S. Grabo, eds., American Thought and Writing, vol. 2, The Revolution and the Early Republic (Boston: Houghton Mifflin, 1965). Harry R. Warfel's biography and scholarly editions are the most comprehensive treatments of Noah Webster, but see also Ellis, After the Revolution, pp. 161-212, and Richard Rollins, The Long Journey of Noah Webster (Philadelphia: University of Pennsylvania Press, 1980).

14. "The United States Elevated to Glory and Honor," cited in Nye and Grabo, pp. 81-82.

15. Letters of Noah Webster, ed. Harry R. Warfel (New York: Library Publishers, 1953), p. 415.

16. James Fenimore Cooper, The American Democrat (1838; reprint ed., New York: Minerva Press, 1969), pp. 111-12.

17. Marcus Cunliffe, George Washington: Man and Monument (1958; rev. ed., New York: Mentor, 1982); Garry Wills, Cincinnatus: George Washington and the Enlightenment (Garden City, N.Y.: Doubleday, 1984); Keith Berwick, The Federal Age, 1789-1829 (Washington, D.C.: American Historical Association, 1961); Wesley Frank Craven, The Legend of the Founding Fathers (New York: New York University Press, 1956).

18. Margaret Alterton and Hardin Craig, eds., Edgar Allan Poe: Representative Selections, American Century ser. (New York: Hill and Wang, 1935, 1962), pp. 312-16.

19. Henry Nash Smith, Mark Twain: The Development of a Writer (Cambridge, Mass.: Harvard University Press, 1962), pp. 151-52; Justin Kaplan, Mr. Clemens and Mark Twain (New York: Simon and Schuster, 1966), pp. 274, 299; Marcus Cunliffe, "Mark Twain and His 'English' Novels," London Times Literary Supplement, December 25, 1981.

20. Charles Royster, A Revolutionary People at War: The Continental Army and American Character, 1775-1783 (New York: Norton, 1981), gives examples of American allusions to Henry V, pp. 9, 325. On Morgan, see the essay by Don Higginbotham in George A. Billias, ed., George Washington's Generals (New York: Morrow, 1964), p. 312, and the same author's Daniel Morgan: Revolutionary Rifleman (Chapel Hill: University of North Carolina Press, 1961).

21. Anthony F.C. Wallace, The Death and Rebirth of the Seneca (New York: Knopf, 1970), pp. 231-32.

22. From Chester Easum, The Americanization of Carl Schurz (1929), pp. 89-91, cited by Godfrey Blodgett, Reviews in American History 11 (March 1983): 77.

THE CIRCUITOUS CAREER OF LOYALIST PLANS FOR
COLONIAL UNION IN AMERICA AND CANADA, 1754-1914

Ann Gorman Condon

The Treaty of Paris produced a permanent cleavage on the North American continent. The older and richer portion of the British colonial empire was sheared off, detached from Europe, freed to pursue a new career that would be nationalistic and westward-looking. The other, northern half of the empire, consisting of some small English settlements and an alien peasant society of French Canadians, remained under the British Crown. The fertile plains area between the Ohio and Mississippi rivers was ceded to the Americans, while Britain retained the vast fur-bearing regions to the north and west for commercial exploitation. According to the Canadian historian W.L. Morton: "No one in London dreamt of founding a second North American empire."[1]

This drastic reorganization of the continent had profound imlications for the 30,000 - 40,000 Loyalists who chose to leave America at the end of the Revolutionary War and resettle in the northern British colonies so as to maintain their connection with the Crown. Both before and after the American Revolution, the Loyalists stand out as an anomalous group in the history of the continent, a group that resists easy categorization. Mary Beth Norton has termed them the "British-Americans"; Esmond Wright speaks of "Men with Two Countries"; they themselves often used the label "American Englishmen."[2] Each term conveys the ambivalence, the mid-Atlantic tug that lay at the heart of the Loyalist experience.

Originally, the Loyalists were the children of what Lawrence Henry Gipson has called "the triumphant empire."[3] They achieved maturity in the exceptional decades of the 1750s and 1760s, when the British Empire became a powerful engine of victory that drove France from the North American continent and then proceeded to organize its vast holdings so as to maximize trade, military power, and revenue. In a multiplicity of ways, the men who eventually became Loyalist leaders served originally as the middlemen of this new, triumphant empire. They were the Americans tapped to fill the governorships, chief justiceships, customs posts, and masting surveys. They were the colonial veterans who had fought under Bradford or Amherst to rid the continent of the hated French. They were the land speculators with proprietary rights in the vast spaces of Nova Scotia and Trans-Appalachia, which the victory of 1760 freed for peaceful development. They were the Anglican clerics sent over by an ambitious SPG to pave the way for a bishopric in America. Their stake in the empire was as deep as their aspirations for America, and their unswerving goal was to unite the two in an imperial partnership that shared equally in the institutional strength of Great Britain and the bountiful resources of North America.[4]

The American Revolution imposed upon these Loyalists an unwanted choice. The more senior among them went to Great Britain, to propose to the king new modes of reconciliation or coercion, or both. The majority spent the long, dismal war in America and then, in the despair and uncertainty generated by defeat and the weak language of the Fifth Article of the peace treaty, they made their individual decisions whether to go into exile or try to return home.[5] Of the total number of Loyalists, well over 80 percent, or about 400,000 people, remained in America. Of those who left, about half, or 30,000 - 40,000, went to British North America in company with a significant group of their original military and political leaders.[6]

The Loyalist leaders brought with them to the northern colonies their peculiar and cherished vision of empire. It had been forged in the heady atmosphere of the 1750s and 1760s. It was expressed principally in a series of plans for Anglo-American union that called for the federation of the 13 colonies into a cohesive, centralized unit and for the admission of this new colonial organ to a substantive role within the imperial decision-making process. The Loyalist proponents also sought to endow this imperial partnership with some kind of collective commitment to political and cultural institutions that would constitute a common civilization or way of life—a new Anglo-American style. While all these plans served immediate military or political necessities, their fundamental goal was to amend the second-class status of the colonies within the empire so that the Americans' escalating sense of self-sufficiency could be contained within imperial channels.[7]

The imperial government failed to heed these Loyalist signals in time to prevent a break with the 13 oldest colonies, but the exiles who settled in British North America remained convinced of the validity of their vision. During the process of resettlement, Loyalist proposals for colonial federation and for a well-defined Anglo-American establishment in North America flooded Whitehall. Once again, the British government turned a deaf ear to all such schemes, even though it would have granted as much to its revolted colonies in 1778. The empire sought instead to avoid further disorder in America by strengthening the power of the royal governor and replicating the English social order in the northern provinces. The Anglican Church and the Loyalist military and civil leaders in each colony were given offices, property, and other privileges that, it was hoped, would in time lead to the development of an indigenous aristocracy.[8]

In this curious way, the Loyalists' most penetrating reflections on the government of the colonies were rejected, but the
Loyalists themselves were installed by imperial patronage as the
principal officeholders, landowners, and social leaders in their
individual colonies. They were an elite, but an elite wholly dependent on Great Britain for their status. British favor alone
distinguished them from the property-holding farmers and small
merchant-tradesmen who lived around them, whether these excluded
groups were British or French Canadian in origin.[9]

But they could not rely on British favor. For the Loyalist
elite found to their dismay that their old valued position as middlemen of a triumphant empire had been exchanged in 1783 for minor
posts on the periphery of an empire that had decisively shifted its
priorities from settlement to commerce.[10] In these artificial and
highly vulnerable circumstances, the Loyalist elite revived their
old plans for colonial federation and put them to a new defensive
purpose. During the four decades from 1800 to 1840, the heirs of
Loyalist privilege sought to apply colonial union to ends that
were antidemocratic and anti-French Canadian. In the political
sphere, this effort was terminated when Lord Durham dismissed out
of hand Loyalist pretensions to an oligarchic role. Although Loyalist social and cultural values would continue to shape Canadian
life for a much longer period, their final proposal for colonial
federation was promulgated in 1849, just after the British government had embraced free trade and responsible government for the
colonies. It was, as Jacques Monnet has written, a "last cannon
shot."[11] Twenty years later Canadian Confederation would embrace
the original Loyalist ideals of colonial union and a positive partnership with the empire. The success of the principle of colonial
federation in 1867 only became possible, however, when it was shorn
of the accretions of elitism and racism the Loyalist tradition had
acquired over the previous century.

The following section will review Loyalist proposals for colonial federation in order to delineate the continuities, alterations,
and reversals they exhibited from 1754 to 1849. A postscript will
note the fate of this impulse after Canadian Confederation. The
objective is not to reveal any significant new information about
the plans per se, for they are well known in the historical literature.[12] Rather, it is hoped that by pursuing this single, familiar
theme through the totality of Loyalist history, one can begin to
glimpse a conceptual framework for understanding the Loyalist
experience. Several fine studies have been produced in the last
two decades about the Loyalists' role in the American Revolution.
More recently, these have been complemented by investigations of
their resettlement in pre-Confederation Canada and their place in
the Canadian political tradition.[13]

Still missing, however, from our understanding of the Loyalist experience is the continental and imperial dimension. Richard Koebner has credited the Loyalists with keeping alive in their "corners of the British empire" a positive notion of the empire based on identity of interest, a notion rejected by Britain in the Constitutional Act of 1791 and Irish Union of 1800, but one that had inspired many men since the 1750s to dream of a "national solidarity of a higher order."[14] This positive notion of empire is the Loyalists' most enduring political contribution, and several Canadian historians have recognized its force.[15] The notion stands in striking contrast to the descriptions of imperial policy most prevalent in modern historical scholarship. In particular, Bernard Bailyn, Stephen Saunders Webb, and J.G.A. Pocock have depicted an empire where colonial subordination is the ironclad rule, and where manipulation and exploitation of dependencies is a matter of course. Bailyn describes an empire that is so unstable, so capricious as to legitimate the most extreme colonial fears that the British ministry was trying to subvert colonial liberties.[16] Webb suggests, even more ominously, that the territorial conquests of 1763 induced Great Britain to return to an old, favored policy of garrison government by military governors-general in which "coerciveness and power-hunger, paternalism and militarism" became the hallmarks of British policy in the American colonies.[17] Pocock sees these examples of pronounced discrimination against the colonies as illustrative of a fundamental distinction within all British history: between the inner kingdom or "domain," where constitutional forms are observed, and the peripheral areas or "marches," where military rule is the norm.[18] In none of these recent interpretations can the Loyalist ideal of Anglo-American union based on partnership and identity of interests find a home.

Yet it did persist. And it did produce in Canada a very different resolution of the relationship between empire and colony than that followed by the United States. After Canadian Confederation it would bubble up again in the Imperial Federation movement and in the outpouring of men and monies from the old Loyalist centers to support the empire in South Africa in 1899 and France in 1914. The very durability and strength of this notion suggests there was another approach to imperial relations that was being mooted in 18th-century North America.[19] The Loyalist plans for federation may permit a preliminary estimate of its dimensions.

The plans divide into three sets: those proposed for the 13 colonies before the American Revolution, those designed during the resettlement process after the war for the remaining British colonies, and those made between 1800 and Canadian Confederation in 1867. While a great assortment of plans for colonial union dot American colonial history beginning in the early 17th century, the proper starting point for the present inquiry is the Albany Plan of Union, sponsored by Thomas Hutchinson, Benjamin Franklin, and several other colonial leaders.[20] The essential prologue for understanding the mentality that produced the Albany Plan is Franklin's 1751 essay "Observations concerning the Increase of Mankind, Peopling of Countries, &c."[21] This famous, much-reprinted document struck a new, highly assertive context for viewing America's role within the empire. After noting that the colonial population was doubling every 25 years and creating a "glorious market wholly in the power of Britain," Franklin concluded with a romantic vision of the empire's future and the role of the North American colonies. They would, he predicted,

> in another century be more than the people of England, and the greatest number of Englishmen will be on this Side the Water. What an Accession of Power to the British Empire by Sea as well as Land! What Increase of Trade and Navigation! What numbers of Ships and Seamen! We have been here but little more than 100 years, and yet the force of our Privateers in the late War, united, was greater than that of the whole British Navy in Queen Elizabeth's time.[22]

The pride, the fecundity, and the sense of burgeoning power expressed here gave birth to a colonial patriotism that would eventually be termed "Loyalist" or "imperial nationalist."[23] Men like Franklin and Hutchinson, operating professionally within the interstices of empire, were acutely sensitive to both the imperatives of British policy and the nascent nationalism of their fellow Americans.[24] They detected in the early 1750s the need for a reformed imperial structure that would produce closer cooperation between the colonies and strengthen their collective voice within the empire. Albany was their first attempt to forge such a structure.

The Congress had been originally convened at the behest of the Board of Trade to deal with Indian defense, but the colonial leaders radically transformed this mandate. They proposed the creation of a general government that could surmount the "extremely jealous" attitudes of the colonies toward each other and at the same time persuade the empire "that the prerogative should relax a little" in matters relating to civil and military appointments in America, "for the King's benefit and the general benefit of the nation."[25] The new general government would be permanent; its president general would be appointed by the king; its Grand Council, elected by the colonial assemblies in proportion to population, would meet annually. Three specific but substantial powers were to be vested in this federation: to tax the member colonies, to provide for Indian defense, and to regulate settlement on the lands purchased from the Indians west of the Appalachian and Allegheny mountains. In defending the plan Franklin stressed the commissioners' belief that such a union "would best suit the circumstances of the colonies...and most effectually promote his Majesty's service and the general

interest of the British empire." It was therefore sent to the colonial assemblies for consideration and to Parliament for enactment.
"This was as much as the Commissioners could do."[26]

That such a sweeping, innovative proposal for the development
of North America was rejected out of hand by both the colonies and
the imperial bureaucracy does not detract from its merits.[27] The
concept of welding the colonies into a single superstructure and
enabling them to participate as real partners with the empire in
the settlement and government of the continent was imaginative,
appropriate, and potentially momentous. William Smith of New York
reported that the speakers at the Congress were "'inflamed with a
patriotic spirit...[and that] this Assembly...might very properly
be compared to one of the ancient Greek conventions, for supporting
their liberty against the power of the Persian empire....'"[28]

Such is the stuff of which empires are made. But neither Great
Britain nor the colonial assemblies could detach themselves from
their traditional perspectives long enough to see the magnitude of
this vision. For a dozen years, except for some isolated proposals
made by men like President Samuel Johnson of King's College, New
York, the notion of colonial federation lay dormant.[29] Franklin
spent these years in England, where he fluttered between advocacy
of colonial federation and possible American representation in the
House of Commons.[30] Thomas Hutchinson was by 1769 so repulsed by the
"'absurd notions of government...[that] have entered unto the heads
of Americans' that he turned against all federation schemes."[31] In
their stead two new champions arose to make colonial federation
their personal means of saving the empire: William Smith, Jr. of
New York and Joseph Galloway of Pennsylvania.

Both men were in fact protégés of delegates to the Albany Congress. Smith's father had attended and sat on the committee responsible for drafting the plan of union; Galloway served for many years
as Franklin's lieutenant in Pennsylvania.[32] Both saw themselves as
uniquely positioned to understand colonial grievances and interpret
them to imperial authorities. Although they worked separately,
their approach to the problem of imperial reorganization was remarkably similar. Intensely patriotic, they shared the same majestic
view of America's future, the same anger at the ministry's illiberal
policies in the 1760s and 1770s, and the same conviction of the
need for a radical reconstruction of the empire. Their commitment
to the empire was based in part on a deep attachment to British
institutions; and it was based in part on an even deeper fear of
America's vulnerability to mob rule.[33]

In plan after plan churned out in the decade before the Revolution, these two lawyers groped toward the establishment of an American branch of Parliament.[34] Their proposals were logical extensions
of the original Albany formula. Both set up an American legislature
and gave it exclusive taxing powers: Smith made the British Parlia-

ment supreme in all other legislative matters, while Galloway wanted colonial consent to extend to nontaxation matters as well. Colonial equality, in such areas as the tenure of judges and economic and commercial regulations, was a top priority. To balance these assertions of colonial autonomy, the Galloway and Smith plans called for a royally appointed president and a bicameral legislature in which appointments to the upper house were made by the Crown for life and some sort of distinction was accorded to its members "as a lure to prevent the office from falling into contempt." The two men were not, of course, in complete agreement. Galloway, the more conservative of the two, made room in his plans for an Anglican establishment and other prerogative practices that Smith, "a Whig of the old Stamp," could not countenance.[35]

Both of these carefully calibrated redistributions of power assumed the necessity of America's remaining within the empire and the consequent necessity of the colonies' remaining subordinate to Parliament. Both plans were submitted to the First Continental Congress in 1774. Smith's got sidetracked by a technicality and was never discussed. Galloway's became the centerpiece of a debate in which the possibility of a peaceful reconciliation was discussed, publicly and rationally, for the last time. Although some of the delegates described Galloway's plan as "almost a perfect Plan," the majority could not accept the principle of subordination. It was not merely voted down: it was expunged from the congressional record.[36] The empire was equally intransigent. The Loyalists' role as middlemen of the empire gave way to the generals, and their vision of a grand Anglo-American federation "uniting one people of the same mind" went into eclipse.[37]

When it reemerged in the 1780s in the brilliant but harsh northern light of Canada, circumstances were very different.[38] The loss during the intervening years of the 13 colonies and of the Loyalists' own personal homes and positions of power was, of course, shattering. The plans produced were thus tinged with sorrow and desperation, quite unlike the optimistic, assertive formulations made before 1776. These postwar plans still envisioned a bright, prosperous future for the British colonies in North America and demanded a large degree of autonomy for them within the empire. They contained as well, however, a much stronger insistence upon the need to build up the power of the governor general and local royal executive, and to shore up prerogative power in the individual colonies by extensive royal support of colleges, libraries, an independent judiciary, and, in some proposals, the Anglican Church. The exiles to British North America made numerous recommendations for its government, and their contents varied according to author. Some dealt with an individual colony or issue; some spoke for a particular interest like the clergy or the military; others prescribed for the whole.[39]

An inflation of rhetoric and ideal forms in these plans was

one effect of the Revolutionary experience. A far more important consequence was a new note of ambivalence. On the one hand, grand statements were made about the role British North America could play on the continent and within the empire: there were numerous predictions, for example, that more Loyalists could be drawn out of the United States to resettle in these new, better-governed colonies and that the natural resources of the North offered vast new sources of wealth for the empire. On the other hand, the plans were shot through with pessimistic warnings about the need to curb the latent democratic tendencies of the continent and protect royal government against the specter of republicanism. Only two of the many plans put forward after the war offered a full-scale scheme of colonial federation. These were by William Smith, appointed in 1785 to be chief justice of Quebec, and Jonathan Sewell, judge of the vice admiralty court at Halifax and member of the council in the newly created Province of New Brunswick.[40]

Smith, of course, had been devising plans for colonial union since the 1760s. Sewell made only one contribution to the genre, about the year 1785, but his training as attorney general of Massachusetts and close adviser to Governor Thomas Hutchinson during the most strife-filled period of American colonial politics amply qualified him for the job. The plans drawn up by both men were in a very real sense reflections on the Revolution, but, to their credit, they were not bitter. Rather, they were an inquiry into what went wrong and a reassertion of Sewell and Smith's belief in the viability of British colonial government in North America. The language on the whole was that of legal draftsmen; only occasionally did these well-trained Crown officials permit their anguish to surface. As Smith put it: "We ought to profit in our future conduct, by the sad Experience of the late troubles."[41]

In both cases their specific recommendations were based on a profound, lifelong commitment to the virtues of civilized life and their conviction that strong, positive government was the only instrument capable of creating civilized communities in North America. Equally, they were committed to the principle of internal self-government and to some popular participation in government. The defect in the governments of the former 13 colonies, as they saw it, was an _excessive_ degree of democracy coupled with a failure to give sufficient countervailing power to "the better sort of people" and the royal institutions of government. Out of this imbalance came republicanism, which rejected the positive notion of government and would lead, they were sure, to anarchy: "thirteen petty nations with jarring interests controlled by a majority that leaves sovereignty to none."[42]

To rectify this, Sewell and Smith laid out two lines of attack. The first was familiar and surely regressive for this point in the 18th century: the reform of colonial society by making its political and social institutions more like those of the mother country.

Such familiar nostrums as raising the property qualification for voters, giving more offices and preferment to persons with property, and establishing royal colleges and libraries were called for to establish a firm hierarchical structure in the individual colonies. Interestingly, neither Smith nor Sewell would endorse an Anglican establishment, feeling there should be full toleration among Protestants, although many of the partial plans submitted by other Loyalists, especially Anglican clergymen, considered a bishopric vital.[43]

These portions of their plans were clearly based on European models. The second line of attack was more progressive and more pertinent to the geography and mores of the continent. This was the call of Smith and Sewell for a "general" or federal government with extensive powers over all the remaining colonies. William Smith wanted a sweeping reorganization and integration of the remaining colonies. The keystone of his arch was an all-powerful governor general whose authority and distinction would make the royal prerogative a living reality in North America. He would be both governor general and captain general, with power over the militia, the individual lieutenant governors, Indian affairs, and relations with the United States. All communications with the imperial government would go through him; all colonial patronage would flow through him. Smith also called for a bicameral legislature with an appointed upper house and an elected lower house, to be established with the concurrence of Parliament. He expected this strongly led federal government to "stand as a permanent bond of Union, between these Countries and the Rest of the Empire."[44]

Sewell, too, wished to transfer a large quantum of royal power to North America and vest it in a federal union. His scheme called for a president or lord lieutenant, but sought principally to strengthen the middle branch of government: "a Council of persons, duly qualified for the trust, on which everything depends...." These privy counselors would hold their appointments on condition of good behavior and be empowered by statute to advise the president on all laws and matters of consequence. Like Smith, Sewell wanted this federal government to have "ample general powers" and through it to establish multiple positive links among the colonies and with the empire.[45]

The fate of the Loyalist elite in serving as the leaders of the northern colonies was given its peculiar shape when Great Britain adopted the more regressive aspects of these plans but dismissed the more progressive, imaginative parts. Some in England, however, were more sympathetic, particularly Lord Shelburne and Charles James Fox. Indeed, at one point in 1784, Ward Chipman reported excitedly from London that a federal government under a governor general had been approved. In the end, an older and narrower view prevailed. The colonies were to serve as "nurseries of seamen"; military governors were sent out to rule them as individual units; each was given an assembly and an upper house. The prestige and privileges of the Loyalist elite were reinforced and subsidies given to the Anglican Church. The only innovation was the grant of full political rights to the French Canadians in hopes they would become integral members of colonial society. In this way, the Loyalist notion of government as a positive, cohesive force was given substantial support by the British government, as was their demand for a social and political hierarchy. But their concomitant notion of an expansive, general government that would reach out to the continent and form a coordinate British community in North America proved no more acceptable in the 1780s than it had in 1754.[46]

The wonder is that the plans reemerged so soon. Typically, colonial settlements require a full generation or more simply to get settled in, to lay out their political and economic sight lines, and to give form to their social goals. This in fact proved true in the Maritime provinces and, to a lesser extent, in Upper Canada. In these colonies there was, to be sure, constant internal bickering from the start.[47] Particularly worrisome to the transplanted American populations was the gap between the power of the Assembly and the new, highly augmented power of the governors and their Loyalist advisers, who reported only to London.[48] In all these colonies, however, the consuming business of survival and the establishment of trade links with the outside world necessarily made such concerns secondary.

In Lower Canada, the truncated French Canadian province carved out of Quebec, the luxury of a long gestation period was not possible. A small group of Loyalist and British officials were appointed the executives of this, "the first large European Colony to be incorporated into the British Empire." The deeply rooted habitant population was granted the vote and the right to sit in the Assembly in the sublime expectation that they would voluntarily embrace "anglicization": English laws, English institutions, and English language. To the astonishment of colonial officials at home and in the province, the French Canadians instead began to use these powers to protect their way of life. Thus developed "two hermetic social structures without interaction of any kind, one English- and the other French-speaking, each seeking to impose its primacy by political means."[49] No one felt more alarmed by this unexpected political polarization than the local community of Loyalist officials and merchants who had seen enough of nationalism and revolution in their immediate past to dread its consequences. Faced with this apparent threat to Loyalist hegemony, the most eminent local Loyalist official, Jonathan Sewell, Jr.--Sewell's son and Smith's son-in-law-- dusted off the plans of his father and father-in-law and applied them to a new political purpose--swamping the French.

Sewell's plan was disingenuous. It acknowledged the loyalty of both the French Canadian people and their Roman Catholic Church, but maintained that the structure of government in British North

America was deficient on two important counts. No mechanism existed to provide for the collective defense of all five provinces. Moreover, the proper hierarchical nature of government was not being achieved, for although "the legislatures are assimilated to the legislature of the mother country...the Crown has but little influence in the democratic branches of either of these provincial legislatures; and it...has none which can enable it to carry a single measure ([no matter] how expedient or indispensably necessary for the whole of the provinces, or for the empire) in opposition to any local provincial interest...." To correct these defects, Sewell proposed to eliminate all five provincial assemblies and create a legislative union of them so that no single province would dominate and "mere local prejudices would be sunk." Sewell's plan was so brief and so general, it is difficult to tell how the delegates to the new legislature would have been chosen. Its intent, nonetheless, was clear: to suppress French Canadian nationalism by eliminating their provincial assembly and submerging them in a highly authoritarian federal government.[50] This use of the federal principle to discriminate against a portion of colonial society and to reduce the role of democratic assemblies to an auxiliary status was a radical departure in Loyalist thought. While it certainly did not represent the views of all the Loyalist elite, it would appeal to many in the strife-ridden years ahead.

In fact the federal plans proposed over the quarter century between 1815 and 1840 tended to divide on this question of ethnicity. On one side was the expansive plan of John Beverley Robinson, attorney general and later chief justice of Upper Canada, who in 1822 opposed another attempt to deprive the French Canadians of their Assembly. Robinson belittled the racial argument, saying the French Canadians were merely expressing "that desire which is found in all assemblies to assert to the utmost that share of power which they think the constitution gives them, a disposition which I think the descendants of English, Irish and Scottish will be found as likely to persevere in, as descendants of Frenchmen."[51] Robinson's plan provided for a federal union that would preserve all the provincial assemblies, thereby confirming French Canadian institutions, and that would enhance the status of the British North American colonies in the empire. He called for a "grand confederacy," a common defense system, and a strong central government. With an imperial sense worthy of William Smith and other Loyalist progenitors, Robinson expressed the hope that in time the other "colonial possessions of the empire" might group "into six or seven Confederacies," each with their own representative in Parliament, "making known their wants, their interests, and their desires, in the great Council of the Nation...."[52]

Robinson's enlightened and sweeping views have won him praise as a prophet of both Confederation and Commonwealth. He clearly did have an idealistic vision of the empire, but it was based, it should be noted, on a solidly hierarchical structure. Part and parcel of his 1823 plan was a high property qualification for elected delegates to the new government and the expressed hope that, in time, "the semblance of monarchy might be made more exact" by creating hereditary ranks to "add to the dignity and support of government...."[53]

Other plans by colonial officials who were closely associated with Loyalist governing circles followed similar lines. Richard John Uniacke, attorney general of Nova Scotia, was the only Maritimer to offer a plan of federation. Uniacke wanted to respect all governments and religions, and was mainly concerned with strengthening the common defense against the Americans and improving commercial links within the empire. Like Robinson, Uniacke felt the governor and council should be independent of popular control, but he was warmly sympathetic to the French Canadians.[54] John Strachan, an early Scottish immigrant whose conversion to both the Anglican Church and the credo of the Loyalist elite led to enormous power in Upper Canada, clearly perceived the threat republicanism posed to his most cherished institutions, and in the 1820s he proposed a plan of union designed to coerce the French into assimilation, substantially increase the powers of the appointive council, and give the Anglican Church more preferment.[55]

These were the principal plans of federation proposed by the Loyalist elite before 1837, when both the French Canadians of Lower Canada and the farmers and shopkeepers of Upper Canada rose up in rebellion against the "Chateau Clique" and the "Family Compact," the Loyalist provincial oligarchies that had deprived them for so long of access to land, church revenues, and a full political voice. The rebellions were put down quickly, but they forced a thorough reappraisal of the government of the northern colonies. The British government sent John George Lambton (Lord Durham) to conduct this review, and his published findings in the Durham Report permanently altered the course of Canadian political development. Durham is rightly remembered for his endorsement of the principle of responsible government, which unblocked the logjam in which Canadian democracy had been trapped, and permitted the rapid realization of colonial self-government. Durham's impact on the Loyalist elite's plans for a federation of British North America is only slightly less momentous.[56]

Of the three key principles that characterized Loyalist plans—positive government, federalism, and hierarchy—Durham embraced two and demolished the third. The one he demolished, of course, was hierarchy. The "irresponsible cliques" and a "monopoly of power so extensive and so lasting," he said, "[would] excite envy, create dissatisfaction, and ultimately provoke attack." Despite this onslaught, Durham was sufficiently persuaded of the other two Loyalist principles, federalism and positive government, that he thanked Jonathan Sewell, Jr. in the text of his report for letting him see Sewell's old plan. In the end, Durham did not recommend a federal government for British North America, opting rather for a legislative union of Upper and Lower Canada. He felt that the most urgent priority was to anglicize French Canada and that any more general union must await their assimilation and the establishment of better communication with the eastern provinces. Nonetheless, Durham clearly felt that federalism should be the eventual basis of government and predicted it would give the colonies the strength, the dignity, and the sense of nationality they deserved and needed.[57]

Thus the old Loyalist proposals were cut in two. The hierarchical half was discarded, the federal half sent into limbo for a decade while responsible government was implemented and French-English relations brought into some kind of working balance. A rump of the Loyalist elite, now deprived of their privileged status, made one final stab at reviving their old schemes in 1849. Calling themselves the British American League, they expressed their deep sense of betrayal over the empire's policies: the admission of the French Canadians (with their cultural institutions intact) to full political participation during the 1840s, the adoption of free trade in 1846, and the acceptance of colonial democracy in 1848 not only annulled the principle of elite government but seemed to doom the imperial connection. In the course of three successive meetings, the distraught members of the league managed to call for a federal union of British North America, annexation to the United States, and Canadian representation in the House of Commons! What the league really wanted, of course, was restoration of the old English-speaking hierarchy. Its cause was stillborn, and with its demise the old Loyalist elite faded as a significant political force.[58]

The authentic revival of the federalist notion came in the 1850s. This time it was backed by men of an entirely different stamp, men interested in railroads, intercolonial trade, and western development. Except for William Hamilton Merritt, a railroad entrepreneur, none of the old Loyalist governing elite played a prominent part in the move toward Confederation. It did receive strong support from British investors in North America and increasingly from the Colonial Office and the British Army, which began to worry about its defense commitments as it observed the awesome power of the United States in the course of the American Civil War. In the 1860s, this coalition of economic and military interests dragged the Maritime provinces kicking and screaming into the union, and in 1867 Canadian Confederation was born.[59] It combined the new device of responsible government with the century-old device of federalism to create "Dominion government." It was democratic, centralized, yet respectful of local provincial interests. It was internally self-governing, yet subordinate to Parliament. In imperial terms, it divided power much the way Joseph Galloway had in his proposal to the First Continental Congress in 1774. The Americans had rejected this compromise. Yet for Canada in 1867, still less than

100 years old and confronted by a much more ominous world, it was entirely satisfactory.

Thus two vast federations spanned the North American continent in the late 19th century. Both became increasingly nationalistic, but thanks to the Loyalists, "British nationalism" ("imperial nationalism") continued to play an important role in Canadian life. Political privilege, of course, was out. The intelligence and cohesiveness of the old oligarchies had to give way to the endemic democracy of the North American environment, although it is unclear whether the Loyalists ever understood this truth. Their attempts to reproduce European forms simply had no basis in a social structure when all had access to property. The groups they chose to exclude from power were not peasant and proletariat, but the other half of the middle class. Moreover, even in Britain itself, hierarchy was being dismantled by 1867.

The Loyalist ideal of empire had a much longer life. Indeed, the final, ironic twist in this circuitous history of Loyalist plans for colonial federation was their adoption by Britain itself. Though Britain had rejected this principle in 1754, 1774, 1791, 1807, 1823, and 1840--and only accepted it in 1867 to divest itself of economic and military responsibilities--the empire experienced a remarkable conversion in the 1880s. Inspiration clearly came from the new power and technological skill of Germany and the United States. With new zeal, the empire embraced the "kith and kin" approach to its colonies, and the Imperial Federation League was born.[60] In Canada, descendants of the old Loyalist elite distinguished themselves as publicists for this movement. Plans for a common tariff, common defense, and educational exchanges were bruited about, and a new concern developed for the state of Canada's military preparedness. The most notable result was a rising tide of imperial sentiment in the English-speaking sectors. Volunteers were sent to the Boer War. Imperial unity became a major plank in the Conservative Party platform. The call to arms in 1914 evoked a substantial response from all sectors of Canadian society, but in the old Loyalist enclaves it felt more like a crusade.

World War I changed Canada's role within the empire, and Loyalist categories of thought did not survive this transition. The men who went on after the war to construct the British Commonwealth of Nations had a different perception of the relationship between empire and colony than did the old colonial elites. Nonetheless, in their 150-year history, Loyalist political ideas represented an important current of conservative thought in North America: they provided the continent with a corporate alternative to republican individualism and with a sense of membership in a larger world.[61] In the 18th century, Loyalist proposals had proved too adventurous for the mother country. In the 19th, they had been too remote for the raw, alien environment into which the Revolution had thrust them. Yet, while Loyalist leaders went into decline, their ideal of union was realized by others.

NOTES

1. William Lewis Morton, The Kingdom of Canada, 2d ed. (Toronto, 1969), p. 173; Vincent T. Harlow, The Founding of the Second British Empire, 1763-1793 (London, 1952-64), 1: 223-311.

2. Mary Beth Norton, The British-Americans: The Loyalist Exiles in England, 1774-1789 (Boston, 1972); Esmond Wright, "Men with Two Countries," in The Development of a Revolutionary Mentality (Library of Congress, Washington, D.C., 1972), pp. 151-57; Richard Koebner, Empire (Cambridge, England, 1961), p. 108; Thomas Hutchinson, "A Dialogue between an American and a European Englishman [1768]," Bernard Bailyn, ed., Perspectives in American History, vol. 9 (1975), pp. 343-410.

3. Lawrence Henry Gipson, The British Empire before the American Revolution (New York, 1936-70), vols. 9-11.

4. Two fine collective biographies of these Loyalist leaders are William H. Nelson's classic, The American Tory (Oxford, 1961), and Robert McCluer Calhoon, The Loyalists in Revolutionary America, 1760-1781 (New York, 1973). The role of these Loyalists as both imperial middlemen and members of a colonial elite is explored in Thomas C. Barrow, "The American Revolution as a War for Colonial Independence," William and Mary Quarterly, 3d ser. 25 (1968): 452-64.

5. As yet, no comprehensive history of the Loyalists who stayed on in America or returned after has been made. Two local but instructive treatments are: Adele Hast, Loyalism in Revolutionary Virginia: The Norfolk and Eastern Shore Area (Ann Arbor, 1979), pp. 111-70, and Neil MacKinnon, "The Changing Attitude of the Nova Scotia Loyalists to the United States, 1783-1791," Acadiensis 2 (1973): 43-53. The best general accounts of the exiles are Wallace Brown, The Good Americans: The Loyalists in the American Revolution (New York, 1969), pp. 147-221, and Norton, British-Americans, pp. 155-249.

6. These calculations are derived from Paul H. Smith, "The American Loyalists: Notes on Their Organizational and Numerical Strength," William and Mary Quarterly, 3d ser. 25 (1968): 259-77. Thre is no general history of the Loyalist experience in Canada. An introductory statement is William Stewart MacNutt, "The Loyalists: A Sympathetic View," Acadiensis 6 (1976): 3-20.

7. Koebner, Empire, pp. 105-18; George T. Lichtheim, Imperialism (New York, 1971), p. 57.

8. Harlow, Second British Empire, 1: 10, 2: 723-73; William Lewis Morton, "The Local Executive in the British Empire, 1763-1828," English Historical Review 78 (1963): 436-57.

9. "Our Gentlemen have all become potato planters and our shoemakers are preparing to legislate," reported Edward Winslow from New Brunswick in 1793: William Obder Raymond, ed. The Winslow Papers, A.D. 1776-1826 (Saint John, 1901), p. 399. The fluidity of Quebec's social structure is described in Fernand Ouellet, Lower Canada, 1791-1840 (Toronto, 1980), pp. 2-20.

10. Harlow, Second British Empire, 1: 1-11; J.G.A. Pocock, "The Limits and Divisions of British History: In Search of an Unknown Subject," American Historical Review 87 (1982): 311-36.

11. Jacques Monet, The Last Cannon Shot: A Study of French Canadian Nationalism, 1837-1850 (Toronto, 1969).

12. For American plans of union during the colonial period: James H. Hutson, "Tentative Moves Toward Intercolonial Union," in George W. Corner, ed., Aspects of American Liberty (Philadelphia, 1977), pp. 81-94. For pre-Confederation Canada: Leslie F.S. Upton, "The Idea of Confederation, 1754-1858," in William Lewis Morton, ed., The Shield of Achilles (Toronto, 1968), pp. 184-207.

13. For a comprehensive bibliography of the American experience, see Wallace Brown, "The View at Two Hundred Years: The Loyalists of the American Revolution," American Antiquarian Society, Proceedings 80 (1970): 25-47. There is no equivalent in Canada, but a most helpful general guide is Del A. Muise, ed., A Reader's Guide to Canadian History, vol. 1, Beginnings to Confederation (Toronto, 1982). Recent and significant interpretations of the Loyalist contribution to the Canadian political tradition are Gad Horowitiz, "Conservatism, Liberalism, and Socialism in Canada: An Interpretation," Canadian Journal of Economics and Political Science 32 (1966): 147-71; Carl Berger, The Sense of Power: Studies in the Ideas of Canadian Imperialism, 1867-1914 (Toronto, 1970), pp. 78-108; Murray Barkeley, "The Loyalist Tradition in New Brunswick," Acadiensis 4 (1975): 3-45.

14. Koebner, Empire, p. 275.

15. Leslie F.S. Upton, ed., The United Empire Loyalists: Men and Myths (Toronto, 1967), for a sampling of this predominant view.

16. Bernard Bailyn articulates this interpretation in two works: The Origins of American Politics (New York, 1968), chaps. 2-3, and the introductory essay to his edition of Pamphlets of the American Revolution, 1750-1776 (Cambridge, Mass., 1965), pp. 3-203.

17. Stephen Saunders Webb, The Governors General: The English Army and the Definition of the Empire (Chapel Hill, 1977), pp. 465-66. For evidence supporting this shift in imperial policy, see the trade statistics in Peter Marshall, "The First and Second British Empire: A Question of Demarcation," History 49 (1964): 12-23.

18. Pocock, "Limits and Divisions of British History," pp. 319-36.

19. For British adherents to these quasi-Commonwealth ideas, see David Fieldhouse, "British Imperialism in the late Eighteenth Century: Defence or Opulence?" in K. Robinson and F. Madden, eds., Essays in Imperial Government Presented to Margery Perham (Oxford, 1963), pp. 22-45, and Harlow, Second British Empire, 2: 783-84.

20. The historical background of the plan may be traced in Harry M. Ward, 'Unite or Die': Intercolony Relations, 1690-1763 (Port Washington, N.Y., 1971), and Hutson, "Tentative Moves Toward Inter-colonial Union." The Albany Plan of Union, and a long note by the editors summarizing the controversy over its authorship, may be found in Leonard W. Labaree et al., eds., The Papers of Benjamin Franklin (New Haven, 1962), 5: 374-92.

21. Ibid., 4: 225-34.

22. Ibid., p. 233.

23. For a penetrating discussion of these terms and their rela-tionship to the plans and the Loyalist mentality, see Keith Ferling, The Loyalist Mind: Joseph Galloway and the American Revolution (University Park, Pa., 1977), pp. 88-92.

24. For English perceptions of these "explosive possibilities," see Jack M. Bumsted, "Things in the Womb of Time: Ideas of American Independence, 1633 to 1763," William and Mary Quarterly, 3d ser. 31 (1974): 544-64. The state of the colonies is summarized in more critical terms in Jack P. Greene, "An Uneasy Connection: An Analysis of the Preconditions of the American Revolution," in Stephen G. Kurtz and James H. Hutson, eds., Essays on the American Revolution (Chapel Hill, 1973), pp. 32-80. Greene clearly feels that by 1750 the indi-vidualistic ethnic was far more prevalent than the imperialist ethnic described by Ferling.

25. Labaree, Benjamin Franklin Papers, 5: 400, 416.

26. Ibid., p. 400.

27. For the rejection of the Albany Plan, see Gipson, British Empire before the American Revolution, 5: 143-66, and Alison Gilbert Olson, "The British Government and Colonial Union, 1754," William and Mary Quarterly, 3d ser. 17 (1960): 22-34.

28. Gipson attributes this phrase to William Smith the elder, who attended the conference from New York. Leslie F.S. Upton is convinced that William Smith, Jr. wrote this description of the plan in an essay printed in 1757. In either case, it seems fair to assume this expressed the Smiths' common view of this effort at intercolonial

union, particularly in view of their close filial and working relationship. See Leslie F.S. Upton, <u>The Loyal Whig: William Smith of New York & Quebec</u> (Toronto, 1969), p. 36.

29. Randolph G. Adams, <u>Political Ideas of the American Revolution: Britannic-American Contributions to the Problem of Imperial Organization, 1765 to 1775</u> (New York, 1922), p. 71.

30. Koebner, <u>Empire</u>, pp. 109-17.

31. Labaree, <u>Benjamin Franklin Papers</u>, 5: 379.

32. Benjamin H. Newcomb, <u>Franklin and Galloway: A Political Partnership</u> (New Haven, 1972).

33. The following paragraphs are drawn primarily from the two principal biographies: Ferling, <u>The Loyalist Mind: Joseph Galloway and the American Revolution</u>, and Upton, <u>The Loyal Whig: William Smith of New York & Quebec</u>. Fine brief sketches of these two men may be found in Calhoon, <u>Loyalists in Revolutionary America</u>, pp. 85-104.

34. For Smith's plan during the Stamp Act crisis, see Robert McCluer Calhoon, "William Smith jr.'s Alternative to the Revolution," <u>William and Mary Quarterly</u>, 3d ser. 22 (1965): 105-18. For successive plans of Galloway, Julian P. Boyd, <u>Anglo-American Union: Joseph Galloway's Plan to Preserve the British Empire</u> (Philadelphia, 1941), pp. 112-77. The reader should note that the 1785 plan included in Boyd's volume, pp. 155-72, was in fact written by Jonathan Sewell. For this attribution, see William H. Nelson, "The Last Hopes of the American Loyalists," <u>Canadian Historical Review</u> 32 (1951): 40-42.

35. Upton, <u>Loyal Whig: William Smith of New York & Quebec</u>, pp. 93, 110.

36. Ferling, <u>Loyalist Mind: Joseph Galloway and the American Revolution</u>, pp. 36-37.

37. Ibid., p. 97.

38. This essay has not included plans written during the Revolutionary War period because their focus on the Revolutionary situation makes them appropriate for separate study. Galloway's plans written during the war are included in Boyd, <u>Anglo-American Union</u>. The many Loyalist proposals written in America and England during the war may be traced in Gregory Palmer, ed., <u>A Bibliography of Loyalist Source Material in the United States, Canada, and Great Britain</u>, pp. 585-857. Also of interest is Mary Beth Norton, "John Randolph's Plan of Accommodations," <u>William and Mary Quarterly</u>, 3d ser. (1971): 103-120.

39. Ann Gorman Condon, "'The Envy of the American States': The Settlement of the Loyalists in New Brunswick, Goals and Achievements" (unpublished Ph.D. thesis, Harvard University, 1976), pp. 69-100.

40. Leslie F.S. Upton, The Diary and Selected Papers of Chief Justice William Smith, 1784-1793 (Toronto, 1965), 2: 189-91, 270-76, for Smith's original plan for British North America and his subsequent amendments to the Constitutional Act of 1791. Sewell's plan is contained in Boyd, Anglo-American Union, pp. 157-72 (see n. 34). It is discussed in Ann Gorman Condon, "Marching to a Different Drummer: The Political Philosophy of the American Loyalists," in Esmond Wright, ed., Red, White & True Blue: The Loyalists in the Revolution (New York, 1976), pp. 1-18.

41. Upton, Diary of William Smith, 2: 190.

42. Condon, "Envy of the American States," pp. 18-19; Upton, Loyal Whig: William Smith of New York & Quebec, p. 142.

43. Condon, "Envy of the American States," pp. 31-36.

44. Upton, Diary of William Smith, 2: 185-91, 270-77.

45. Boyd, Anglo-American Union, pp. 157-59.

46. Raymond, Winslow Papers, p. 170; Harlow, Second British Empire, 2: 766-67.

47. For the early Maritime provinces, see the two volumes by William Stewart MacNutt: New Brunswick: A History, 1784-1865 (Toronto, 1963) and The Atlantic Provinces: The Emergence of Colonial Society, 1712-1857 (Toronto, 1965). For the colonial period in central Canada: Gerald M. Craig, Upper Canada, the Formative Years, 1784-1841 (Toronto, 1963). More monographic are Condon, "The Envy of the American States"; Robin Burns, "God's Chosen People: The Origins of Toronto Society, 1793-1818," Canadian Historical Association, Historical Papers, 1978, pp. 213-228; and two articles by Neil MacKinnon: "Nova Scotia Loyalists," Social History-Histoire Sociale 4 (1969): 17-48, and "'This Cursed Republic Spirit': The Loyalists and Nova Scotia's Sixth Assembly," Humanities Association Review 27 (1976): 129-41.

48. Morton, "Local Executive," pp. 436-57.

49. Harlow, Second British Empire, 2: 771-73; Ouellet, Lower Canada, p. 61.

50. Jonathan Sewell, Plan for a Legislative Union of the British Provinces in North America (London, 1807; reprinted in Jonathan Sewell, John Beverley Robinson, and James Stuart, Four Pamphlets on the Confederation or Union of the Canadas, Toronto, 1967), pamphlet

no. 1, pp. 1–14. For the vehemence of Sewell's hostility to the French Canadians, see his letter in Arthur G. Doughty and Duncan MacArthur, eds., <u>Documents relating to the Constitutional history of Canada, 1791–1818</u> (Ottawa, 1914), pp. 400–405.

51. Adam Shortt and Norah V. Storey, eds., <u>Documents Relating to the Constitutional History of Canada, 1819–1840</u>, 2d ed. (1918), p. 316.

52. John Beverley Robinson, <u>Letter to the Right Honorable Earl Bathurst, K.G., on the Policy of Uniting the British North-American Colonies</u>, reprinted in Sewell et al., <u>Four Pamphlets</u>, pamphlet no. 2, pp. 38, 39–40.

53. Ibid., p. 32; Craig, <u>Upper Canada</u>, p. 104; William Ormsby, "The Problem of Canadian Union, 1822–1828," <u>Canadian Historical Review</u> 39 (1958): 282–90.

54. Brian Cuthbertson, <u>The Old Attorney General: A Biography of Richard John Uniacke, 1753–1830</u> (Halifax, 1980), pp. 58, 120–21.

55. J.L.H. Henderson, <u>John Strachan: Documents and Opinions</u> (Toronto, 1969), pp. 142–70.

56. Of the numerous accounts of this period in Canadian history, the most comprehensive are Craig, <u>Upper Canada</u>, pp. 188–275, and Ouellet, <u>Lower Canada</u>, pp. 211–341.

57. Charles P. Lucas, ed., <u>Lord Durham's Report on the Affairs of British North America</u> (Oxford, 1912), 2: 304–23.

58. Upton, "The Idea of Confederation," p. 194; Morton, <u>Kingdom of Canada</u>, p. 285.

59. The most thorough accounts of this transition are James Maurice S. Careless, <u>The Union of the Canadas: The Growth of Canadian Institutions</u> (Toronto, 1967), and William Lewis Morton, <u>The Critical Years: The Union of British North America, 1857–1873</u>. For the shift in imperial attitudes, see Bruce A. Knox, "The Rise of Colonial Federalism as an Object of British Policy, 1850–1870," <u>Journal of British Studies</u> 11 (1971–72): 92–112.

60. Donald Southgate, "Imperial Britain," in C.J. Bartlett, ed., <u>Britain Pre-Eminent: Studies in British World Influence in the Nineteenth Century</u> (London, 1969), pp. 159–65.

61. Berger, <u>Sense of Power</u>, esp. chap. 3, and Barkeley, "Loyalist Tradition in New Brunswick." These works have stimulated a lively debate as to how nationalistic the upsurge of imperialism in Canada was in fact. Representative are Ramsay Cook, "Nationalism in Canada or <u>Portnoy's Complaint</u> Revisited," <u>South Atlantic Quarterly</u> 69 (1970): 1–19, and Graham Carr, "Imperialism and Nationalism in Revisionist Historiography: A Critique of Some Recent Trends," <u>Journal of Canadian Studies</u> 17 (1982): 91–99.

COMMENTARY

J.G.A. Pocock

Adam Smith came just in time. He persuaded British opinion that even if colonies were not actually unnecessary to a system of commerce, an authoritative system of imperial control was not needed to safeguard the flow of trade. From this could follow many consequences; there was the utopia of free trade, which permitted John Bright--that quintessential country ideologist--to stigmatize all exercise of national power as a species of aristocratic corruption; and there was the imperialism of free trade, in which the flag, often reluctantly and against its better judgment, followed trade into distant and peculiar markets.

But the problem of loyalism, not of much account to Smith, is another matter. This issue engaged the attention of Josiah Tucker, whose deepest political belief was the urgent necessity that Britain should declare itself independent of its colonies, not only on grounds of political economy, which he shared more or less with Adam Smith, but because colonists were an undesirable set of dissenters and republicans, slaveholders and followers of John Locke, into whose archaic and unsavory system the demographic changes charted by Franklin threatened Britain with absorption.

What then was to be done with those colonists who, for reasons best known to themselves, wished to retain the connection with the Crown? Tucker considered the question during the years of the American Revolution, and reluctantly conceded they would have to be granted some area in which they could maintain the imperial relation as long as they wanted it, which he neither expected nor desired to be for long. It looked, at the time he wrote, as if that region would be the Chesapeake. It turned out to be the Saint Lawrence. Tucker was not a representative thinker but a prophetic one. The problem of loyalism had been born.

Ann Gorman Condon's paper leaves it beyond doubt that the Treaty of Paris was a starting point of Canadian as well as U.S. history, and that the history of British North America ranks beside that of the independent federal republic as an aspect of the history of Anglophone politics and culture. We can no longer think of Loyalists as uprooted and wasting away in exile; they founded an America of their own.

The political ideas and projects of Loyalists who settled in Canada had an American pedigree traceable to the Albany Plan. Condon has taught us that they can also be viewed in a dual context, English as well as American. In the latter context, Condon's Loyalists sound remarkably like a generation of émigré Federalists, not only because of their ideas about how to associate a plurality of colonies under a common sovereignty, but because they so evidently figure in the doomed (but quite long) rearguard action of aristocracy in the politics of this continent. In the English context, at the same time, they were Whigs of the counterrevolution, whom we misname Tories; they belong, that is to say, to that long half-century from Pitt to Peel, when in the wake of the American and French revolutions the parliamentary monarchy was maintained by a harder and perhaps more astute oligarchy than that of even the first Hanoverian reigns. It seems a pity that Tocqueville could not delay his trip long enough to visit Canada after the Durham Report, and describe the processes of democratization at all three corners of the North Atlantic triangle.

When Condon emphasizes the dual perspective of Anglo-Canadian history--and defines her Loyalists as those intent on being both American and British--she opens up yet another historical scene: that usually classified (not to say excluded) as "Commonwealth history" or "the history of the self-governing Dominions," but better thought of, I submit, as a major paradox of extension in British history. This, too, derives its beginnings from the Treaty of Paris. The American Revolution--described by one of Condon's New Brunswick colleagues as "the first North American civil war"--was the disruption of the largest and potentially the most expansive empire of settlement that Britain ever ruled. It is a historical commonplace that the so-called Second British Empire that succeeded it was an empire of trade rather than of settlement, which in India and elsewhere rested less on colonization than on what is rather inaccurately termed "colonialism."

The paradox is that settlement and colonization continued. The Loyalist hegira to the Maritimes and Upper Canada was reinforced, in the early decades of the 19th century, by a steady stream of English, Scottish, and Irish emigration, which was also beginning to establish colonies in three regions of the Southern Hemisphere. The paradox deepens when we consider that British and Irish emigration to the colonies was numerically outweighed by emigration to the independent United States; it deepens again when we consider that while British (but not Irish) immigrants to this republic were so rapidly assimilated as to leave not a hyphen behind them, the peoples of the self-governing dominions retained, as fundamental to their historical existence, the problem of dual identity that Condon has specified as the essence of loyalism.

The history of loyalism after 1783 enlarges steadily to become the history of the overseas British and their political and cultural

problems in maintaining a plural identity. I want, therefore, to
enlarge the British context of Condon's reading to emphasize such
American components of Canadian history as the attempt to prolong
the existence of aristocracy or the ineradicable presence of the
French Canadians. A Loyalist may be defined as one who asserts a
British identity for reasons not always apparent or agreeable to
the makers of policy and opinion in the United Kingdom. The original Loyalists had cause to wonder just how much the British were
doing for them at Paris, just as the British had cause to wonder
just how much they should do for the Loyalists. And on the side-
lines, Josiah Tucker insisted that Britain was better off without
colonies, the sooner they became independent the better. His
opinion has never since lacked either moralist or realist defenders.

What I would suggest is that all the experiments and projects
Condon described were attempts to solve this problem by way of compromise. An empire of free settlement must be defended, but settlers must not be free to determine when defense is necessary.
This was the theme A.P. Thornton detected as crucial to British
imperial history, but one that not even Texans ever made crucial
to the history of the United States.

In a model for British history Condon mentions in her paper,
I made much of a distinction between a settled society's civil
heartland and the military march upon its borders. But I also
advanced the concept of the secondary polity, into which the march
might evolve when its inhabitants and those of the domain or heartland could agree that local frontier problems were best handled by
local civilian means. Loyalist history obliges us to recognize
that there are two ways of looking at the growth of such agreements
and such polities. When Westminister and Whitehall rejected Loyalist schemes for local federation and kept the colonies divided into
military governorships, it was not only for fear that the growth of
representative government would lead to local independence; it was
also because there was a constant perceived threat of war with the
United States, and no imperial government was going to leave the
management of this threat in Loyalist hands. This was a matter of
perception as well as of prudence. It is in Ontario historiography
that the War of 1812 is named "the American War" or "the Canadian
War" and remembered as a struggle for survival; and in United Kingdom historiography that it is presented as a war of no significance.
The two viewpoints do not embrace one another.

And when from the middle of the 19th century Westminster began
to encourage the growth of representative government and colonial
consolidations, it was not because the dangers of war had grown
less; there was the threat of union or Fenian invasions in North
America, and there was the reality of internal war in New Zealand.
It was because, with the growth and relative prosperity of settler
economies, the best way of avoiding war was beginning to appear to
be making the colonies responsible for their own government and

their own defense, always with the almost unspoken provisos that there would now be limits to what they could expect the United Kingdom to do for them, and that if they chose to set up for themselves in independence, this would not be altogether unwelcome. But so long as the Loyalist imperative of dual identity ensured that they never would seek independence, there was need for an understanding of the military obligations on both sides of the relationship.

It is notorious that this problem was not rationally solved but left to the very powerful (if not always ambiguous) operations of sentiment. This accounts for the crusading spirit with which all the dominions, and not only Canada, went to war in 1899 and 1914 and 1939, and it accounts for the bitterness they now feel when the ideology of Europeanism informs them that their very heavy casualties were historically meaningless. But as late as 1982, the peoples of the United Kingdom surprised themselves by the instinctive reaction that took them to war for the Falklands; there instantly ensued projects for making the islands self-governing, however-- that is, responsible for their own defense in the future. And the United Kingdom remains at miniwar for the only component of its own structure where Loyalists insist on being British for reasons of their own.

The Treaty of Paris introduces into British history the problems of a complex kind of plurality, which American Loyalists were the first to assert and to suffer. In the history of British political thought, the phenomenon of loyalism introduces a theoretical problem that, as far as I know, has been dealt with by deliberate silence and deafness: the problem of diffidatio, the repudiation of the tie of government by the sovereign rather than the subject. When may Loyalists who desire to remain British be told that they may no longer remain so? Can even Hobbes's Leviathan deny protection where it no longer suits him to accept allegiance? If the American Civil War has settled it that a state may not secede from the Union, is it conceivable that the Union might expel a state? These are problems that have never been explored in theory. May they never be confronted in practice.

Congress established the Woodrow Wilson International Center
for Scholars in 1968 as an institute for advanced study and
the nation's official "living memorial" to the 28th president,
"symbolizing and strengthening the fruitful relation between
the world of learning and the world of public affairs."

The Center opened in October 1970 and was placed in the
Smithsonian Institution under its own presidentially appointed
Board of Trustees. Its chairmen of the board have been
Hubert H. Humphrey, William J. Baroody, Sr., Max M. Kampelman,
and, currently, William J. Baroody, Jr.

Open annual competitions have brought some 915 fellows, guest
scholars, and short-term grantees to the Center since 1970.
All carry out research, write books, and join in dialogue
with other scholars, public officials, members of Congress,
journalists, and labor and business leaders.

The Center is housed in the Smithsonian's original building,
the castle, on the Mall in Washington, D.C. Financing comes
from both private sources and an annual congressional appro-
priation. The Center seeks diversity of scholarly enterprise
and of points of view.